**BUILDING GOD'S HOUSE
IN THE ROMAN WORLD**

*The ASOR Library of
Biblical and Near Eastern Archaeology*

Building God's House in the Roman World

▲ ▲ ▲

Architectural Adaptation
among Pagans, Jews, and Christians

L. MICHAEL WHITE

Published for
The American Schools of Oriental Research

THE JOHNS HOPKINS UNIVERSITY PRESS
BALTIMORE AND LONDON

© 1990 The Johns Hopkins University Press
All rights reserved
Printed in the United States of America

The Johns Hopkins University Press
701 West 40th Street, Baltimore, Maryland 21211
The Johns Hopkins Press Ltd., London

The paper used in this publication meets the minimum requirements of American National Standard for Information Sciences—Permanence of Paper for Printed Library Materials, ANSI Z39.48-1984.

Library of Congress Cataloging-in-Publication Data
White, L. Michael.
  Building God's house in the Roman world : architectural adaptation among pagans, Jews, and Christians / L. Michael White.
      p.   cm.—(ASOR library of biblical and Near Eastern archaeology)
  Bibliography: p.
  Includes index.
  ISBN 0-8018-3906-8 (alk. paper)
  1. Architecture, Early Christian. 2. Basilicas. 3. Temples, Roman. 4. Mithraea. 5. Synagogues. 6. Buildings—Rome—Remodeling for other use. I. Title. II. Series.
NA4817.W55   1989
726'.5'093709015—dc20   89-32588 CIP

For Gloria, Jessica, and Travis

Contents

▲ ▲ ▲

Figures — ix
Preface — xi
Abbreviations — xiii

1. Introduction — 1
   Landmarks of Early Christian History — 2
   Archaeology and Christian Architecture — 6

2. The Beginnings of Christian Architecture: Models and Perspectives — 11
   House Church and Basilical Origins: Theories and Models — 12
   House Church and Christian Architecture: Adaptation and Environment — 20

3. "Private" Cults in a Constructive Context: The Adaptive Environment — 26
   The Constructive Context — 27
   Private Cultic Activity in the Roman World — 31
   A Roman Phenomenon: the Mithraeum — 47

4. Synagogues in the Graeco-Roman Diaspora: Jewish Adaptation and Accommodation — 60
   Houses and Synagogues in the Diaspora — 62
   The Role of Patrons: Social Factors in Adaptation — 77
   Adaptation, Development, and Accommodation — 85
   Jewish Communities in the Adaptive Environment — 93

CONTENTS

5. From House Church to Church Building: Phases of Christian Growth and Adaptation — 102
   - The House Church — 103
   - The Domus Ecclesiae — 111
   - Beyond the Domus Ecclesiae — 123
   - The Aula Ecclesiae — 127

6. Conclusions: Christian Adaptation and the Social Environment — 140

Notes — 149

Index — 207

Figures

▲ ▲ ▲

1. The "Terrace of the Foreign Gods" overlooking the Theater Quarter at Delos — 33
2. Plan restoration showing construction of Insula 91 and Sarapeion A at Delos — 34
3. Plan reconstruction of the Temple of Gadde at Dura-Europos during Period IV — 42
4. Plan reconstruction of the Temple of Gadde at Dura-Europos during Period III — 42
5. Plan restoration of the *Mitreo della pareti dipinti* ("Mithraeum of the Painted Walls") at Ostia — 51
6. Plan restoration of the Aventine Mithraeum at Rome — 52
7. Plan restoration of the Early Mithraeum and Parthian period house at Dura-Europos — 54
8. Plan restoration of the middle and late stages of renovation of the Mithraeum at Dura-Europos — 55
9. Schematic plans of the Diaspora synagogues at Sardis, Priene, Dura-Europos, Delos, Ostia, and Stobi — 63
10. Plan restoration of the synagogue at Delos — 65
11. Plan restoration of the synagogue at Priene — 68
12. Plan restoration of the synagogue at Ostia — 70
13. Plan restoration of the synagogue complex at Stobi — 72
14. Plan restoration of the synagogue at Sardis — 73
15. Plan restoration of the Early and Later Synagogue at Dura-Europos — 75

FIGURES

16. Plan restoration of Block L7 and the synagogue at Dura-Europos — 76
17. Plan reconstruction before and after the Christian Building at Dura-Europos was renovated into a domus ecclesiae — 108
18. Isometric reconstruction of the Christian Building at Dura-Europos — 109
19. Plan restoration of renovated insula in *titulus Byzantis* at Rome — 112
20. Isometric reconstruction of *titulus Byzantis* at Rome — 112
21. Plan restoration of the Basilica SS. Giovanni e Paolo at Rome — 113
22. Schematic section of the Basilica San Clemente at Rome — 115
23. Isometric reconstruction of the Roman villa with Christian chapel at Lullingstone — 116
24. Isometric reconstruction of the First Church (aula ecclesiae) below San Crisogono at Rome — 132
25. Siting plan of the fourth- to sixth-century church beneath the medieval basilica of San Crisogono at Rome — 132
26. Plan restoration of San Crisogono and aula ecclesiae at Rome — 133
27. Plan restoration of the fourth-century hall church and heroon beneath the Octagonal church complex at Philippi — 135

Preface

▲ ▲ ▲

The present study is based on the collection of archaeological and documentary materials first assembled in the author's Yale dissertation, and now published separately under the title *The Christian Domus Ecclesiae and Its Environment*. Many of the conclusions of that work have been incorporated into the organization of this study, which focuses especially on the process of architectural adaptation as a way of understanding the environment for development of early Christian buildings. The change from house churches to public basilicas coincided with crucial developments in both social aspects and religious practices in the Christian movement. Yet Christians were not the only group to adapt and renovate private buildings for worship. Thus, special attention must also be paid to the larger cultural context of construction and adaptation, especially in Diaspora Judaism and Roman Mithraism. While this study depends on primary archaeological and documentary research, the approach is ultimately multidisciplinary. It relies equally on insights from numerous fields of New Testament and early Christian study as well as Hellenistic and Roman social history. The result is finally intended to contribute as much to the social history of the early Christian movement as to architectural and theological issues.

The author wishes to express appreciation to those who have helped to make this study a reality. First, I am grateful to Oberlin College and to the American School of Classical Studies at Athens for travel and research support relating to the archaeological materials. Much of the social history research and writing was completed with the support of a fellowship from the National Endowment for the Humanities. Finally, I wish to

PREFACE

express personal appreciation to Eric M. Meyers and Ramsay MacMullen for their encouragement on different aspects of this project. My deepest gratitude and respect go to Wayne A. Meeks and Abraham J. Malherbe, who taught, stimulated, and encouraged. The study of the house church in earliest Christianity is certainly indebted to them.

Abbreviations

▲ ▲ ▲

AJA	*American Journal of Archaeology*
ANRW	*Aufstieg und Niedergang der römischen Welt*, ed. H. Temporini and W. Haase. Berlin, 1972–
BJS	Brown Judaic Studies
CBCR	*Corpus Basilicarum Christianarum Romae*, 5 vols., R. Krautheimer. Vatican City, 1939–1956
CCCA	*Corpus Cultus Cybelae Attidisque*, 6 vols., ed. M. Vermaseren. Leiden, 1977–
CDEE	*The Christian Domus Ecclesiae and Its Environment: A Collection of Texts and Monuments*, L. Michael White. Harvard Theological Studies 36. Minneapolis, 1990.
CIAC VI	*Atti del VI Congresso Internazionale di archeologia cristiana, Ravenna, 1962*. Vatican City, 1965
CIAC VIII	*Atti del VIII Congresso Internazionale di archeologia cristiana, Barcelona, 1969*. Vatican City, 1972
CIG	*Corpus Inscriptionum Graecarum*, 4 vols., ed. A. Bockh et al. Berlin, 1825–1877
CIJ	*Corpus Inscriptionum Judaicarum*, 2 vols., ed. J.-P. Frey. Rome, 1936–1952
CIL	*Corpus Inscriptionum Latinarum*, 16 vols., ed. T. Mommsen et al. Berlin, 1893–
CIMRM	*Corpus Inscriptionum et Monumentorum Religionis Mithriacae*, 2 vols., M. J. Vermaseren. The Hague, 1956–1960
CPJ	*Corpus Papyrorum Iudaicarum*, 3 vols., ed. V. Tcherikover. Cambridge, MA, 1957

ABBREVIATIONS

CRINT I.1   *Compendium Rerum Iudaicarum ad Novum Testamentum*; section one, *The Jewish People of the First Century*, volume one, ed. S. Safrai and M. Stern, Philadelphia, 1974

CRINT I.2   *Compendium Rerum Iudaicarum ad Novum Testamentum*; section one, *The Jewish People of the First Century*, volume two, ed. S. Safrai and M. Stern, Philadelphia, 1976

DEP VI   *The Excavations at Dura-Europos, Preliminary Reports: Sixth Season, 1932–1933*, M. I. Rostovtzeff, A. R. Bellinger, C. Hopkins, and C. B. Welles. New Haven, 1936

DEP VII–VIII   *The Excavations at Dura-Europos, Preliminary Reports: Seventh and Eighth Seasons, 1933–1934 and 1934–1935*, ed. M. I. Rostovtzeff, F. E. Brown, and C. B. Welles. New Haven, 1939

DEF V.1   *The Excavations at Dura-Europos, Final Reports: Volume V, Part I: The Parchments and Papyri*, C. B. Welles, R. O. Fink, and J. F. Gilliam. New Haven, 1959

DEF VIII.1   *The Excavations at Dura-Europos, Final Reports: Volume VIII, Part I: The Synagogue*, C. H. Kraeling. New Haven, 1956

DEF VIII.2   *The Excavations at Dura-Europos, Final Reports: Volume VIII, Part II: The Christian Building*, C. H. Kraeling. New Haven, 1967

ECBA   *Early Christian and Byzantine Architecture*, 3rd ed., R. Krautheimer, New York, 1977

EPRO   *Études préliminaires aux Religions orientales dans l'Empire romain*. Leiden, 1961–

HE   *Historia Ecclesiastica*, Eusebius

HTR   *Harvard Theological Review*

ID   *Inscriptions de Délos*, 4 vols., ed. F. Durbach et al. Paris, 1926–1937

ABBREVIATIONS

IG	*Inscriptiones Graecae*, ed. A. Bockh et al. Berlin, 1873–
IGRR	*Inscriptiones Graecae ad res Romanas pertinentes*, 5 vols., ed. R. Cagnat et al. Paris, 1911
ILS	*Inscriptiones Latinae Selectae*, 3 vols., H. Dessau. Berlin, 1892–1916
JRS	*Journal of Roman Studies*
LCL	Loeb Classical Library. London and Cambridge, MA, 1912–
LD	*Donateurs et Fondateurs dans le Synagoges juives*, B. Lifschitz. Cahiers de la Revue Biblique VII. Paris, 1967
OGIS	*Orientis Graeci Inscriptiones Selectae. Supplementum Sylloges Inscriptionum Graecarum*, 2 vols., ed. W. Dittenberger. Leipzig, 1903–1905
PBSR	*Papers of the British School at Rome*
P. Oxy, etc.	for abbreviations for papyri, see *A Greek-English Lexicon*, compiled by H. Liddell and R. Scott, revised by H. Jones. Oxford, 1925–1940
RDAC	*Rivista di archeologia cristiana*
REG	*Revue des Études Grecques*
RER	*Review of Religion*
TSC	*The Second Century: A Journal of Early Christian Studies*
VC	*Vigilae Christianae*
ZNW	*Zeitschrift für die Neutestamentliche Wissenschaft*

BUILDING GOD'S HOUSE
IN THE ROMAN WORLD

1
Introduction

▲ ▲ ▲

Behold the relics of Rome, the image of her pristine greatness! Neither time nor the barbarian can boast the merit of this stupendous destruction: it was perpetrated by her own citizens.
(Petrarch, 1304–1374)

Nothing, it would seem, so evokes a consciousness of history, of time and change, than the monuments of ages past, which by their very time-boundedness comment upon old and new, then and now. Thus, Petrarch's lament over Rome's fallen glory festered in Gibbon to a more bitter condemnation of the culprits of decline.[1] The Emperor Augustus himself boasted that he "left in marble that which he found made of brick."[2] He also left therein a bit of historical commentary seen from the optimism of progress. Yet such imperial quips too evince the sense of change, of old and new, which the monuments themselves evoke. "Laugh, O Caesar," exclaimed Martial, mocking relics of a past glory, "at those kingly wonders, the pyramids."[3]

We may contrast the awe of nineteenth-century romantics, neoclassicism falling on the heels of Gibbon as poets and antiquarians alike rediscovered that past glory. Lord Byron felt its tug as he contemplated the ruins of majestic Sounion (*Childe Harold's Pilgrimage*, Canto II, 86):

> Save where some solitary column mourns
> Above its prostrate brethren of the cave;
> Save where Tritonia's airy shrine adorns
> Colonna's cliff, and gleams along the wave;
> Save o'er some warrior's half-forgotten grave,
> Where the grey stones and unmolested grass
> Ages, but not oblivion, feebly brave,

> While strangers only not regardless pass,
> Lingering like me, perchance, to gaze and sigh "Alas!"

With the first blush of archaeological discovery came newly found antiquities in increasing numbers. Egyptian statuary and Greek marbles awed and inspired, and yet stirred the emotions of mutability and human finitude. In Shelley, like Byron or Keats, the refrain echoes:

> Worlds on worlds are rolling ever
> From creation to decay.[4]

It is in retrospect that human consciousness labels and interprets such change as progress or decline. But such is perhaps the natural inclination of self-conscious historical retrospection, which looks to the past for "landmarks" to the present.

Landmarks of Early Christian History

Finding such landmarks in earliest Christian history is a difficult task, but one that is more and more in demand with the greater availability of texts and monuments to be examined and interpreted. In a series of lectures entitled "Landmarks of Early Christianity," the church historian Kirsopp Lake essayed a self-critical sentiment toward such a task:

> At first sight the historian of religions appears to be faced by a number of clearly distinguished entities, to each of which he feels justified in giving the name of a separate religion; but on further consideration it becomes obvious that each one of these entities has been in a condition of flux throughout its history. Each began as a combination or synthesis of older forms of thought with comparatively little new in its composition; each ended by disintegrating into many elements, of which the worst disappeared, while the best were taken up into new life in some new religion.[5]

INTRODUCTION

The historian looks for landmarks that chart a course of development in discernible stages in order to posit description and analysis of that development.

Establishing these landmarks becomes the first step in interpretation. It is much like the archaeologist who, after sifting through jumbled, seemingly indistinguishable, remains of human activity, delights in the discovery of an ashlayer. Rather than some macabre perversity, this delight in finding signs of destruction is in the recognition that it marks clear stages of ending and beginning; a clear break in occupational history and stratigraphy. It is a landmark from which other historical developments, both before and after, can now be discerned more clearly. Yet, as Lake correctly observes, such landmarks are not always evident, either in the history of religions or in social history and archaeology. Indeed, in many cases what pass for landmarks of human history are rather symbols of larger developmental courses or phases, and are often imposed by retrospective consciousness. There are few ashlayers in the history of early Christianity, and the scholar is left to ponder the best ways to mark off its development. Still, monuments stand to the changes that have occurred and call out for attempts to hear them.

The basic landmark that will be the focus of this study is the beginning of Christian church building and the establishment of an institutionalized religion in the Roman world. Religion is more than a message, and the appeal of the early Christian movement did not lie in its offer of salvation alone. There were savior gods aplenty in the Graeco-Roman world, and many a cult following to promote them. The competition and interaction of religions occurred in the social world as well as the intellectual. The history of the early Christian movement cannot be written without addressing the fact that growth, worship, theology, ethics—in short, every aspect of religion in human experience—were centered in communal experience, in assembly. The Christian movement did not begin as a separate religion but as one of several reforming currents in first-century Judaism. By the fourth century, however, it had become an official religion of the Roman state.

It seems, then, that one of the best ways to see this historical progression is in the development of the place of assembly and church building. In the beginning of the movement, the followers of Jesus met in the homes of members. According to Acts, the primitive Jerusalem community gathered "from house to house" (Acts 2.46; 5.42; cf. 12.12). The domestic "upper room" (Acts 20.8) perpetuates the tradition of Jesus' Last Supper (cf. Luke 22.12; Acts 1.13). It is likely that the author of Luke-Acts has idealized or romanticized the picture somewhat, and this may in some ways reflect the first self-conscious historiography.[6] Yet, the earliest Christian sources confirm the basic elements; Paul regularly addressed letters to and from "the church in the house [*hē kat' oikon ekklēsia*] of so-and-so."[7] Recent studies have shown how this "house church" setting conditioned the nature of assembly, worship, and communal organization. It was first and foremost an urban phenomenon. The constituency and social location of Pauline communities reflected the character and conditions of urban households and other private domestic activities.[8] It is most significant, moreover, that the place of assembly was unchanged from its original domestic function. There were as yet no church buildings. At this stage the house church was primarily a social phenomenon of the history.

Within three centuries, however, the situation, and with it the character of assembly changed radically. In sharp contrast to the catch-as-catch-can house churches depicted in Acts stands the monumental church building. One is seemingly random and informal; the other is hieratic and fixed. From the fourth century onward the basilica (the epitome of Christian church architecture) became a norm of style. Patronage by the emperor Constantine and his mother Helena Augusta account for the proliferation of monumental church buildings both at Rome and in the Holy Land.[9] Besides endowing new construction, they also supported the restoration and renovation of existing buildings in basilical style.[10] This monumentalization under the aegis of Constantine offers the historian a landmark for many facets of development in early Christianity.[11] The Christian basilica took its place alongside the monumental public archi-

INTRODUCTION

tecture of the state, the imperial fora and palaces, and the temples of the gods. At the same time one cannot help but notice the enormous differences within the Christian movement marked by the changes of the architecture of the fourth century from the period of origins.

In the history of Christianity, then, two landmarks stand out from the architectural tradition: on one side the house church of the Pauline period; on the other, the basilica of the Constantinian age. One marks the period of primitive beginnings and sectarian identity; the other, an age of emergence into the mainstream of Roman society and acceptance as a state religion. The landmarks themselves present few problems of recognition on the surface. Through their overt contrast they are identifiable, measurable signs of change. But historical refinement and sophistication also show them to be symbolic moments in a more gradual process of change. For as Lake would call us to observe, neither stage is unique in and of itself for its own time. The problem for the historian, then, is reconstructing in more detail the subtle lines of development, the process of change, with an eye toward both social and historical components.

Both the process and the time period of development from house church to basilica are crucial to understanding the history of earliest Christianity. It was the period of formation and crystalization of most aspects of worship, theology, ethics, and organization, during which the Christian movement came to have its recognizable shape and identity. It was the period during which Christianity achieved a unique self-definition away from Judaism, and further internal self-definition with regard to heterodoxy and orthodoxy. By some it is viewed as a period of triumph and maturation toward the great Church of the early medieval era. By others it is viewed as a period of decline and apostasy from the pristine purity of the New Testament. Fundamental changes in the nature and setting of Christian assembly, therefore, are of more significance than for the development of architecture alone. They are inextricably tied to all aspects of Christian practice, precisely because assembly and worship were at the center of the religious experience as well as the social expansion of the movement.

Archaeology and Christian Architecture

Generally, the development of church building has been the province of historians of art and architecture, and only secondarily of use to social and intellectual historians. Despite New Testament references to household assemblies, since the Renaissance the normative character of basilical planning has served as the starting point for discussions. Investigations of architectural development were predicated on static conceptions of aesthetic and style, with little or no consideration of critical issues from the earliest periods, before there was a Christian architecture.[12]

Much of the raw material for this discussion came from the burgeoning archaeological discoveries at Rome and in the Near East during the eighteenth and early nineteenth centuries. Post-Renaissance neoclassicism and aesthetics were bolstered by the emergence of the Roman school of early Christian archaeology, associated especially with the name of Giovanni Battista de Rossi (1822–1894).[13] This period brought initial exploration of both the catacombs and subterranean levels beneath churches and cathedrals. Indeed, many of the basic discoveries of early Christian antiquities that continue to be discussed were brought to light at this time. While basic issues and theories had been debated for several centuries, the archaeological field was opened up afresh with profuse new discoveries commencing at the end of the nineteenth century, and new shape and definition were given to the raw data and the critical interpretation of that data.[14]

So profound were some of these new discoveries, that they fundamentally reshaped basic assumptions about Christian architecture made by (among others) the most influential church historian of the early twentieth century, Adolf von Harnack (who died in 1924).[15] Albeit concerned with social issues, Harnack was primarily an intellectual historian and theologian. He professed little competence in primary archaeological data, and relied on the prevailing architectural theories of his generation. The essential problem of this early scholarship was that no early church buildings were known that could be securely dated prior

INTRODUCTION

to Constantine. Indeed, some that were dated to this early period (such as churches at Rome and the basilica at Emmaus) were found to be quite erroneous.[16] New discoveries prompted fresh approaches and solutions to the perennial issues.

Two areas of archaeological work conducted after World War I proved to be especially important. The first began with new work to refine and expand analysis on the subterranean levels beneath the oldest churches at Rome. This project was led by Richard Krautheimer beginning in 1934, and continues to the present.[17] The singular achievement of Krautheimer and his school has been the comprehensive scale of analysis brought to bear on each archaeological site as its use is traced from earliest strata of pre-Christian construction to the building and rebuilding of medieval basilicas in successive styles. Each case, then, becomes (to whatever degree possible) a stratigraphic archaeological record of that particular building site. In this process a more cautious and thoroughgoing assessment of traditional or legendary claims for earliest Christian usage at certain sites has been attempted. Especially important are the claims, from tradition or from earlier archaeological sites at Rome, that some represent pre-Constantinian house churches or church buildings going back to as early as the first century C.E. The most notable case in this regard is the Basilica of San Clemente, which traditionally is thought to be the property donated for a church building by Clement of Rome, who died around 95 C.E. Krautheimer's work makes it possible to assess these traditions more carefully and to bring into sharper focus the archaeological progression of the site (from Republican buildings to Christian basilicas, layered on top of one another and continuing through the Baroque period).

Even more interest was precipitated by the discoveries at Dura-Europos (a Roman garrison on the Syrian frontier) beginning in 1921–1922.[18] In 1931 a house was unearthed that had been renovated for use as a place of Christian assembly. Because of the destruction of that city in Sassanian incursions of 256 C.E., the Christian edifice is securely dated and remains both the earliest and most completely known pre-Constantinian church building. Due to these unique circumstances the joint archaeological expedition of Yale University and the French Academy of Inscriptions and Letters yielded evidence for the physical shape of the building and its renovation for Christian usage.[19] Perhaps more than any other modern discovery the Dura Christian building has precipitated new emphasis on pre-Constantinian church buildings and reopened the question of development from the earliest house church period.

It cannot be forgotten, however, that on the same street at Dura two other cultic facilities were found that had been renovated from private houses. One was a mithraeum, the sanctuary of the romanized cult of the Persian god Mithras. The other was a heavily decorated synagogue, by far the most extraordinary discovery, causing scholars to rethink traditional assumptions about the origins and development of the synagogue and Diaspora Judaism.[20] It was at first a house, and only through subsequent renovation had taken on more of the trappings of a formal synagogue structure. In many ways, then, the development of a normative synagogue architecture through the fourth century paralleled (rather than preceded) that of Christian church building. Interestingly enough, the earliest strata of possible Christian occupation beneath San Clemente also indicated that the building was immediately next door to a house which had a small Mithraic establishment installed in the ground-floor cortile. From the archaeological evidence, the earliest Christian activities can hardly be disengaged from those of the immediate social context. Significantly, in all three cases at Dura, the initial renovation for religious usage did nothing to transform the basic domestic character of the existing building, yet, the Dura Christian building was no longer used as a residence after renovation. It had become a church building in some more formal sense. It cannot, therefore, be pushed back as an example or model of the house churches of the New Testament period. There are difficulties in trying to date the archaeological evidence back to the first or second century at San Clemente and numerous other sites as well. Thus, these discoveries require fresh assessment within the framework of the landmark development from the house church to the basilica, and suggest that we cannot look at the Christian evidence in isola-

INTRODUCTION

tion from the religious use of private architecture in the larger Roman environment.

What is needed, then, and what the present volume seeks to offer, is a more comprehensive analysis of the beginnings of Christian development in church building—the progression from house church meetings to basilical architecture. On the one hand this volume is largely concerned with archaeological and documentary collection, to assess the available evidence. On the other hand, it is analytical; it seeks a historical reconstruction and interpretation of the developmental process. From this perspective, it is not an architectural history as such, and the further lines of analysis will sharpen this distinction. It is instead a social history that depends on the most careful reconstruction possible of the evidence (both archaeological and literary) in its historical context.[21]

A catalogue of relevant texts and monuments is assembled in a companion volume (*The Christian Domus Ecclesiae and Its Environment: A Collection of Texts and Monuments*).[22] In addition to both Christian and pagan literary references it includes as much as possible of the Christian archaeological evidence. The types of evidence range from excavation reports on buildings (usually rewritten to reflect the phases of construction history for each site) to inscriptions and papyri. Also included are some selected comparative monuments (largely buildings and inscriptions) depicting the diffusion of Mithraism and Judaism in the Graeco-Roman environment.

By looking at the history of scholarship we see some of the traditional models and issues in the understanding of the beginnings of Christian church building. By integrating new information and perspectives from archaeology and social history, we are able to establish analytical issues for reconstruction. In particular we may examine the environment for patterns of adapting and renovating private buildings for religious and communal usage in greater detail. We focus on the diffusion of the numerous oriental cults in the Hellenistic and Roman periods. This offers insights into the way Christianity spread and developed. Of special interest are two such groups. First is the cult of Mithras, one of Christianity's main competitors for official acceptance by Rome. The second is Judaism itself as it spread in the Diaspora and served as a conduit for the emergence of the Christian movement. These groups offer a social context for the transition from house churches into church buildings, as a barometer for the development of the Christian movement into a major force in the culture of the Roman world.

2
The Beginnings of Christian Architecture

Models and Perspectives

▲ ▲ ▲

The earliest and most enduring interest in early Christian church buildings and their development has come from the realm of architectural history. Until recently scholars of New Testament and Christian origins have devoted little attention to the topic. This lack of attention was probably because, apart from the literature, there was no clear evidence from the first or second centuries with which to work. The perspective was largely textual and theological. The available archaeological evidence came from later periods and was often used merely to support and illustrate theological ideas from the literature. Architecture, too, was a later development. Because the basilical plan had become so integral to assumptions of all church building, it served as the starting principle for investigations into the origins and development of Christian architecture. Recognizing the New Testament references to household meetings, therefore, only raised the question of how church buildings moved from the house setting to basilical form. Of course, more than just architectural form was at stake, since theological assumption integral to basilical planning presupposed normative patterns of assembly and liturgy. Thus, standard elements in the iconography of basilical architecture were read back into the earliest periods, into the New Testament itself. Such assumptions, therefore, have given fundamental definition to the study of church building which must be considered and evaluated before moving on.

House Church and Basilical Origins: Theories and Models

The earliest theories of the beginnings of Christian architecture arose in the nineteenth century and tended to discount the New Testament house church.[1] They placed a basilical ideal at the very beginning of the process of erecting church buildings in the pre-Constantinian period. The origins of the basilical form, then, were sought either in classical models of Roman public architecture or in the pattern of underground "chapels" in the Roman catacombs. The latter attempt has been fostered by the continuing popular appeal of the Roman tradition. It is vested in the romantic notion of the earliest Christians hovering among the tombs of the martyrs in order to worship during times of persecution. Such suppositions have long been dismissed as viable explanations for the origins of the basilica, both on historical and archaeological grounds. It is doubtful that the catacombs were ever used for regular assembly and worship, though they do represent a significant element in early Christian piety.[2] Other early theories looked to halls, such as the *scholē* of Paul at Ephesus (Acts 19.9).[3] Others still looked to the Jewish synagogue as a model.[4] In this case, the assumption was that basilical synagogue architecture had already become fixed and normative in Jesus' day. In particular, the basilical lines of "Galilean type" synagogues found at Capernaum and elsewhere seemed to offer a model easily accessible to the emergent Christian church. Only more recently has it been recognized that none of the supposed examples of this synagogue type can be dated securely before the fourth century C.E.[5] Indeed, the discoveries at Dura-Europos shook up many standard assumptions about both Jewish and Christian architectural norms and development during the earlier periods.[6]

The "Atrium House" and Basilical Theories

Some theories began to include the New Testament tradition of private household meetings around the middle of the nineteenth century. In large measure these attempts were stimulated by burgeoning archaeological finds, especially at Rome and in the rediscovery of Pompeii. Here, frozen in time, were firsthand examples of housing from the Roman world. An early proposal by A. C. Zestermann (1847) was followed by G. Dehio's comprehensive theory in 1882.[7] Dehio's theory recognized the importance of the New Testament house church, going so far as to make it the primary setting for assembly throughout the first three centuries. It was thereupon proposed that one should look to the form of the typical Roman "atrium house" for the basic architectural scheme from which the basilica evolved.[8] Dehio believed that Christians assembled in the central atrium of the house, which became the model for the nave of the basilica. Likewise, the entrance to the tablinum (the main living room) off the atrium, where the household shrine would have stood in pagan families, became the prototype of the apse and altar. Finally, the symmetrical alae flanking the atrium were viewed as the model for the transept.

Although a proposal with immediate appeal and, as we shall see, lasting effects, Dehio's basic theory was questioned on some points. Chiefly it was charged that his typical Roman house was based on the simpler, more regular plan of Republican villas and did not adequately account for diversity in the early Principate.[9] Second, the formal analogies were incomplete, as there was nothing to serve as the model for the atrium-forecourt of the typical Christian basilica. Despite such criticism of detail, the basic view persisted. The growing assumption was that the private house assembly of the New Testament period evolved directly and genetically into the plan of the monumental basilica.

As archaeological work continued Dehio's original house theory was taken over by M. Schultze (1895) and further modified by R. Lemaire (1911). Schultze[10] attempted to account for more diversity in housing and basilica plans, which he traced to the influence of the Hellenistic peristyle house in the east as reflected in Syrian church architecture. In the west basilical architecture followed the more elaborate style of Italian housing found at Pompeii, which introduced a peristyle in the tablinum, while the atrium served as an entry area. Schultze's model attempted thereby to account for all the standard elements of the basilica (colonnaded nave with apse and forecourt) by analogies to the components of the Italian villa. He argued, moreover, that the evolution from house to basilica was already complete by the mid-third century.

Lemaire[11] basically followed Schultze's model in all respects save one. Seizing on the influence of the Hellenistic peristyle house, he argued that its elaborated oecus (*oecus* is equivalent to the Latin *tablinum*) became the repository for altar and clergy. Customary elaborations of the Roman period included raised exedrae, and thus made it a natural precursor for the apse and the bema. Perhaps more significantly, Lemaire made detailed use of literary sources to correlate with the architectural plans. He postulated the usual practices of worship in the house setting by extrapolation backwards from literary texts and the liturgy of the basilica. Finally, Lemaire concluded that this atrium house setting continued into the second century, but that by the beginning of the third century the evolution to church house (which he termed *domus dei* from liturgical texts), was well on the way to becoming the basilica.

These early house theories never gained wide acceptance among archaeologists and architectural historians, but they have continued to exert considerable influence in some areas connected with the history of earliest Christianity.[12] This may be due largely to the basic evolutionary model espoused in a direct progression from house to basilical church building. The emphasis lay on the continuity of the tradition through theology and liturgy, and evidence was sought to support this view. The central place given to liturgical factors has provided the linchpin for many in this field. It is perhaps nowhere more clear at the turn of the century than in the work of Henri Leclercq, Walter Lowrie, and others seeking archaeological and artistic evidence of early Christian belief and practice.[13]

The House Theory and Models of Christian Development

Continued archaeological work necessitated further modifications in the basic house theory. Thus, by the time Lowrie's revised work[14] on early Christian art and architecture appeared, the arguments against atrium house origins were sufficiently

THE BEGINNINGS OF CHRISTIAN ARCHITECTURE

strong to make his earlier stance untenable. Chief among the discoveries of this era was the Dura-Europos Christian building. To account for this new evidence Lowrie's modified house theory proposed a four-stage evolution from house to basilica: A short-lived first stage occurred at the beginning of the Jerusalem church as reflected in Acts 2–5, when assembly was "from house to house." In the second stage, synagogues served as the primary setting for missionary preaching, while worship proper was set in private homes (cf. Acts 20.7–8). Thus, the first two stages account for the New Testament evidence. The third stage extended from the end of the first century "well into the third century," during which time private houses came to be transformed into church buildings, and here Dura is cited as an early case. The fourth stage, Lowrie concluded, began before the middle of the third century, especially in larger cities where growth and expansion of Christianity would have necessitated construction of large-scale buildings. In this way the basilica, modeled directly after houses and mystery cult chapels (and supported by archaeological examples), was already in use by the third century.[15]

The house theory has persisted especially among ecclesiastical historians, long after it ceased to be used by architectural historians and archaeologists. Its survival has proven particularly influential, though at times implicit, in the area of liturgical development, which as we saw went hand in hand with some of the early house theories. Primary application can be seen in the works of L. Duchesne and Dom Gregory Dix.[16] Starting with the New Testament evidence Dix assumed the private, domestic character of Christian assembly into the second century. On this basis he attempted to detail the typical pattern of worship in the atrium house as the beginning point for liturgical development of later centuries. Here development assumes a high degree of continuity. Already for the New Testament period Dix asserted a fundamental separation between the eucharist and the agape meal. While both would have been set in private homes, only to the former as the corporate assembly of the entire congregation, would he allow the term *church* to be applied.[17]

According to Dix this corporate assembly of the entire congregation would most likely have been held in the houses of wealthier members in order to accommodate the crowds.[18] Consequently, he equated such houses with the elaborate peristyle-atrium houses of Pompeii. From this point he goes on to adopt an implicit formulation of the house theory in order to describe the liturgical practices in this house setting. Thus, Dix said:

> Here ready to hand was the ideal setting for the church's "domestic" worship at eucharist, in surroundings which spoke for themselves of the noblest traditions of family life. The quaint old images of the household gods and the altar must go, of course, along with the sacred hearth and its undying fire. All else was exactly what was needed. The chair of the *pater familias* became the bishop's throne; the heads of the families were replaced by presbyters, and the clansmen by the laity, the members of the household of God. Virgins and widows and others for whom it might be desirable to avoid the crowding in the *atrium* could be placed behind the screens of the *alae*. At the back [of the *atrium*] near the door, where the clients and slaves of the patrician house—attached to it but not of it—had stood at its assemblies, were now to be found the catechumens and enquirers, attached to the church but not yet members of it. The place of the stone table was that of the Christian altar; the tank of the *impluvium* would serve for the solemn immersion of baptism in the presence of the whole church.... The dining room of the house (*triclinium*) which usually opened off the *atrium* could be used when needed for the Christian "love feast" (*agape* or "Lord's Supper"; by the second century this had lost its original connection with the eucharist, if indeed it had much connection with it even in later apostolic times).[19]

It is significant that the liturgical practices and ecclesiastical organization ascribed here to the house church are retrojected from third century (or later) sources. Dix argues, for example, that there would be nothing in Hippolytus' eucharistic order that would have been "repudiated" by this earlier period.[20] He concludes, therefore, by suggesting that the form of worship from this atrium house setting evolved naturally and directly into the liturgical and architectural forms of the basilica by the third century, for which he also cites archaeological support from Dura-Europos and Rome.[21]

The atrium house theory embedded implicitly (for Dix never refers to architectural historians by name!) in the theological substructure of this description has had a pervasive influence down to current scholarship.[22] It portrays a unified landscape of continuity from the New Testament house church worship to the liturgical and architectural development of the basilica. At the same time various historical studies for the New Testament period call into question some of the individual assumptions: the meeting in the atrium, radical separation of eucharist from agape meal, and the social organization of household meetings. The physical and social setting assumed for Paul's discussion of eucharist in 1 Corinthians 11.17–34 is now recognized to be a mixed assembly around the common table of the house after the pattern of typical dinner parties.[23] It is a far cry from the hieratic liturgy assumed by Dix. There is nothing in such a picture of the physical setting on which to pin a direct evolution of architectural elements to basilical form. Contemporary architectural historians and archaeologists consider this notion of basilical origins an issue hardly worth mentioning.[24] Consequently, a new perspective needs to emerge for a historical starting point in the house church setting.

House Church and Basilica: The Problem

The rejection of the atrium house theory as the source pattern for basilical architecture has subtle but fundamental implications for the study of the house church and church building in the pre-Constantinian period. Historical critical problems pinch in from both ends of the developmental spectrum. On one end, a basic assumption of the atrium house theory was that a typical plan (usually drawn from Pompeian villas) existed for Roman housing across the Empire.[25] On the other end, it has been too readily assumed that there was uniform implementation of basilical architecture by the fourth century. Archaeological work has proven both of these assumptions false. For the early period, diverse housing and widespread adaptations of private domestic edifices will prove extremely important in our study of the religious environment.[26] At the other end, current architectural consensus sees the Christian basilica as a direct result of Constantinian policy in the years following the *Edict of Milan*.[27] It was based on standard forms of monumental public architecture at Rome. Derived from civil halls, imperial palaces, or classical hypostyle architecture,[28] it was self-consciously adapted to the new social position of the Christian Church under imperial patronage.[29]

Basilical form, then, was imposed on—rather than evolving genetically from—patterns of church building that existed before the Constantinian era. J. B. Ward-Perkins concluded that there was no monumental Christian architecture before 313 C.E. to serve as a model, and that the first basilica (in the strict sense) was the Church of St. John Lateran, built from an imperial palace donated in 314.[30] The house church and pre-Constantinian church building must be seen from a new perspective. While one may look for historical continuity, norms of spatial articulation and liturgical form from basilical architecture cannot simply be retrojected onto the earlier periods. In one sense this divorces the beginnings of normative Christian architectural development from the earlier periods.[31] By its very nature the house church defies normal canons of architectural history and iconography, since there was as yet no template of plan and style. It took the Constantinian revolution to provide such a template. For the earlier periods, literary, archaeological, and documentary evidences must be allowed to speak on their own terms, in their own historical and social context.

The most comprehensive effort to address and examine pre-Constantinian archaeological evidence from the perspective of architectural history has come in the work of Richard Krautheimer at Rome.[32] This enterprise began with the study of the extensive building levels (first discovered in the eighteenth and nineteenth centuries) beneath many of the medieval churches. It had been claimed that a number of such discoveries reflected

Christian usage of houses and baths which were then taken over as basilical church buildings. The archaeological remains and traditions connected with these early parish churches, usually called *tituli* ("title-churches"), have received special attention, resulting in a more critical and nuanced portrayal of the architectural progression there.[33] Based on this work at Rome, Krautheimer's broader survey of the early Christian and Byzantine periods has suggested an architectural periodization ranging from the New Testament to the fourth century.

In the first period (ca. 50–150 C.E.) assembly and worship (following the pattern in Acts) would have been held in the homes of wealthier members. The common meal setting would have meant a location in the dining room (triclinium) or perhaps other larger rooms as that were available. No architectural specialization occurred, however, to provide spatial articulation for religious use. Consequently, as to the general course of development of church building, Krautheimer concludes:

> Until A.D. 200, then, a Christian architecture did not and could not exist. Only the state religion erected temples in the tradition of Greek and Roman architecture. The saviour religions, depending on the specific form of their ritual and the finances of their congregation, built oratories above or below ground, from the simplest to the most lavish but always on a small scale. Christian congregations prior to 200 were limited to the realm of domestic architecture, and further to the inconspicuous dwellings of the lower classes. This limitation and particularly the evasion of the architecture of official worship, is something that becomes decisive for the early development of Christian architecture.[34]

It is most significant, here, that in the absence of purely architectural categories, Krautheimer evaluates development on the basis of two intersecting scales of social context: other "savior cults," and socioeconomic status. Even if one were to quibble with details or implications (such as a strict limitation to the lower classes) this turn to the environment offers important methodological considerations, and it is one which, it will be argued, occurred throughout the pre-Constantinian development.

Krautheimer's second period (ca. 150–250) is correlated with changes in the position and composition of the Christian movement. In this period the place of assembly began to develop more specialized structural needs. While some congregations might still have been meeting in private homes, others began to own property to meet the manifold needs of community life. The structure itself remained "within the local tradition of domestic building in the Roman-hellenistic world, yet adapted to the new needs of the Christian congregations."[35] Such specialized needs could no longer be met by an unaltered private house or apartment. A regular place of assembly adapted to community use was required, and for this Krautheimer adopts the term *domus ecclesiae* (the "house of the church") as a technical designation.[36]

In the third period (ca. 250–313) Krautheimer sees a continuation of the domus ecclesiae pattern, but allows for a gradual introduction of larger buildings in individual cases. These larger buildings, such as the first church of San Crisogono at Rome, were not yet basilical in form or monumental in size.[37] The fourth period commenced (313), therefore, with the Constantinian revolution and the founding of the Lateran basilica (314).[38]

House Church and Christian Architecture: Adaptation and Environment

Krautheimer's architectural history suggests a developmental model in stages. It posits two fundamental definitions: that the beginning of basilical form in 313 is distinct from what went before, and that the architectural determinants for worship are distinct from those of the cult of the dead. The growth of Christian cemeteries and memorial practices especially associated with martyrs and saints followed its own path. Thus one should not look to the catacombs or the beginnings of Christian funerary architecture as primary models of assembly, as had been traditionally assumed at Rome. The most significant step

THE BEGINNINGS OF CHRISTIAN ARCHITECTURE

in the prebasilical development of assembly architecture, therefore, is the emergence of the domus ecclesiae. Through physical adaptation an existing edifice, such as that at Dura-Europos, became formally a church building and functionally, at least, the property of the church.[39] Yet, it must be conceded that Krautheimer's study remains limited to the field of architectural history, and his treatment of prebasilical Christian buildings is quite brief. A more detailed historical treatment is still in order for this development.

In so doing some definitions are needed. A key point arises from the fact that there can be no archaeological evidence for the earliest household meetings (the house church proper). By definition, then, there was no architectural adaptation and, consequently, nothing distinctively Christian about the physical setting.[40] By definition, too, domus ecclesiae comes to designate any building specifically adapted or renovated for such religious use. Some typical assumptions regarding the development also need to be tested and reexamined. On the social level, it is regularly assumed that the earliest Christians met in houses in order to avoid the idolatrous practices of Greek and Roman temples, and because the Christian movement came from among the poor and dispossessed.[41] On the architectural level, it is too often assumed that there was little or no direct line of continuity from the domus ecclesiae to the basilica,[42] and that after 314 basilical form universally and almost immediately superseded all existing church buildings.[43] In the course of the present study we shall see that none of these assumptions can be upheld. These definitional matters set the question in a historical perspective and call for further attention to the development and its context. What is needed is a more detailed model for the process of architectural adaptation.

Archaeological Evidence of Adaptation and Development
The Dura-Europos Christian building remains our clearest example of a domus ecclesiae; however, it cannot simply be projected backward onto the house church situation of an earlier period.[44] It owes its form as a church building to specific points of adaptation predicated on the form of the existing edifice.

Architectural development from house church to domus ecclesiae assumes adaptation and renovation. An aspect of development that has not received adequate notice is partial adaptation or renovation in successive stages. Archaeological evidence for this is rare. Even at Dura there is no evidence whatsoever that the building was used for Christian worship prior to its present renovated form. Still, some evidence exists that suggests the possibility of partial adaptation, especially in the villa beneath the basilica Euphrasiana at Parentium, Istria and in the Roman villa at Lullingstone, England (Roman Britannia).[45]

There is also evidence for subsequent stages of renovation from the domus ecclesiae, which might suggest transitional development or enlargement prior to the basilica. To Krautheimer's prime example, San Crisogono at Rome, we may add two cases from Roman Syria/Arabia, at Qirqbize and the "Julianos' Church" at Umm el-Jimal.[46] Less certain, but worth noting, are the North Hall of the church of Bishop Theodore at Aquileia and a newly discovered hall under the octagonal Byzantine church at Philippi.[47] In each case, the adaptation or construction resulted in a rectangular hall plan, but with none of the formal trappings of basilical architecture. The dates range from the mid-third century (Dura) throughout the fourth century (Umm el-Jimal and Lullingstone). Moreover, there are other indications of buildings which, having already undergone adaptation to domus ecclesiae, were subsequently remodeled as large hall structures. Included are the sites at Parentium and both SS. Giovanni e Paolo and San Clemente at Rome.[48] These cases suggest that the process of adaptation and renovation continued throughout the early period and that an additional transitional category might be recognized. For this move to a more formally defined hall structure (though still not a basilica per se) we may suggest the term *aula ecclesiae* as a technical designation.[49]

In addition to offering a more detailed picture of pre-Constantinian development, this notion of adaptation may also help explain the transformation from domus ecclesiae to basilica. Some lines of continuity have been suggested, as in the work of Jean Lassus on the great Syrian ecclesiastical complexes.[50]

THE BEGINNINGS OF CHRISTIAN ARCHITECTURE

While the house was not a genetic model for the architecture as such, its rooms, turned to specific religious functions, grew into the specialized buildings (some of them basilicas) of the larger church complex. For Lassus, then, *church* becomes the designation for the entire complex (as it would for the Dura Christian building), not just the main basilica. He has also argued this perspective from more recent archaeological evidence in other parts of the Roman world. For example, at Hippo Regius (Roman Numidia) he maintains that a Christian quarter had grown up around the cathedral by Augustine's day; however, the complex had evolved naturally from a peristyle house earlier used as a church and found contiguous to the episcopal basilica.[51] This suggestion offers further insights into social issues connected with the growing Christian population of the empire and the emergence of Christian quarters in larger cities.[52]

One must also begin to question the notion, often implicitly presupposed in recent architectural histories, that the church's fortunes under Constantine brought about a universal transformation to basilical architecture virtually overnight. On the contrary, the archaeological evidence indicates that domus ecclesiae and aula ecclesiae forms continued well after that point when basilicas had supposedly become the norm. Thus we find that while monumental basilicas were springing up under the aegis of Constantine, other churches were still being founded following prebasilical patterns. A good example is at Qirqbize, Syria, established in the first third of the fourth century as a rectangular hall. Only later, near the end of the century, did this aula ecclesiae begin to assume interior basilical trappings, when basilical architecture was penetrating the region between Antioch and Aleppo.[53]

The process is not limited to outlying provinces; it can be seen at Rome as well. There, several of the earlier titular churches continued to operate untouched by the new style of the Lateran or Saint Peter's. The first plain hall structure of San Crisogono was modified to basilical form only in the fifth century.[54] The same is evident at both SS. Giovanni e Paolo and San Clemente, two of the earliest known sites from Rome. In neither case was basilical form introduced before the beginning of the fifth century. In SS. Giovanni e Paolo the year was 410, and the construction represented a sharp change in plan.[55] In both cases, then, existing church buildings, which had emerged through the adaptation of domus ecclesiae, continued to operate alongside and untouched by monumental Constantinian basilicas for several generations.

In other areas of the empire, especially outlying regions of the provinces, the emergence of basilical church buildings appears to have been scattered, and often quite late. In his survey of the archaeological remains of Libya (Roman Tripolitania) Ward-Perkins notes that almost all the surviving churches are of classical basilical type. But none can be dated before the fifth century, while the majority belong to the sixth century. In an effort to account for the data, he points to the slow progress of the spread of Christianity in the region due to its predominantly nonurban character. In other words, the architectural development was dependent on the social environment. Then, he suggests (almost as an afterthought) that the evidence of Christianity down to the fifth century probably presupposes a continued use of the domus ecclesiae.[56] These suggestions for North Africa (like Syria) find analogies in the provinces of Hispania and Britannia as well.[57]

From this preliminary survey of the archaeological evidence some observations may be drawn. Once we have severed any genetic evolution from house church to basilica, we must look to the progression from house to domus ecclesiae on its own terms. While the Dura Christian building remains the only clear and uncontested example prior to Constantine, the growing archaeological data suggest models of development in two ways. First, we must recognize a subtle process of architectural adaptation through incremental renovation of existing structures. Second, we must broaden our field of vision to account for the continuation of this pattern after the basilica has been introduced.

The body of data is annoyingly diverse and does not readily allow systematization, especially in traditional architectural terms. Of the cases known from archaeological remains no two are quite alike. There is no domus ecclesiae type as such. Instead, each one derives its form through adaptation (to greater or lesser degrees) of an existing edifice. Thus, local conditions relating to the type of building and the social circumstances of the Christian community played a more central role than abstract notions of architectural style. Indeed, in the absence of a normative architecture by which to evaluate archaeological peculiarities, social or communal factors tend to bear the weight of conjectural restoration among archaeologists, architects, and historians alike.[58] Krautheimer suggests three areas of historical development that affected architectural decisions: first, liturgical formalization, second, organization of the clergy, and third, other community functions (e.g., baptism).[59] Yet this array of factors falls largely in the category of worship needs, while attendant social factors are not considered. Carl Kraeling concurs in the light of the Dura Christian building. He suggests that continued adaptation and renovation were necessary to accommodate new needs and changing circumstances of Christian communities, especially prior to Constantine. He consciously looks to the character of particular physical adaptations as a clue to function and social-historical context.[60]

At this point the focus shifts away from architecture in the strictly aesthetic sense. We are concerned, rather, with the architectural definition and elaboration of communal worship space through adaptation and renovation of existing buildings. We must be concerned with both how and why such changes occurred, insofar as the archaeological evidence allows us to speculate. In the final analysis, it may be axiomatic that any decision on the part of a religious community to alter its place of assembly implies correlative and conscious needs or changes within the group itself. Thus, the recognition of architectural adaptation shifts the focus to the social circumstances and the environmental factors in this process.

3

"Private" Cults in a Constructive Context

The Adaptive Environment

▲ ▲ ▲

For any given city in the Roman Empire the religious landscape (literally and figuratively) was dominated by monumental public temples. At Rome itself and throughout the provinces—from Palmyra on the east to Colchester on the west—the remains bear witness to the position of such temples in civic life.[1] Festivals and processions were public affairs open to all. They attracted crowds from near and far. Of course the local magistracy attended in their official capacities, alongside the pious who came for personal religious reasons alone. In addition, depending on the renown of the temple, the locale, or the festival itself, there came an inevitable array of curiosity seekers and good-timers. The monumental public temples served as social centers, banks, markets, and seats of welfare distribution. Nor was their role entirely diminished by the end of the fourth century, when the Empire had become officially Christian.[2] Still, it would be misleading to see this religious landscape as too static and monolithic. These public temples were often undergoing renovation and rebuilding, and new projects for this or that Emperor's patron deity were constantly popping up. Furthermore, in the exchange and overlay of cultures from the Hellenistic period onward new religions came into play—cults and sanctuaries dedicated to Isis, Sarapis, Magna Mater Cybele, Attargatis, Mithras, and more. Eventually they took their places alongside the classical temples of old Rome, often copying classical forms. In some cases, however, new modes of cultic activity emerged in rather stark contrast to the monumental public domain. These more private cultic forms often grew out of the household setting or adapted domestic architecture for their activities.

"PRIVATE" CULTS IN A CONSTRUCTIVE CONTEXT

The Constructive Context

Construction work must have been a common sight and sound for anyone walking through the city streets of the Hellenistic-Roman world. It can fairly be said that almost everything in Rome is built on or from something earlier. The same is true, of course, of most mediterranean cities, where urban growth was upward more so than outward. Yet, the emperors of Rome especially tried to outdo one another in extravagant building programs both in the capital and in the provincial cities. A good example comes from the single fateful year 79–80 C.E. beginning with the eruption of Vesuvius and the destruction of Pompeii, Herculaneum, and the other resort cities of the Neapolitan coast. The historian Cassius Dio records events in Rome:

> In the following year [after the eruption of Vesuvius] another fire, this one on the surface of the earth, spread over much of Rome while Titus was away from the city dealing with the disaster which had occurred in Campania. The fire destroyed the temple of Sarapis, the temple of Isis, the *Saepta*, the temple of Neptune, the baths of Agrippa, the Pantheon, the *Diribitorium*, the theater of Balbus, the stage-front of the theater of Pompey, the buildings of Octavia with their books, and the temple of Jupiter on the Capitoline along with the surrounding temples.[3]

This list of major public buildings destroyed conveys a rather clear sense of the magnitude of construction that was required to maintain the marble splendor of an imperial facade.

Concerning this same episode Suetonius describes Titus' reaction:

> During the burning of the city Titus made no public statement other than a comment to the effect that he himself was "in ruins," and he set aside the ornaments of his country houses for use [in reconstruction] on the public buildings and temples; he also put several men of the Equestrian order in charge of the rebuilding, by which

appointments he was assured that everything would be done with unusual promptness.[4]

Construction, renovation, and remodeling were the order of the day in the Roman world; they were social realities of urban life. There were ample opportunities for building and rebuilding, both natural and contrived.[5] Whereas the fire of 80 was seen as divinely ordered, the one in 64 was more suspicious in origin. Nero, it would seem, had his means of stimulating urban renewal and building up Rome's glory, not to mention his own.[6] At a ceremony in 80 to dedicate the rebuilding, the poet Martial drew a satirical contrast between the construction of Nero and that of Titus. The scene was the newly completed Flavian amphitheater (the Colosseum), which had been built over pools and gardens of Nero's Domus Aurea, by filling them in with concrete to serve as foundations. One can just imagine Martial scanning around and pointing to the Forum, the Palatine, and, in the distance, the Caelian as he observes:

> Here where the glittering solar colossus views the stars more closely, and where in the central road lofty cranes (*pegmata*) rise aloft, the hateful hall of the beastly king [Nero's Domus Aurea] used to radiate its beams, at the time when a single house used to occupy the whole city. Here where the mass of the conspicuous and revered amphitheater rises up, the pools (*stagna*) of Nero once stood. Here where we marvel at the swiftly built donation, the baths [of Titus], an arrogant field had deprived the poor of their homes. Where the Claudian portico spreads its shade afar, the farthest part of the palace came to an end. Rome is restored to herself, and under your direction, O Caesar, those delights now belong to the people which once belonged to the master.[7]

Martial's piqued panorama of the new Rome under the Flavians is also a commentary on the social reality of construction in daily life. The constant pace of monumental public building, especially under imperial patronage, was the hallmark of a con-

"PRIVATE" CULTS IN A CONSTRUCTIVE CONTEXT

structive context both at Rome and in the major cities of the provinces.

If the sounds of construction echoed in the broad thoroughfares and public spaces of the capital, they must have reverberated through the narrow little streets and alleyways. In the lesser cities of Italy and throughout the provinces as well, imperial aegis stimulated massive construction programs. There were huge machines, cranes for hoisting this or that and architectural devices for accomplishing magnificent feats.[8] The prominence of guilds and collegia dedicated to various types of construction workers (*fabri*) suggests that they were an important social component in city life, matched by the wealthy civic benefactor (hailed *fabricator*) who underwrote public building programs.[9] The same is true at the meaner levels of social life in the cities. The mixed jumble of buildings—houses, shops, tenements, warehouses—were a din of daily activity and constant upkeep. They were also a constant fire hazard and a profitable marketplace for speculators.[10] The satirist Juvenal caricatures the state of residential life at Rome:

> Here we inhabit a city supported for the most part by slender props; for that is how the baliff patches up the cracks in the old wall, telling the inmates to sleep at ease under a roof ready to tumble about their ears. No, no, I must live where there are no fires, no nightly alarms. Ucalegon [the neighbor] below is already shouting for water and moving his chattels; smoke is pouring out of your third-floor attic above, but you know nothing of it; for the alarm begins on the ground floor.[11]

It cannot have been very different from the typical scene in Manhattan or London. Here on a main street stands a government building statuesque in granite and marble, now enveloped in a topsy-turvy maze of scaffolding as it undergoes renovation. Watch out for falling debris as you pass by. There next door in equal splendor is the monumental religious edifice representing the dominant or official cult of city and state. Here on a side street is a once fine apartment, now a squalid tenement. There in another part of town a modest, multilevel brownstone facade conceals a lavishly modernized townhouse; a warehouse has become chic loft apartments. Once out of the official sector of monumental and public buildings, the original architectural design of the exterior often belies an interior turned to an entirely new form and function. Construction continues as part of social life, much as Strabo lamented for his day:

> The building of houses goes on unceasingly in consequence of collapses and fires and repeated sales (these last, too, go on endlessly); in fact the sales are intentional collapses, so to speak, since the buyers keep razing the houses and building new ones, one after another, to suit their desires.[12]

These were not just idle quips. They reflect genuine fears and a bustle of building and construction that must have animated everyday urban life.[13]

Literature and inscriptions are full of data for public building programs enough to make fair guesses about public expenditures and construction costs.[14] What these economic data suggest as well is the range of social factors that accompanied the building process, not the least of which was the impulse toward individual acts of public benefaction, such as that of the younger Pliny toward Comum, his hometown. He gave funds for a new library along with an endowment for its upkeep (a total of 1,100,000 sesterces).[15] He also gave funds for the decoration and *tutela* (upkeep) of the public baths (HS 500,000), if not for the actual building of them (probably around another million).[16] To the town of Tifernum Tiberinum Pliny gave a set of imperial statues and, naturally, an appropriate temple to house them. It was dedicated at a public feast given at his own expense, at which Pliny was publicly declared patron and benefactor of the town.[17]

One can also glimpse similar social factors at work in connection with foreign religions. One such case records repair and renovation work on the Isis temple at Pompeii after it had been damaged in an earthquake. The construction was dedicated in the name of Numerius Popidius Celsinus, and it secured his enrollment in the local decurionate, even though he was only a boy of six. Over the gate from the street the inscription, obliged in the endowment of course, honors his piety:

> Numerius Popidius Celsinus, son of Numerius, rebuilt from its foundations with his own funds the temple of Isis, which had collapsed in an earthquake. On account of his generosity, even though he was six years old, the decurions of the city received him without cost into their own order.[18]

In this case, then, construction and dedication offers a commentary on the social position and connections of the boy's family both in Pompeian society and in the Isis cult. The elder Numerius was an aspiring freedman of the prominent *gens Popidii*, but former slaves were normally prohibited from the decurionate. By public acts of benefaction it was possible for the son to rise into the ranks of the local elite. It was a social exchange bartered in construction, by which the family traded the *humilitas* of slave and *libertus* for the *dignitas* of a decurion. This case also suggests issues in the spread and establishment of foreign religions in the Roman world, since an act of beneficence toward the temple complex of the Egyptian cult resulted in an honorary grant of public rank and status.

Private Cultic Activity in the Roman World

It is interesting that when A. D. Nock commences his discussion of the spread of oriental religions he focuses on the establishment of cult groups in local urban settings, developing his social description through archaeological and epigraphic evidence. Two inscriptions that attract special attention involve the Tyrian merchants' association at Puteoli and the early Sarapis cult of Delos.[19] One cannot ignore the fact that in these cases of oriental religions the evidence of diffusion emerges from social, political, and economic concerns, particularly those relating to the disposition of religious facilities, the cult buildings. As a measure of the spread of oriental religions, what can be discerned from the way the various groups went about establishing their cultic facilities?

The case of the Tyrian merchants at the port city Puteoli comes from the same year as the destruction of nearby Pompeii and the fire at Rome. An inscription dated 29 May 79 C.E. records the establishment of the cult of a god called Helios Saraptenos, a deity of the Phoenician coast. The name, a syncretistic amalgam, is the hellenized designation for the local "Ba'al of Sarapta," who was brought to Puteoli on divine command by a certain Elim (perhaps a priest).[20] The cultic association was made up largely of Tyrian merchants residing in Puteoli; there they formed their own commercial agency which also served as the center for their ancestral worship and ethnic identity. Later, however, dwindling numbers and other financial drains made upkeep of their rented quarters difficult. While we do not know what these quarters were like, they probably included some sort of collegial hall and a sanctuary for the god, though both could have been accommodated in rather modest space. The cultic association did not grow and expand with time; a century later the sanctuary was still housed in rented quarters. A second inscription from 174 C.E. preserves the text of a letter from the Puteoli merchants (now called *statiōnos*) to their native city. In it they requested financial assistance to pay the annual rent (*misthōsis*) of 250 denarii. The plea was urgent as the agency's treasury was strapped in preparing to honor the Emperor's birthday, probably by means of a banquet. Like other foreign groups, acceptance and patronage meant that they in turn were obligated to give an elaborate celebration, no mean fete.[21] The request was heard favorably by officials at Tyre, who agreed to divert revenues from another Tyrian agency at Rome as a continuing subvention of the rent. In this case, then, there was open and official recognition of the practice of establishing and maintaining foreign cultic activities in rented quarters. It seems that the Tyrian cult and commercial agency never made the move to monumental public architecture.

Hellenistic Precedents

The Tyrian merchants of Puteoli were continuing a process in the Roman period that had begun much earlier in the Hellenistic age. One of the earliest examples comes from the penetra-

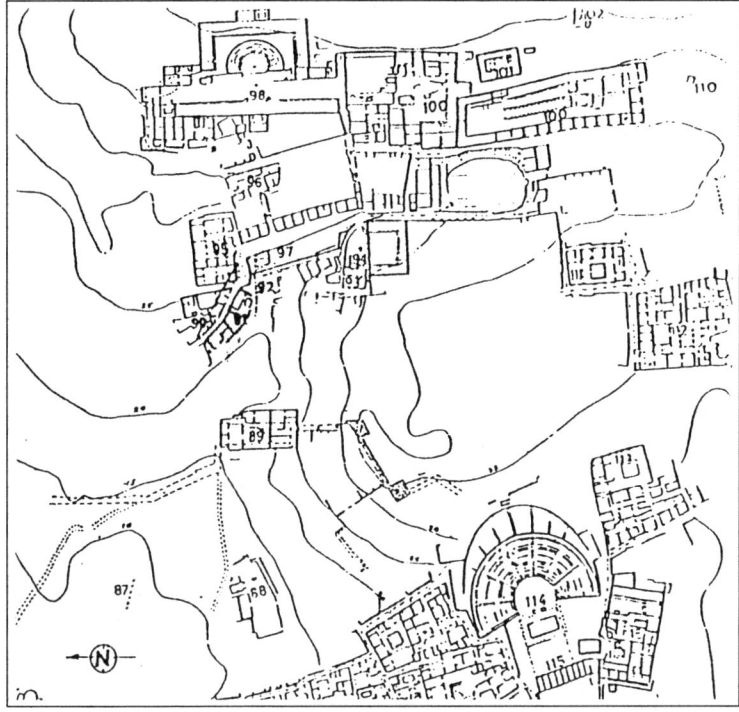

Fig. 1.
The "Terrace of the Foreign Gods" overlooking the Theater Quarter at Delos.

tion of the Egyptian cults into the Aegean during the Ptolemaic period.[22] According to the lengthy aretalogical inscription from Delos[23] the worship of Sarapis was brought to the island (early third century B.C.E.) by a hellenized Egyptian priest, who established the cult in his own apartment. There in rented domestic quarters the cult stayed for two generations, even though it attracted new adherents.[24] Finally, under the third priest, Apollonius (grandson and namesake of the founder), a proper temple (Sarapeion A) was built at the behest of the god Sarapis himself. Afterward the Egyptian cults grew in popularity, with three different temples and a position of prominence in that region of the island known as the "terrace of the foreign gods" (fig. 1).

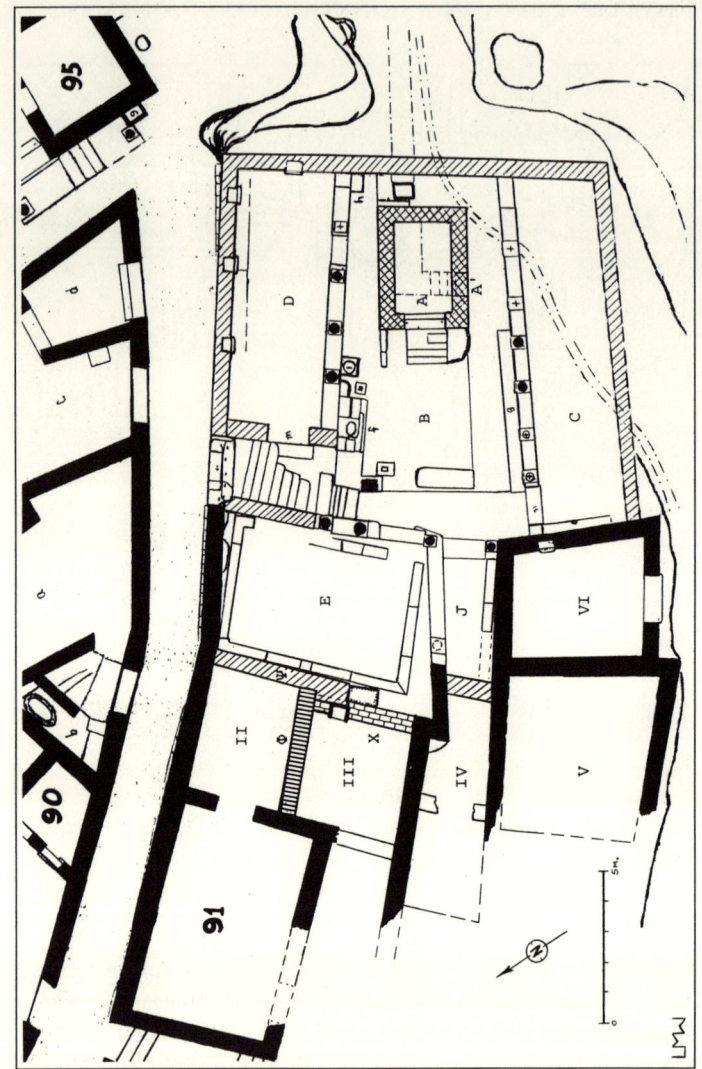

Fig. 2.
Plan restoration showing construction of Insula 91 and Sarapeion A at Delos.

The very name suggests the course of social history that ensued.[25]

It is striking that the early cult came under legal fire (having existed unimpeded for years) only after it built a formal temple, a house for the god. Why? Nock suggests that the conservative reaction rested on legal precedent: that Apollonius (II) had not obtained official authorization for establishing a temenos to a foreign god.[26] The basis for this interpretation followed recently by H. Engelmann and F. W. Danker,[27] lies in the claim of the inscription itself that the ground on which the Sarapeion was built was a "dung heap" (line 18f.: *topos . . . en koprou mestos*), a despised location (line 53: *aklea chōron onta paros kai asēmon*), that had long been undeveloped. On this interpretation, one would have thought that Apollonius was providing a social service (an ancient equivalent of urban renewal) by building the temple. The opposition is thereby assumed to have objected to the introduction of the foreign cult out of religious conservatism and prejudice. There is, however, another way of understanding the social circumstances of the Sarapis cult when one reads the inscription in the light of new archaeological data. A clue comes from the topographical history, by which P. Bruneau has questioned the literal rendering of the "defiled ground."[28] A more careful look at the building itself and its construction history raises further questions. (See fig. 2.)

Archaeological analysis of the construction reveals that Sarapeion A was built by architectural extension of an existing insula (GD 91)[29] of private buildings in the depression below the Inopos reservoir (GD 97). The ridge overlooking this depression was occupied by two existing domestic buildings (Houses 95 and 90). The precise lines of construction can be seen in three areas of the Sarapeion: first, in the extension of the north wall (beginning at the stairs) to form the east perimeter of the temenos;[30] second, in the construction of the west wall of Room E (the dining hall)[31]; and third, in the orientation of the naos (A) and the crypt (A′) beneath it on the axis of depressed area J of the earlier structure.[32] From these findings I conclude that Room E (originally part of insula 91) was taken over during construction of the temple on the undeveloped tract to the east, and that the Inopos drain was a focal point for the location of the naos. Dining room E, however, was the main area of social activity of the cultic community.[33]

These observations lead me to suggest that the "dung heap" refrain in the aretalogy is not literal but hyperbolic. After all, people lived on all sides without reservation, and a Nymphaion and Samothrakeion had already been established just up the hill (GD 92 and 93). Bruneau[34] links House 95 ("La Maison de l'Inopos") with epigraphic evidence for an office known as the *Inopophylax* or *krēnophylax*, the "guardian of the [sacred] spring of the Inopos." If, as Bruneau suggests, the reference is to the Inopos drain, then we begin to see that construction of the Sarapeion encroached on a local landmark, the sacred spring of personified Inopos, of which the neighbor in House 95 was the hereditary guardian. Not only did construction of the Sarapeion divert the drain from the reservoir (so important during the dry summer months), it also transformed its religious symbolism. For the naos crypt (A') of the Sarapeion, tied into the drain, served as a Nileometer, the sacred wellspring of the Nile.[35] The hyperbole may be seen, then, as a rhetorical device intended to offset the real charge against Apollonius, that the building of the Sarapeion had subverted or defiled sacred ground. By a clever reversal, Apollonius claims that the land was defiled (neglect by the *Inopophylax?*) and had been sanctified by the command of the god, a circumstance not unknown in the ancient world even on defiled ground.[36]

A second indictment against Apollonius may well have come from the fact that he had acquired and adapted private domestic property (Room E) for public cultic use.[37] In terms of the social circumstances of the land purchase and the plan of construction, one suspects that the adaptation of the dining hall and the new temple was more than just an expedient. I would suggest that Room E, as part of the existing area of GD 91, was the original location of the cult, the rented quarters (line 15f.: *en misthōtois*) where the elder Apollonius had lived and housed the god.[38] The worshippers of Sarapis would surely have known this, and it would have served as a symbol of the god's presence in their history, at their cultic meals,[39] and in the miraculous

"PRIVATE" CULTS IN A CONSTRUCTIVE CONTEXT

deliverance of Apollonius.[40] Thus, the history of the establishment of the cult in private quarters and the adaptation of these quarters into a sacred site are a powerful commentary on the social progress of the worship of Sarapis on Delos.

Roman Accommodations

Local establishment of small cults, both foreign and domestic, often used similar private settings throughout the Hellenistic and Roman periods. In some cases, however, the legal and social status of these groups must have changed. In his study, *The Hellenistic World and the Coming of Rome*,[41] Erich Gruen examines the nature of Roman imperialism in the Hellenistic world and its effects on Rome itself. One of the primary avenues of romanization was accommodation to Hellenistic conventions of diplomacy and personal interaction. Rome simply took over both formal (treaties, contracts, etc.) and informal (associations, etc.) models from the Greeks, commencing in the third century B.C.E. Thus, the Hellenistic conventions of friendship (Greek: *philia*) were adopted and adapted to suit Rome's design of creating political dependencies.[42] By equation with the Latin *amicitia, philia* was subjoined to the Roman model of *patrocinium* (patronage), growing out of Roman domestic practice. Yet patron-client relationships with Rome were readily cultivated by the Greeks as a way of exploiting Rome's power.[43] Thus, Rome did not simply mold the Greek world to its own ends; rather, Hellenistic structures provided the framework in which interrelationships developed in the Greek east. The impact of this social impulse on civic life and construction may be seen, for example, at Athens in the construction of Roman temples, the Hadrianic library, and other public buildings in and around the monuments of the classical city, the Agora and Acropolis. Under Hadrian the Roman senator Herodes Atticus built and dedicated the Odeon on the slope of the Acropolis itself.[44] The philhellenic patron Herodes bestowed similar benefactions on Corinth, Delphi, and Troas.

Through this same mechanism we find the variegated religions of the Greek east adopted into the Roman world as well. If we return for the moment to the history of Delos, now under

Roman control, we see the process continuing apace. Sarapeion C (GD 100; see fig. 1) on Delos was an expansive complex dominating the summit of the terrace of the foreign gods (beside the Temple of Syrian gods—GD 98).[45] It was built and maintained in direct contact with the provincial administration at Athens, under Rome's watchful eye, to become the official sanctuary to the Egyptian gods.[46] Here the relationship with the older Sarapeion (A) became turbulent. After around 166 B.C.E. there seems to have been a move by the official Egyptian cult (the priests and patrons of Sarapeion C) to shut down the more private associations of Sarapiasts that continued to use the sanctuary of Apollonius. The situation shows no religious conservatism, as there was open and direct competition between separate strands of Egyptian worship. Demetrius Rhenaius, the new priest of Sarapeion A and a descendent of the founder, Apollonius II, was forced to appeal for and receive a *senatus consultum* from Rome.[47] The reply was an official document transmitted by the Athenian *stratēgos* to the governor (*epimelētēs*) of Delos which upheld the rights of the private cultic *thiasoi* attached to Sarapeion A, the principle stated being nothing more than the prior history of the sanctuary.[48]

The irony is that a private Egyptian cult, imported to Greek soil, meeting in rented domestic quarters, with a hellenized Egyptian as priest, should be granted a formal, public charter by Rome on the basis of ancestral custom. Apparently in Rome's administration of the Greek east, local custom and the precedent of tradition, even recent tradition, counted for much. Architectural adaptation of an existing structure and the continued activities of the cultic association constituted a de facto public charter. Still it must be reckoned that the private cultic association of Sarapeion A did not have huge success in the public context. Instead, it was superseded locally by the introduction of a more public cult of the Egyptian gods under the patronage of Athens itself. Thus, even within related religious expressions there was competition for growth and support at the level of benefaction and building. The more adaptive cult, the pan-Egyptian Sarapeion C with its greater accommodation to romanized tastes, ultimately triumphed socially on Delos.

"PRIVATE" CULTS IN A CONSTRUCTIVE CONTEXT

It seems to me that we should begin to examine the effects of pluralism and privatization in the diffusion of cults. There is widespread evidence in the Greek east that new or imported religious and ethnic associations set up shop, at least initially, in more private quarters. In some cases, these private meetings occurred alongside public (and official) presence of the cult in the same area. Later on there was often a movement toward a more public, or even monumental, type of building. Sarapeion C on Delos was a monumental public edifice under Athenian patronage built de novo on the prominent summit of the terrace. With this movement on an architectural level, one tends to surmise a social progression as well. Thus, the case of Sarapeion A can be multiplied by a number of foreign groups on Delos, many of whom adopted and renovated domestic-style buildings. Some were elaborate collegial and merchant establishments, such as the House of the Poseidoniasts from Berytus.[49] On entering the hellenistic world of commerce, these Syrian shippers and merchants had equated their local god (a form of Ba'al) with the Greek Poseidon. Their collegial hall was an otherwise typical Delian peristyle house in design, located in the Skardana quarter overlooking the archaic Lion Terrace. On the interior it afforded a large hall for commercial and social functions while an inner court offered access to a sanctuary to their patron deities. Similarly on Delos we also find the Italian corporation of Hermaists, the Tyrian Herakleiasts, and collegial halls of a Jewish synagogue group and a Samaritan enclave.

There are further examples to be noted by glancing briefly at the Egyptian cults in the Aegean. For example, at Corinth in addition to public "temples" (no longer extant but known through literary references) the archaeological evidence reveals the existence of a private "chapel" to Sarapis created by adaptation and renovation of a shop in the South Stoa from the end of the first century C.E.[50] At Epidauros the Sanctuary of the Egyptian Gods, very much like the House of the Poseidoniasts at Delos, is attached to an elaborate peristyle house.[51] Other Egyptian sanctuaries from the Roman period to be studied in this light (as they show signs of adaptation or renovation) include those at Philippi, Ephesus, Priene, and Gortyn, Crete.[52]

One significant feature of the Egyptian cults, especially those associated with the worship of Sarapis, was the practice of communal dining. This was often reflected, as in Sarapeion A at Delos, in the special provision for a dining room attached to the sanctuary.[53]

Privatization and Adaptation

Still more examples can be found on the eastern *limes* of the Roman Empire at Dura-Europos, a Roman garrison and trade stop on the Euphrates. Having grown up under the Hellenistic monarchies (third century B.C.E.) and the Parthian empire (first century B.C.E. through first century C.E.), the city developed a cosmopolitan and syncretistic religious culture, despite its relative isolation. The prominence of monumental public temples in daily life can be seen in the development of a peculiar Durene temple type, which can be found in Greek, Parthian, and Roman construction.[54] One characteristic feature of these temples is the provision for several private dining chambers on the perimeter of the sacred precincts. Three Durene temples are of particular interest, since all were constructed on property previously occupied by private houses and shops: the Temple of Adonis, the Temple of Zeus Theos, and the Temple of Gadde. In each case, the temple achieved its final form during the middle part of the second century C.E., during which time the Romans captured the city (under Trajan), ceded it once again to the Parthians (under Hadrian), and then took final possession of it in the campaign of Lucius Verus (166–168 C.E.). Thus, their history reflects the appropriation and accommodation of Roman rule to the religious and social expressions of Hellenistic-oriental culture.

Most of the earlier houses on the site of the Temple of Adonis were leveled, and the temple complex was superimposed on this foundation. On either end of the complex, however, houses left intact were incorporated architecturally into the construction. On the north end a house became part of the main sanctuary, and on the south end a house became part of a smaller naos, or perhaps a telesterion. Houses continuing in domestic use bounded the entire length of the complex on the

"PRIVATE" CULTS IN A CONSTRUCTIVE CONTEXT

east side.[55] On the west side stood nine small dining "chapels," some of which were dedicated privately by individuals or small cell groups within the larger public cult of Adonis. The dining rooms were individually appointed and decorated as acts of private devotion to the god. One (designated Chapel 38) was dedicated by a confraternity of eight men with Semitic names who are said to have "erected the edifice" (*anegeirentes ton oikon*).[56]

In a similar fashion the Temple of Zeus Theos was built over an insula block of private houses completed around 114–120 C.E.[57] The central portions of the complex contain the usual open-air temenos created by razing the existing houses on the site, and the sanctuary proper (with traditional naos and pronaos) was centered in the western half. On the perimeter, however, the earlier houses were not destroyed, but were systematically refurbished to serve as triclinial dining chapels. Consequently, some of them are a bit irregular, and a number are actually double chambers. Some also have special provisions for seating, such as a thronos, in addition to the more typical benches. These chapels were privately dedicated and decorated. The largest and most prominent double chapel (Rooms 24/31) was dedicated by a major benefactor of the construction of the temple complex.[58]

The Temple of Gadde, a local Palmyrene deity, was begun in Hellenistic times and progressed through four stages of construction to achieve its final form in the early Roman period (ca. 159 C.E.). In the first stage (period I) it was an unpretentious "chapel" in a private domestic complex. Gradually it grew, incorporating the surrounding houses, and underwent a final renovation in period IV. This final plan was unusual even by Durene standards, since it comprised a double temenos, each with its own naos and chapels, connected by an intervening court (cf. fig. 3). Its peculiarities can be explained by the constraints of renovating existing domestic buildings for religious use.[59] In period I the domestic plan seems to have remained largely unchanged. From the remains of periods II and III it can be seen that the final complex incorporated three contiguous houses (fig. 4, designated A, B, C). In periods I and II, then, House B

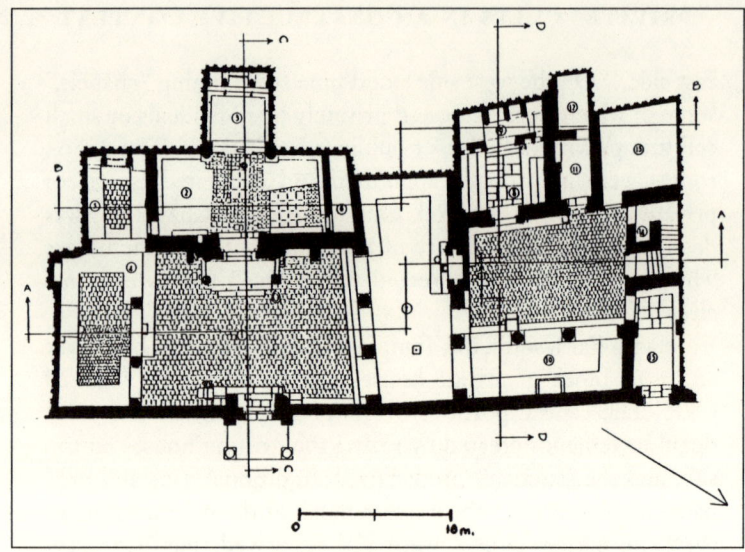

Fig. 3.
Plan reconstruction of the Temple of Gadde at Dura-Europos during Period IV.

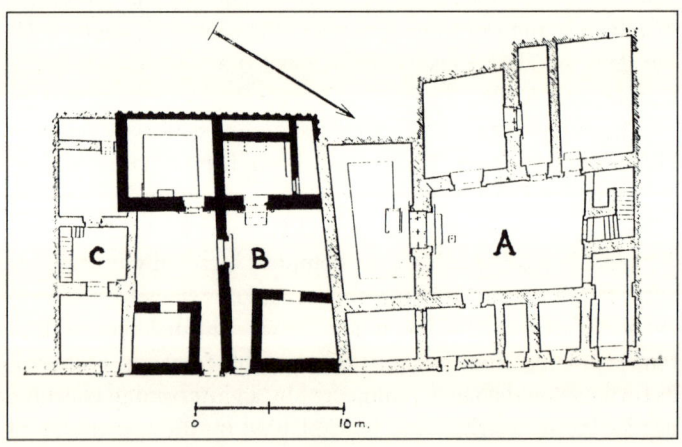

Fig. 4.
Plan reconstruction of the Temple of Gadde at Dura-Europos during Period III.

was the site of domestic activity and a small cult chapel. During the period II renovation (ca. 50 B.C.E.) the interior of House B was demolished to open up a large court, which led to a diwan (living/dining room) and served as the entry chamber for the sanctuary proper.[60] House A was built at this time, probably to serve more of the domestic functions of the family displaced by the expansion of the cultic facility in House B. In period III (ca. 50–150 C.E.) the process of gradual adaptation resulted in the taking over of all of House B for the cult. The diwan was enlarged and segregated, and the sanctuary proper was made more formal and given entry from the court (fig. 4).[61] At this stage House A remained unchanged, a private dwelling. Only in period IV (ca. 150–159 C.E.) was the entire complex transformed into the monumental public temple with a double temenos.[62] House A was then incorporated directly into the temple, while the sanctuary of House B was remodeled into a more formal naos with pronaos and court in the style of Durene temples. House C was taken over to serve as a private dining area associated with the complex.

This architectural progression indicates the growth of the cult from a small domestic setting to monumental public proportions. Through the epigraphic remains it may be possible to correlate this architectural development with the social circumstances of a group of ethnic Palmyrenes, mostly merchants, living in Dura from the second century B.C.E. The temple served as a guild hall and social center as well as a religious sanctuary. One prominent family seems to have held a leading position in the sanctuary's operations through several generations and with substantial benefactions to the temple.[63] We might well guess that the local worship of Palmyrene Gadde was initially established in the private home (House B) of this family, and that eventually the entire house was devoted to the cult. Later, an adjacent property, House A, was probably acquired or built by them, and it too was subsequently given over to the public cult in the final transformation.[64] The ability to trace the process of adaptation through several stages of construction and renovation provides invaluable social data.

A survey of the local religious landscape at Dura-Europos

over time indicates that this process of gradual appropriation and adaptation was commonly followed. A guild of professional scribes took over two houses and renovated them into a collegial establishment[65] in the same block as the synagogue, also renovated from a house. Down the street in one direction stood the renovated domus ecclesiae of the Christians; in the other direction was the house renovated to become a mithraeum. In case after case, year after year, these small religious associations adapted private domestic structures for public religious or collegial use. The ability to acquire such property and adapt it for special use through architectural renovation had significant impact on the social fabric of the city.

In yet another case from Dura three inscriptions, spoils from the mithraeum block, record the establishment of a private sanctuary to an unnamed god.[66] The dedicants were a father and son, who successively held the prominent office of "herald of the city" (*kēryx tēs poleōs*). The father, Epinicus, who called himself priest of the god, founded the sanctuary near the end of the first century C.E. The son, Alexander, renovated and enlarged the sanctuary and its antechambers, and added on an *oikos* (perhaps a dining chapel). Since there was no temple in this region of the city, it is likely that these texts refer to the growth of a private household sanctuary, analogous perhaps to the earlier stages of the Temple of Gadde. Unfortunately, there is no physical evidence of what the inscriptions are describing. It is not impossible that this same house-sanctuary later became the mithraeum.[67]

Such household sanctuaries are rarely discernible from the archaeology precisely because they required minimal adaptation and articulation of the cultic space. For the most part they remained domestic in form and function. Nonetheless, there seems to have been a widespread practice of establishing such household cults. At Priene on the Aegean coast of provincial Asia, for example, a private house-sanctuary dedicated to the deified Alexander was discovered just down the street from another house converted into a synagogue.[68] To create the sanctuary of Alexander the oecus (or living room) of the house was outfitted with religious equipment to serve as the naos, while other rooms in the house seem to have continued in domestic use. Thus, it is not entirely clear whether there was a cult group attached to this sanctuary apart from the household itself. It is not uncommon to find cults constituted entirely of members of one household. Such was the case of the cult of the Bacchantes at Tusculum headed by Pompeia Agripinilla, wife of one of the consuls for the year 127 C.E.[69] The nearly 500 initiates (*mystae*) mentioned in the inscription were ordered according to cultic ranks and offices, but were actually all members of Pompeia's household, including her slaves. Significantly the matron of the house also held the highest office, as priestess and patron. A similar private religious association is known from Philadelphia, Lydia, and dated to the first century B.C.E. A marble stele records the rules of the association given by the patron deity, Agdistis (a form of the Magna Mater). Agdistis, called mistress of the house, delivered the rules to Dionysius, the owner of the house and patron of the cultic association.[70] The rules make provision for "both men and women, both slave and free" to enter, but the designation of slaves as *oiketai* probably means that they too were members of Dionysius' household. The purity rules of the cult, though stated generically, were in fact oaths of conduct to be taken by the paterfamilias and his extended household. In this way the rules and the cultic organization served to reinforce the internal social structure of the household. The text imposes these rules on "all who enter," suggesting that the house was somehow conceived as the sanctuary of Agdistis, although there is no archaeological evidence for the precise nature of the architectural form. Since the text mentions altars to ten "savior gods," it is not unlikely that some sort of architectural adaptation was made. Yet, possible relationships of the cult beyond the family network are unclear.[71]

Several other examples of the cult of the Magna Mater, in its diverse forms, reinforce this view of private household associations that stood alongside the more public and monumental cult. From an earlier period there was a cult group, calling itself a community of initiates (*koinon tōn mystōn*) of the Mother of the Gods at Argos, which held its religious observances (*thrēskeia*) in the garden of a house (*oikia*) dedicated for this purpose.[72]

Dedications of Attis statues are known from domestic shrines.[73] At Rome, in addition to the formal temple of Magna Mater on the Palatine there are indications of other places of cultic activity, such as the so-called Phrygianum on the Vatican and the small tholos on the Via Sacra (near the Arch of Titus) dedicated privately by members of the *gens Haterii*.[74] Another group dedicated to the Magna Mater and *Navisalvia* seems to have assembled in the area of the river Emporium during the early to mid-first century C.E.[75] One of the inscriptions from this context suggests that the group had its own identity as a more private cultic association: *Matri deum / et navi Salviae Q. Nunnius / Telephus mag(ister) / col(legi) culto(rum) eius / d(e) s(uo) d(ono) d(at)*.[76] A late second-century house situated on the Caelian also contained a private household sanctuary for the cult of the Magna Mater. Usually called the *Basilica Hilariana*, the site took its name from the owner of the house, a pearl merchant (*margaritarius*) named Manius Publicius Hilarus.[77] A private room off a recessed atrium served as the meeting place (*schola*) of a private group known as the Association of Treebearers (*Collegium dendrophorum*). Another inscription in mosaic by the entrance suggests that the hall was named in honor of the owner of the house and patron of the cult group: "For those who here approach the propitious gods who are also of the Basilica Hilariana" (*intrantibus hic deos propitios et Basilic[ae] Hilariana*).[78] It is suggested that these individual cult groups also maintained connections with the other, more official or public forms of worship of the Magna Mater, especially at major public festivals;[79] however, it remains significant that they could be organized as collegia in adapted private quarters.

These cases suggest a natural and accepted practice of establishing the social lines of cult organization as a diverse mix of household cults, smaller cell groups, and collegial associations within the broader environment of major cities.[80] The categories often overlap, as cults could be incorporated into collegia. In other cases one finds households organized as cults, or cultic associations meeting in private homes. One particularly interesting case involves the reference to a *Collegium quod est in domu Sergiae Paullinae* (CIL VI, 9148). Attested by six other variants,[81] this inscription represents a well-established collegium made up of the members of an extended family (including slaves and clients). The text has often been cited in discussions of early Christianity because of the similarity with the name of Sergius Paulus in Acts 13.7, and it has been suggested that the collegium was actually a Christian house church at Rome in the second century.[82] While this contention is unfounded, it does suggest a line of comparative analysis as diverse forms of private religious activity were able to adopt and adapt domestic architecture for cultic and social functions. An especially prominent social function, albeit with ritual and cultic significance, was the communal meal. These private cell groups offered greater intimacy and social interaction, whether they were attached directly to public temples or met in more private surroundings.[83] They reflect a model of social interaction that was fundamental to the diffusion and maintenance of religious groups.

A Roman Phenomenon: The Mithraeum

Among the "oriental" religions, Mithraism was a uniquely Roman phenomenon, and so constitutes a special test case with a number of similarities to Christianity.[84] Although evidenced in the west by inscriptions from the end of the first century, the cult of Mithras was still something of an unknown quantity when Plutarch described it in the second century.[85] By the end of the second century, however, it had witnessed a rapid diffusion throughout the empire, especially in and around Rome.

In the romanized cult of Mithras it is possible to speak of a typical layout for the sanctuary, called a mithraeum.[86] The dominant symbolism is of a cave.[87] The underworld connotations seem to have contributed to both its secrecy and its air of supernatural expectancy. Yet the vaulted ceilings of the mithraea were often decorated with stylized stars, a "canopy of the heavens," or other lighting effects designed to appeal and attract.[88] The main room was an elongated hall (the "cave" itself), with the altar or small shrine at the far end. A central aisle stretched the length of the hall with raised benches (*podia*) on either side. Often access to the hall itself was restricted, with entry gained through a vestibule (pronaos) and occasionally through other rooms. A distinctive feature of this layout is its integral placement of the sanctuary proper (the naos in typical temples) within an assembly hall, where initiation, social functions, and communal dining were held. The cult niche and its articles of worship (the altar, cult symbols, and images of Mithras) were the focal point of the communal assembly.[89] Since the halls were usually quite small they were necessarily intimate and private expressions of cultic activity.[90]

Architecture and Adaptation

Despite the typical elements of layout and iconography there was great diversity among mithraea in the Roman world, which suggests factors in both the adaptability and the diffusion of the cult. Thus, we may offer some rough statistical observations on the profusion of mithraic sanctuaries in the Roman Empire. Of fifty-eight mithraea known through architectural remains[91] no more than fourteen (and the number may be closer to ten) can be determined to have been specifically constructed de novo as cult buildings; almost all such cases come from western provinces (Britannia, Gallia, Germania).[92] In Italy, which has by far the greatest concentration of extant mithraea (a total of twenty-five sites), only one (at Angera in Cispadana) was specially constructed de novo as a mithraeum.[93]

It is by far more common (as in all fourteen sites at Ostia and seven at Rome) to find mithraea established within preexisting structures, including warehouses,[94] baths,[95] cryptoportici (of all sorts),[96] vaulted subterranean storage chambers,[97] and (of course) private homes.[98] Architectural adaptation might be nothing more than minimal internal remodeling to demark and segregate the sanctuary from its physical surroundings. In other cases, multiple stages of renovation eventuated in more substantial and elaborate cultic facilities. Thus, while the interior arrangement of mithraea conformed to a typical layout, there was great variety in plans and proportions owing to the diverse structures in and from which they were built. There was not an exterior architectural iconography (and only the merest hint of one for the interior layout as a "cave") that prevailed translocally and that was transmitted as theological content (either explicit or implicit). Thus, too, the process of establishment, adaptation, and maintenance must be reckoned from the social circumstances of each individual Mithraic conventicle.

At Ostia, for example, the Mithraeum of Callinicus was built (after ca. 140 C.E.) in two small, rear chambers on the ground floor of the Casa di Diana insula.[99] The size and shape were compressed because of the small amount of available space, and there was only minor interior remodeling to accommodate the aisle/bench layout. So small and restrictive is the plan that G. Becatti presumed it to be a private family sanctuary;[100] however, in addition to the main donor, M. Lollianus Callinicus (who was designated *pater* and *sacerdos*), and some members of his household,[101] two other prominent individuals made donations to the sanctuary. The fact that this mithraeum did not show more growth and renovation may say something about decline and disuse, since one of the major donors, M. Caerellius Hieronimus (designated *sacerdos*)[102] later showed up in a prominent position in the much larger and more elaborate *Mitreo degli animali* at Ostia.[103]

Other mithraea show much greater levels of adaptation, especially as they went through several stages of renovation. Close examination of the *Mitreo delle pareti dipinit* ("Mithraeum of the Painted Walls"; fig. 5) suggests a progressive enlargement and segregation of the sanctuary in two phases of construction in the rear chambers and cortile of a ground floor domus.[104] The nature of the construction, especially the enlargement of the second phase, suggests numerical growth of the cult group corresponding to the greater diffusion of Mithraism at Ostia, and the progressive segregation of this sanctuary.[105]

At Rome the Aventine Mithraeum (under the present church of Sta. Prisca; see fig. 6) was originally built (ca. 194/195) in one small aisle of a cryptoporticus beneath an imperial palace. A major renovation project during the third century more than doubled its area (through adaptation and outfitting of three adjacent rooms) and provided elaborate decorations.[106] We should not conclude too hastily that the location of a small sanctuary in a basement indicated disadvantaged social placement. At least a moderate degree of wealth and social standing is suggested for Aventine Mithraeum I (during the Severan period), given the acquisition and adaptation of the cryptoporticus of an urban palazzo. Some connection with the imperial household is perhaps indicated. In the renovation to stage II (ca. 220), moreover, considerable numerical growth is indicated and was probably correlated with an overall rise in socioeconomic level to have enabled the use of three additional rooms and to have provided for the construction and elaborate decorations.[107]

The Dura-Europos mithraeum (figs. 7 and 8) provides further clues to its social makeup by the peculiar availability of archaeological and epigraphic data through three distinct phases of renovation. The sanctuary was originally installed in one room of a private house with very little renovation save internal decoration. Since the sanctuary was founded by two Palmyrene *stratēgoi* (Ethpeni and Zenobios) stationed at Dura after the eastern campaign of Lucius Verus (ca. 168–171), it is likely that the first small conventicle was made up of predominantly oriental military personnel of upper and middle rank.[108] Since the rest of the house retained its domestic character in the first stage, it is likely that the owner of the house had connections with the Mithraic group. Perhaps the building was owned or acquired by Ethpeni or Zenobios.[109]

Given the private and restrictive character of the first stage, the alterations of the middle mithraeum were quite dramatic. The physical renovation involved demolishing much of the house's superstructure except in the room of the mithraeum proper. Using the side walls of this room for orientation an addition was erected to create the elongated hall, with one interior chamber and a vestibule. Extension of the side podia along each wall of the hall and vertical articulation of the "naos" suggest heightened economic and social location for a numerically larger conventicle. These changes are correlated with reinforcement of the garrison with *vexillationes* from the IV Scythian and XVI Flavia Firma legions in preparation for Caracalla's Persian campaign (ca. 209–211).[110] Commander of the reinforced garrison was the *centurio princeps* (or head of the military *officium*), Antonius Valentinus, who also dedicated the

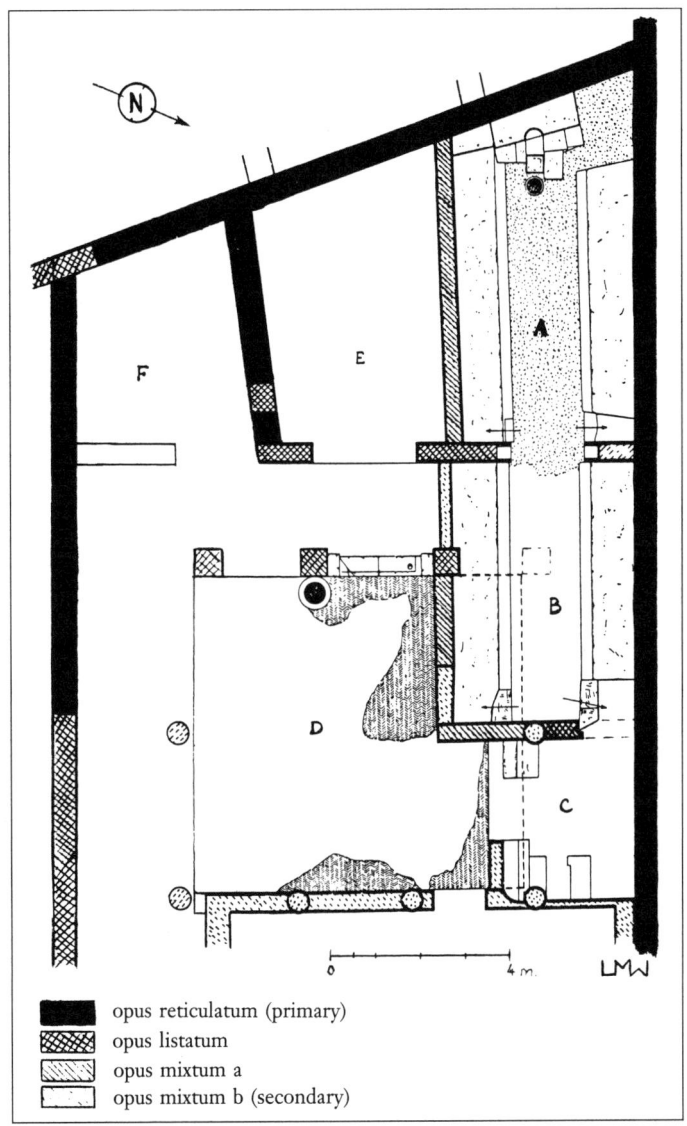

Fig. 5.
Plan restoration of the *Mitreo della pareti dipinti* ("Mithraeum of the Painted Walls") at Ostia.

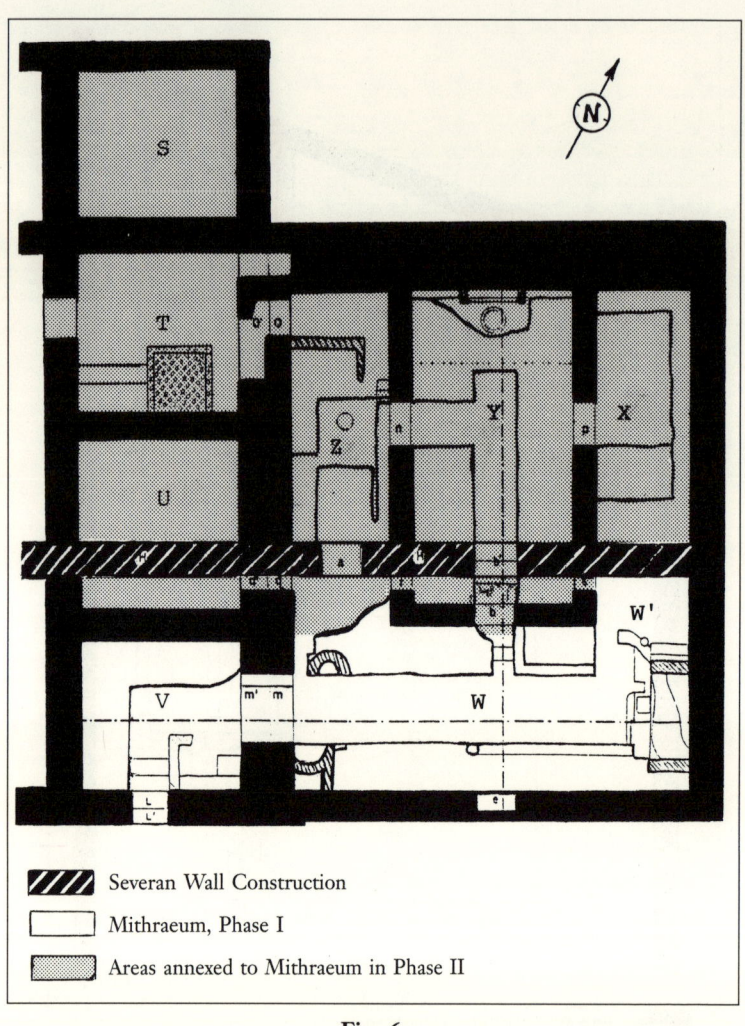

Fig. 6.
Plan restoration of the Aventine Mithraeum at Rome.

construction of the rebuilt mithraeum.[111] The period of the middle mithraeum showed the most vigorous growth and activity, at least insofar as epigraphic remains indicate.[112] At this point the building had become publicly identifiable and, thus, de facto (if not de jure) the property of the local Mithraic cult.

In its third phase (after ca. 240) the sanctuary was enlarged and elaborated further, using the basic plan of the middle mithraeum. This renovation included expanding the seating capacity of the *podia* through an interior structural modification, and an addition in size by annexing external chambers. The more spectacular changes, however, came in the physical enlargement and artistic elaboration of the tauroctone niche to form a vaulted altar platform: a sacred *spelaeum* with a canopy of stars. The elaboration of the last stages indicates further growth with greater wealth and public recognition.[113] The sanctuary gradually moved to a more formal architectural iconography; however, it is clear that basic siting and orientation, as well as certain architectural peculiarities, derived from the original adaptation of a private home.[114] Adaptability, then, is a two-edged sword as the cult adapted to its surroundings and adapted them to its own use.

Adaptation and Diffusion: Social Factors

Conspicuous in the diffusion of Mithraic sanctuaries is the role of patrons and benefactors who acquired and renovated property and supplied decoration. In general the semiprivate cultic associations such as mithraic conventicles do not seem to have purchased property outright in the manner of investors. They obtained it by gift (donation or dedication), sometimes as property itself or as trust backed by property. Major temples and cult centers also amassed considerable resources in this manner.[115] In the case of Mithraism, one of the most common expressions found in the dedicatory inscriptions for building, remodeling, and decoration is *sua pecunia fecit*, "made at his own expense."[116] Indeed, the fortunes of any given facility (seen as long-term growth or decline) are probably correlated with the beneficence and motivation of a few leading individuals. These data, compounded from each local case, may begin to reshape our tradi-

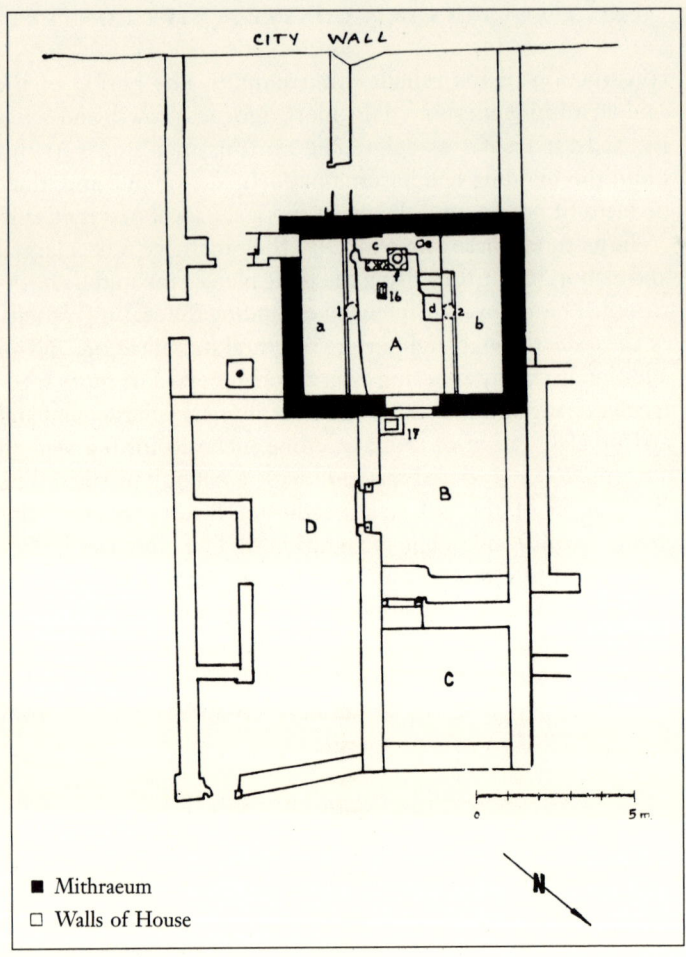

Fig. 7.
Plan restoration of the Early Mithraeum and Parthian period house at Dura-Europos.

Fig. 8.
(opposite page) Plan restoration of the middle and late stages of renovation of the Mithraeum at Dura-Europos.

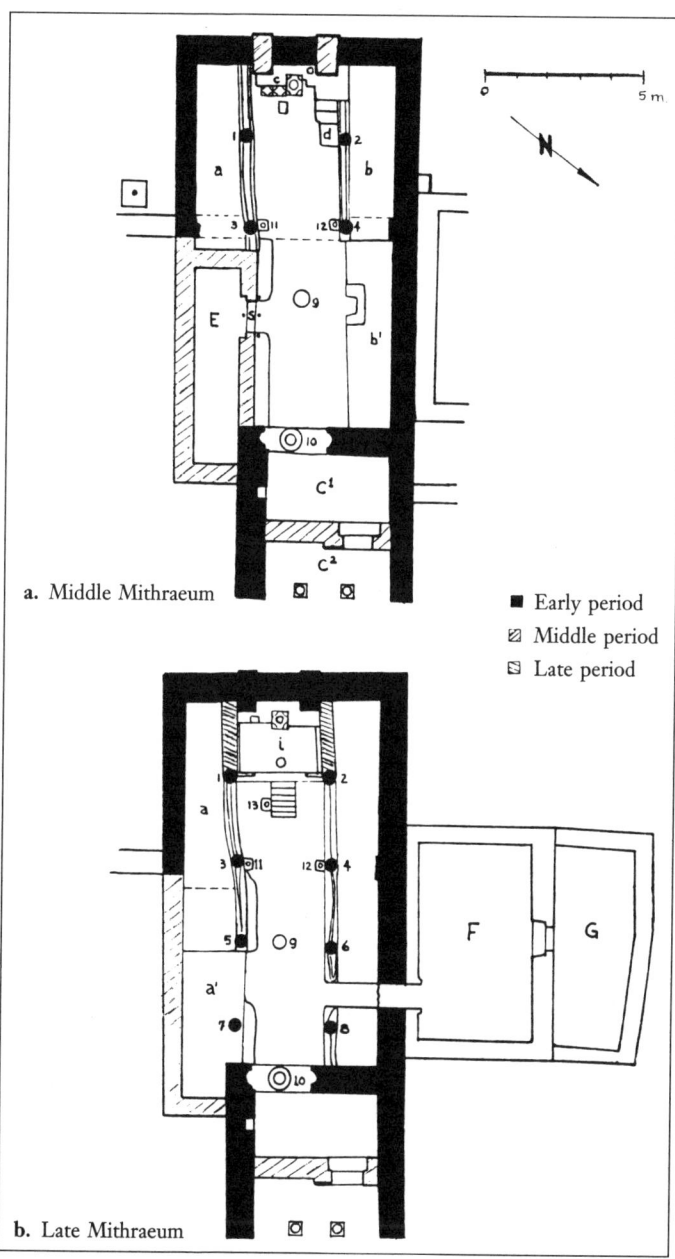

a. Middle Mithraeum

- Early period
- Middle period
- Late period

b. Late Mithraeum

tional assumptions about the social composition, patterns of organization, and translocal diffusion of Roman Mithraism as a religious movement.

Since Cumont's time, it has been thought that Mithraism was primarily a cult of the military and that the army provided the most obvious lines of diffusion and recruitment.[117] In certain cases, to be sure, Mithraism did travel with the legions, particularly on the borders of the Roman Empire.[118] Yet, in other cases, especially the major urban centers where Mithraism gained its greatest following, there seems to have been little direct influence of the military. This is especially evident at Rome and Ostia, but it is also the case in some of the provinces that were not heavily garrisoned. In Pannonia, for example, the administrative seat Poetovio (Ptuj) had three known mithraea, of which only one (Temple III, the latest) was predominantly military. Of the other two, one (Temple II) had a mixed membership of military and administrative officials, while the other (Temple I, the earliest) was founded by an enclave of eastern personnel mostly in the imperial bureaucracy.[119] Similarly, in the lightly garrisoned province of Gaul, it seems that Mithraism was brought in mostly by orientals with Greek *cognomina*, including slaves, freedmen, and members of corporations.[120] The successful establishment of the cult in this region depended upon the continued activity of these oriental transplants, and only gradually did the cult begin to attract romanized Gauls of higher social standing.[121]

In this way, too, architectural adaptation and renovation may be a barometer of the success of diffusion and establishment on a local level. There is ample epigraphic evidence of local mithraea going to "rack and ruin" as a sign of decline.[122] At Virunum, the provincial capital of Noricum, epigraphic remains reflect activities of a mithraic conventicle spanning a little more than a century. The mithraeum went through phases of active use with intervening periods of desertion and neglect as it collapsed and was restored on two occasions separated by some fifty years.[123] Of the extant inscriptions associated with this site, only one seems to have military connections,[124] while four others came from members of the provincial administration: a governor (*praeses*) of equestrian rank,[125] a notary (*tabularius*), a treasurer (*arkarius*), and two department heads (a *dispensatoris arkarius* and a *praefectus vehiculorum*).[126] It is likely, then, that the mithraeum was established by transient members of the imperial bureaucracy, including an occasional legionary officer attached to the provincial *officium*. The roller coaster fortunes of the local Mithraic cell, and with them the architectural fortunes of the mithraeum, were determined by the shifting climate of provincial administration.[127] Growth and adaptation was predicated more on individual acts of patronage and benefaction than on patterns of conversion or recruitment.

Mithraism relied heavily on the support of its wealthy patrons, who made it possible to acquire property and renovate (or construct) a sanctuary. Ongoing acts of individual benefaction and dedication account for further embellishment, decoration, and outfitting of these sanctuaries with everything from incidentals (basins, wicks, etc.) to the essential tauroctones and altars. Time after time they gave in dedication to Mithras, repeating a phrase so often heard that it needed only the merest chiseled hint to recognize these personal acts of piety. On artifacts and walls, the great and small, one observes *DSDD* or some equivalent formula: *D(e) S(uo) D(ono) D(at)*, someone's pious legacy. Thus, more often than not individual religious inclinations were expressed practically through such personal acts of patronage and benefaction. As Ramsay MacMullen puts it: "Paganism, . . . for us to recognize it in its familiar forms, required the patrons who paid for its temples."[128]

In a majority of cases we find mithraic dedications and inscriptions from leading patrons who also held one or more of the higher offices or grades within the cult. Major building donations were commonly made by individuals designated as *pater* or *pater patrorum, pater sacrorum*, and *sacerdos*.[129] Occasionally several leading members, a *pater* and a priest or a coterie of up-and-comers, combined efforts in a given project or donation.[130] Some major donors came from lower grades of initiation,[131] but the rank and status of most within the cult paralleled their rank and status outside, and mithraic organization followed more on the lines of collegia.[132]

The leadership and beneficence of prominent patrons was crucial to acquisition of property, renovation and construction, and ongoing growth and development of the cult. The so-called seven grades of initiation characteristic in our literature on Mithraism were perhaps more socially determined than has been generally recognized.[133] Occasionally, titles such as *corax* and *leo* are found in peculiar combinations with leading cultic roles (*pater* or *prosedente*). More often than not, however, the highest cultic grades (*pater* or *sacerdos*) also belonged to individuals who made significant donations to the cultic establishment, especially for renovation and construction.[134]

There was not a strict translocal homogeneity in the diffusion of Roman Mithraism. Local mithraic communities or individual cells seem to have followed their own internal social organization. Some were regimented more along military lines and probably drew on the army for members. Others observed the social hierarchy of local urban cultures in areas where military garrisons were less evident. Yet in each type of organization, rank and status were bestowed on those who served as patrons of the cult. Especially honored were patrons who contributed to the construction, renovation, maintenance, and decoration of the cult building, "the sacred cave of Invincible Mithras."

The Adaptive Environment

Mithraism, along with most other forms of official paganism, did not survive the onslaught of Christian expansion after the fourth century.[135] Still it is an excellent example of the environment for diffusion of foreign cults in the later Republic and, especially, under the Principate. By way of conclusion, then, two aspects should be noted that bear on the process of diffusion and architectural adaptation. First, the mix of cultures that so annoyed Tacitus and amused Juvenal produced an official tolerance of pluralism and diversity. Wherever foreigners settled they were free to perpetuate their ancestral customs. Of course, countervailing social pressure loomed large to accommodate language, lore, and custom to the patterns and styles of the dominant culture, first Greek and then Roman. Social con-

"PRIVATE" CULTS IN A CONSTRUCTIVE CONTEXT

ventions of patronage and benefaction often provided the avenue for foreigners and those of the lower orders, like Petronius' Trimalchio, to enter the mainstream. Cultic groups also moved into the mainstream by these social conventions. The tendency toward accommodation, however, often resulted in tension concerning preservation of the ancestral ways. Accommodation and integration were not complete. Thus, the other aspect to be noted is a tendency toward what we have termed *privatization* in social and religious activities. Merchants, guilds, collegia, brotherhoods, and cults of all sorts flourished, especially in the major urban centers. There seems to have been a social need for people with a common bond to band together, and this need was most often expressed in organizations that had some sort of religious or cultic identity. Even when there was a public or official cult, there were often private cells dedicated to the same deity. Both in the public cult and in the private cells, moreover, the urge to build, which so enervated the Roman world, was pervasive. Yet, especially among the more private groups, this urge resulted in diverse forms of smaller cultic buildings, often adapted from the architecture of the urban environment. One sees, then, from top to bottom in the Roman world a social context that fostered and honored construction and renovation. Patronage and benefaction were important mechanisms in this process as they offered direct access to the social and economic mainstream.

4

Synagogues in the Graeco-Roman Diaspora

Jewish Adaptation and Accommodation

▲ ▲ ▲

By the early Roman period there were also many Jews traveling the highways and trade routes, to the major urban centers of the Hellenistic east, and as far west as Italy and North Africa. In some cases they may have been taken as slaves, only later becoming freedmen with attendant status and rights. In other cases their mobility was prompted by business or commerce, affairs of state as well as affairs of status. Slaves, merchants, mercenaries, entrepreneurs, and the occasional scholar or public figure; all appeared from time to time in the Diaspora. However they came, Jews carried their ancestral traditions and worship with them, to varying degrees, as they established community life in ethnic enclaves.[1] Many Jews of the Diaspora maintained ties with the Homeland and particularly with the Temple, so long as it stood. Nevertheless, the process of diffusion could not but create diversity and tension. The issue is not a simplistic distinction in theology between Palestinian and Hellenistic Judaism. After all, there was great diversity among the various groups, currents, and sects within Palestine itself, and Palestinian social life had become thoroughly infused with Hellenistic and Roman language as well as cultural ideals.[2]

The main difference for Diaspora Jews was the response to living as aliens, as an ethnic and religious minority, in the dominant culture of urban life first in the cities of the Greek east and then in Rome itself. Trying to balance the equation between tradition and accommodation produced diverse responses in framing Jewish identity. Some Jews, like Tiberius Julius Alexander, Philo's nephew, apostatized altogether in pursuit of Roman culture. How many others chose this path is hard to guess, precisely because their Jewish heritage is so seldom recorded.

SYNAGOGUES IN THE GRAECO-ROMAN DIASPORA

Most others chose some middle path of maintaining Jewish identity while assimilating the Hellenistic-Roman environment. Consequently, there was little inherent unity either in theology or in social organization among the Jewish communities of the Diaspora.

Prior to its destruction in 70 C.E., the Temple served as a central unifying principle in matters of worship, yet it too could produce divergent (and sometimes heated and antithetical) responses.[3] After the demise of the Temple cult, it would take another century and a second abortive revolt before a thorough reconstruction of Jewish religious leadership could begin to establish normative patterns of worship life in Palestine, not to mention extending to the far reaches of the Graeco-Roman Diaspora. Thus, we should expect that community religious life among Jews of the Diaspora varied greatly according to local conditions. In some cases there were probably differences from congregation to congregation within the Jewish population of a given city. In ancient Rome, for example, as many as eleven different synagogue communities are known by name, though no buildings have been identified.[4] The epigraphic remains suggest, however, that these different congregations represented quite distinct social groupings out of the Jewish population at large. They were differentiated by language, social standing, organization, and other factors. Most likely these differences had an impact on the relations of individual groups to the Roman culture and, consequently, on theology as well.

It is now generally thought that the synagogue as the central institution of Jewish community life was a product of the Hellenistic and early Roman period, though it took different forms in the Homeland and the Diaspora. Long-standing assumptions concerning the institution in Roman Palestine during the first century C.E. may have no historical grounding. While references to synagogues are known from late first-century sources, it does not appear that there was a formally ordered rabbinical institution as such prior to the second century C.E.[5] Moreover, there is no archaeological evidence for exclusively synagogue buildings in the Homeland dating to the first century. Prior to the fourth and fifth centuries, then, there was no identifiable standard of synagogue architecture as implied by classifications such as the "Galilean" or "Basilical" types known from later Palestine.[6] The assumptions do not apply in the diverse and often alien environment of the Diaspora. The experience and organization of Jewish groups in the Diaspora offers a distinct, though ultimately convergent, line of development for the synagogue as a result of the social contexts of its diffusion and adaptation.

Houses and Synagogues in the Diaspora

The earliest archaeological evidence for the existence of synagogue buildings, sometimes simply called "prayerhalls" (*proseuchai*), comes not from the Homeland but from the Diaspora. Synagogue communities are known through epigraphic remains from numerous cities of the Graeco-Roman world and from as early as the second century B.C.E.[7] Still only six synagogue buildings from the Diaspora have been excavated extensively (see fig. 9). They include: Priene and Sardis (in Asia Minor), Stobi (in Macedonia), Delos in the Aegean, Ostia (outside of Rome), and Dura-Europos (in Roman Syria).[8] They range in date from the second century B.C.E. through the sixth century C.E. Of these six, five were renovated from private domestic edifices, and in each case they had been houses typical of domestic architecture in that locale. Only the massive Sardis synagogue stands out as a monumental public building, although it is certain that its basilical hall (dating from the third century C.E.) was not originally designed as a synagogue. Nor was it the first edifice in the city to be used for synagogue assembly. Documents preserved by the historian Josephus indicate a Jewish *topos* at Sardis at least from the time of Julius Caesar.[9] This earlier building may well have been of more modest proportions, perhaps a private house at first. Yet it must be reckoned that whatever the nature of these accommodations, they served a Jewish community at Sardis for several centuries before the monumental public building was acquired and adapted to their needs.

In light of such evidence A. T. Kraabel has concluded that

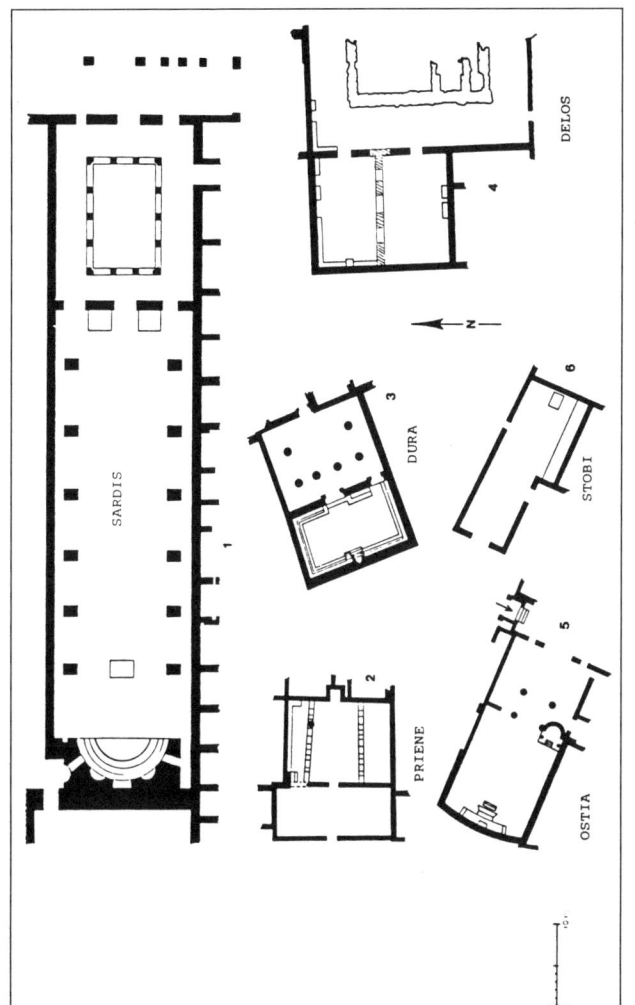

Fig. 9.
Schematic plans of the Diaspora synagogues at Sardis, Priene, Dura-Europos, Delos, Ostia, and Stobi.

synagogues in the Diaspora were determined architecturally more by local customs and influences than by any notion of Jewish theological or architectural norms.[10] Even in matters of orientation there was great diversity as only a few of the later ones ever faced toward Jerusalem. In the earliest diffusion of Jewish communities into the Diaspora, local congregations probably met in the homes of individuals. The earliest synagogue buildings had little or no distinguishing architectural features. Only after the destruction of the Temple, and even then only after the Bar Kochbah revolt failed to restore it, did synagogue buildings begin to take on their symbolic functions through the architectural articulation of sacred space.[11] Thus, to understand the circumstances of local synagogue communities, we should look to the archaeological remains of synagogue buildings for correlative social and economic factors. In so doing, we also recognize that synagogue construction would have been part of the larger environment of adaptation that was operative for the many other foreign groups and religions that had moved into the Greek (later the Roman) world.

Delos

The synagogue edifice on Delos is probably the oldest known either in the Diaspora or in the Homeland.[12] Some scant literary remains, edicts preserved in 1 Maccabees and Josephus, indicate the presence of a Jewish community on the island during the second and first centuries B.C.E.[13] Consequently it is an important case study, since it bears little in the way of distinctively Jewish markings. The building was originally a private house near the shore; it was taken over by a local Jewish community and adapted architecturally as a place of worship and community center. The construction history of the site suggests renovations occurring in two stages, in the late second century B.C.E. and in the mid-first century B.C.E. (see fig. 10). The building probably continued in operation at least through the first century C.E. and into the second.

Renovation to adapt the building to community use did little to alter the domestic form. The major features of the project involved construction of interior partitions in one large room in

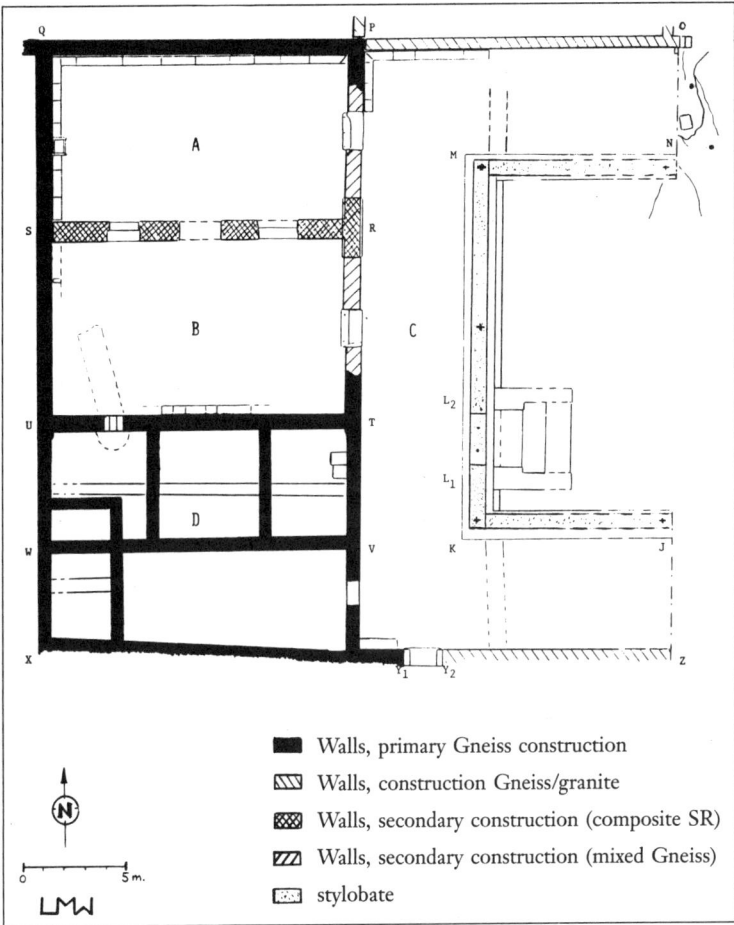

Fig. 10.
Plan restoration of the synagogue at Delos.

order to create a hall for assembly.[14] This could be entered directly from the exterior portico or from an adjoining room with triportal entrance. Around the walls of the main hall were benches; a carved marble chair, a thronos, stood in the middle of the short wall opposite the door from the portico. Apart from some inscribed bases bearing dedications to *Theos Hypsistos*, there was little or no distinctively Jewish decoration. The portico also underwent some embellishment at one point to create a tristoa entrance from the seaside. The nature of these adaptations suggests minimal religious articulation of the space. For other rooms in the building no specific uses can be ascertained, except for the cistern rooms. Most notably missing are a permanent Torah shrine and distinctive Jewish symbols, such as the menorah. Kraabel attributes the lack of typically Jewish embellishment to the fact that the structure was adapted for synagogue use while the Temple was still standing; therefore, it remained little more than a converted residence used primarily as an assembly hall and community center.[15] The nature of the renovations also points in another direction, for the seaside approach to the portico and the community hall suggest similarities to the collegial halls of other foreign groups on the island. The contemporary House of the Poseidoniasts from Berytus, for example, followed an elaborated peristyle house plan. It served not only as a commercial association for the local enclave of shippers and merchants, but also as a sanctuary for their ancestral god.[16] It is quite likely that an early Jewish enclave on Delos, as in other places, would have established such an ethnic association to advance their professional interests and to preserve their ancestral worship, but with little to distinguish their building from other houses and associations in the Hellenistic environment.

These rudimentary findings regarding the social placement and organization of the synagogue community find corroboration from inscriptions of a Samaritan enclave on Delos.[17] The Samaritan remains (from the second and first centuries B.C.E.) are contemporary and located only 100 meters up the shore from the synagogue building. The Samaritans, calling themselves "Israelites who pay homage to Hallowed Argarizein" (i.e., Mt. Gerizim), also had a collegial hall and *proseuchē*. The honorific inscriptions indicate that they had received benefactions over a period of years from Greek patrons for the construction and maintenance of their establishment.[18] While there is evidence that the Samaritan enclave clung to their traditional worship, their edifice has not as yet been identified, perhaps because of a similar lack of religious architectural articulation. Yet their social placement relative to the other Jewish group on the island is significant as it suggests contact and coexistence in the pluralistic commercial environment. Their relations with pagan benefactors may further indicate cultural accommodation and social acceptance, and it is noteworthy that a Roman edict preserved by Josephus seems to have given official notice to the existence of several distinct "Jewish" groups, with differing social status, on Delos.[19]

Priene

At Priene more lines of physical adaptation in the creating of the synagogue are visible.[20] The building was a modest Hellenistic house (with oecus and prostas) of a sort commonly found in Priene domestic architecture. It was located in one block of the domestic quarter, near another house that contained a private sanctuary to the deified Alexander.[21] The renovation from house to synagogue probably dates to the second century C.E. (see fig. 11). It involved a more complete transformation from domestic forms as the courtyard and street-front shops were sacrificed for the construction of the hall of assembly and an entry vestibule from the side street. The original domestic quarters of the house remained largely unchanged on the exterior but were modified on the interior to be used for community functions. These rather modest physical alterations further indicate a public dimension beyond the constituency of the synagogue community. Razing the shops and rebuilding the walls of the court had to attract public notice. The construction of the hall itself also encroached upon other buildings through party walls in the insula block; most notably, physical installation of the Torah niche intruded through the party wall of a neighboring house. The renovation project suggests a larger and more visible Jewish community. Intrusion into neighboring houses suggests acquisition by Jewish residents or the activities of a thriving Jewish quarter, whose status was not generally threatened.[22] Unfortunately there is no documentary evidence to provide further information on the history or constituency of

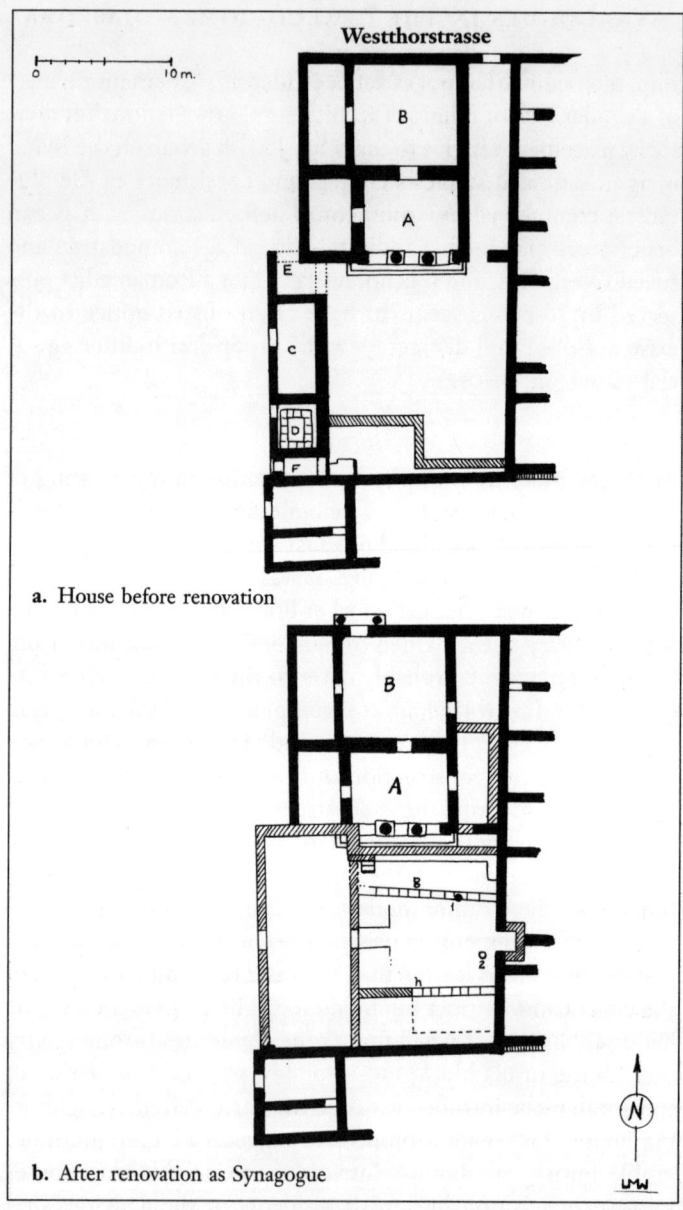

Fig. 11.
Plan restoration of the synagogue at Priene.

the Jewish community. The nature and scale of the building project suggest, however, that the synagogue community had already been active for some time and that this renovation marked a new plateau in the social and religious life of the community.

Ostia

Much more information can be gained in cases where multiple stages of renovation may be observed. Progressive adaptation allows one to track a longitudinal social progression for that particular community. The synagogue at Ostia (ranging from the first through the fourth century C.E.; see fig. 12) is regularly claimed to have been specially constructed as a synagogue edifice, the only such known from the Diaspora.[23] However, recent examination of the remains in light of the archaeological reports raises some doubts. It appears to me that the building was originally a private building of some sort, perhaps a house or insula, which was adapted to its Jewish communal function in at least three phases of renovation. The first renovation resulted in expansion of the building complex by the addition of a large dining hall, probably at the time that it was adapted to synagogue use.[24] The remains indicate two further renovation projects within the building that were designed to adapt it for specific religious functions. One of these involves the extension of the ground floor assembly hall vertically through a second story. To carry the higher ceiling columns were introduced into the hall, thus creating a space of more monumental public proportions. Exterior buttressing was required, and second floor windows were sealed over. This structural modification was coincidental with the second project, the introduction into the synagogue hall of a specially constructed apsidal aedicula to serve as the Torah shrine, suggesting increased liturgical formalization.[25] At least one of the building's earlier stages of renovation can be correlated, through an inscription (combining Greek and Latin), with a private benefaction to the building itself.[26] The inclusion of the opening salutary formula on behalf of the emperor (*Pro salute Aug[usti]*) reflects the social purview of the Jewish residents of Ostia. At Ostia (as at Priene) there is

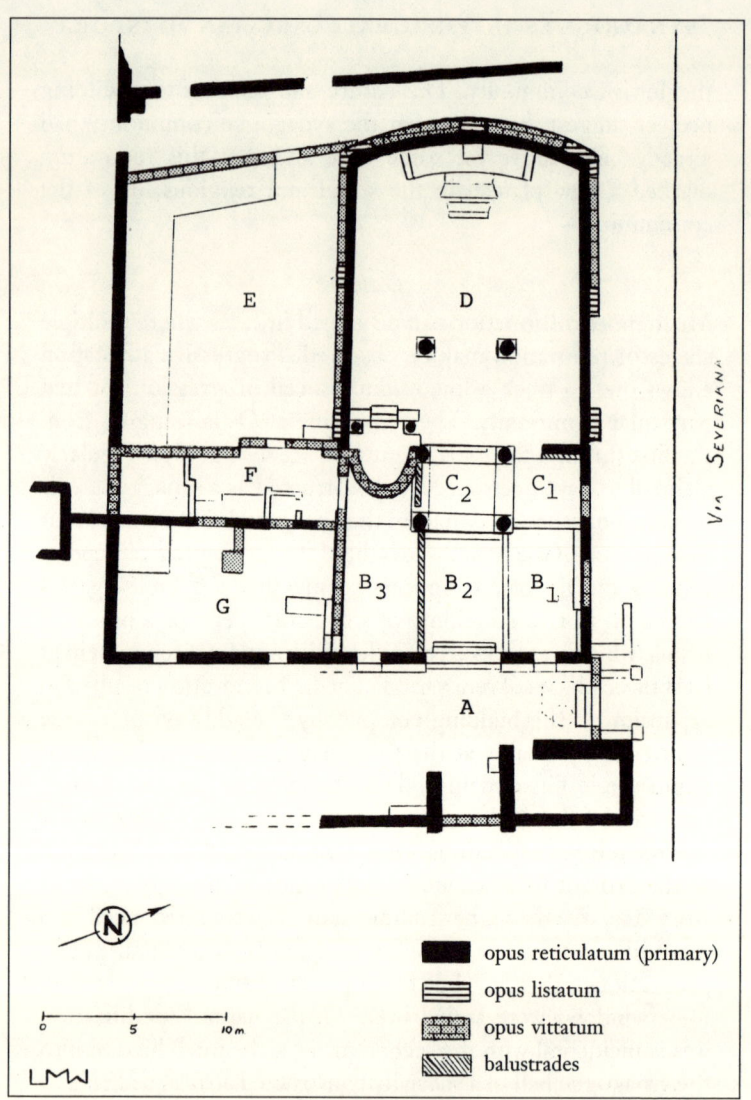

Fig. 12.
Plan restoration of the synagogue at Ostia.

further evidence of conscious articulation for Jewish worship, both with the use of menorah decorations and with the subsequent introduction of a permanent Torah shrine.

Stobi

The Stobi synagogue edifice (see fig. 13) was originally adapted (second or third century C.E.) in one area of a large urban domus owned by Claudius Tiberius Polycharmos, who is called *patēr tēs in Stobois synagogēs* ("father of the synagogue at Stobi").[27] This first synagogue was later rebuilt (by the early fourth century) into a larger synagogue hall structure contiguous to, but physically distinct from, the Polycharmos house. Later still (fifth century) the entire synagogue building was taken over and rebuilt as a Christian basilica.[28] This case is especially important because of the insight on synagogue organization provided by the donor inscription of Polycharmos, which includes (among other provisions) stipulations for the retention of part of the original property for private use of the family. Polycharmos provided that part of his property should become the de facto province of the synagogue community under the religious leadership of a patriarch. Yet, Polycharmos himself continued to exercise leadership in both social and religious matters as *patēr synagogēs*. The upper chambers of the house, however, remained the habitation of Polycharmos and his heirs. The bequest is significant, moreover, because it specified a monetary value of 250,000 denarii for the property, which was to be paid as a penalty to the patriarch of the synagogue should any changes be made. We do not know if such payment was ever made, but changes certainly did occur, both in the renovation of the second synagogue and even more so in the Christian takeover and the construction of the basilica.

Sardis

The Sardis synagogue is one of the most spectacular finds of recent years. There had been an earlier meeting hall for the Jewish community since the time of Julius Caesar, but there is no evidence for what sort of building it might have been. Moreover, there is a sizeable gap in the historical evidence for Jewish

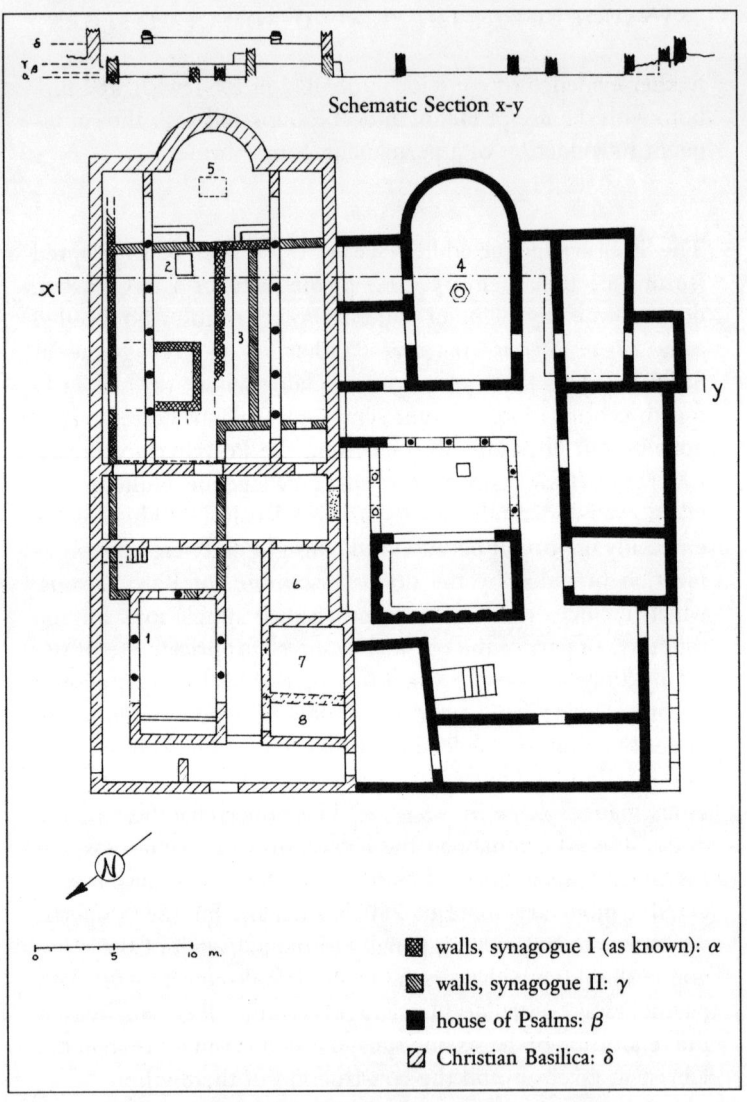

Fig. 13.
Plan restoration of the synagogue complex at Stobi.

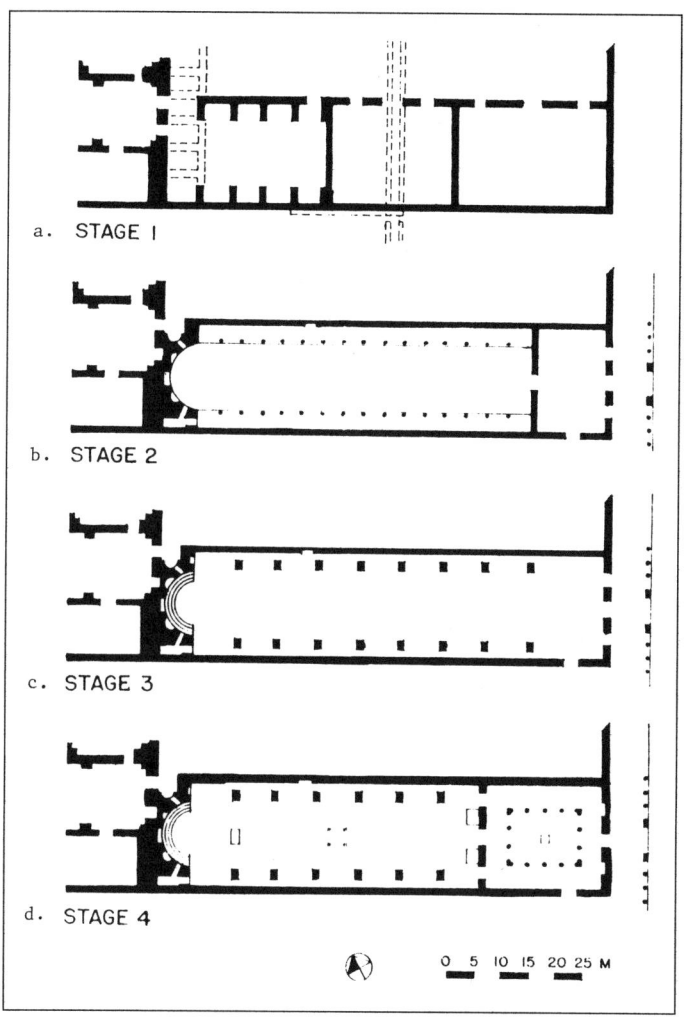

Fig. 14.
Plan restoration of the synagogue at Sardis.

life between those earlier records and the records of the later community attached to the monumental synagogue edifice. This synagogue (see fig. 14) was installed in a long wing, originally divided into three *apodyteria* or dressing rooms, of the municipal bath-gymnasium complex.[29] The area was converted to a basilical hall plan, probably for municipal use sometime in the second century C.E. Shortly thereafter, it came into use as a synagogue hall of assembly. It then went through further interior renovation and redecoration to become an opulent public showpiece for the Jews of Sardis. Its history carried well into the sixth century. The social implications of this architectural history arise from the fact that the Jewish community could come into possession of a prominent municipal property and demonstrate sufficient social and economic resources to maintain it. The prosopographic data from donor inscriptions in the decorations of the last stages indicate that the Jewish community numbered among its members or sympathizers a prestigious list of local leaders. Included are local citizens and members of the decurionate (*sardianoi* and *bouleutai*), clerical workers in the Roman provincial administration (*boēthoi taboulariou*), a former procurator (*apo epitropon*), and a count (*komēs*).[30]

Dura-Europos

The Dura-Europos synagogue shows three distinct architectural phases.[31] Initially it was a typical Durene house in an insula block of ten irregular domiciles. Even though Jews are known to have been in the city prior to this time, use of the house as a synagogue edifice cannot be demonstrated archaeologically. Only in the second stage can such Jewish usage be discerned, when the interior of the house was remodeled. The renovations of the second stage (the Early Synagogue, dated ca. 150–200 C.E.; see fig. 15) were entirely on the interior: particularly, the creation of a hall of assembly and installation of a small Torah niche. From the exterior the building remained typical of domestic architecture. Only in the third stage (the Later Synagogue, dated to 244/245) was the edifice completely transformed. The original area of the house was gutted to accommodate a much larger hall of assembly and entry forecourt. A

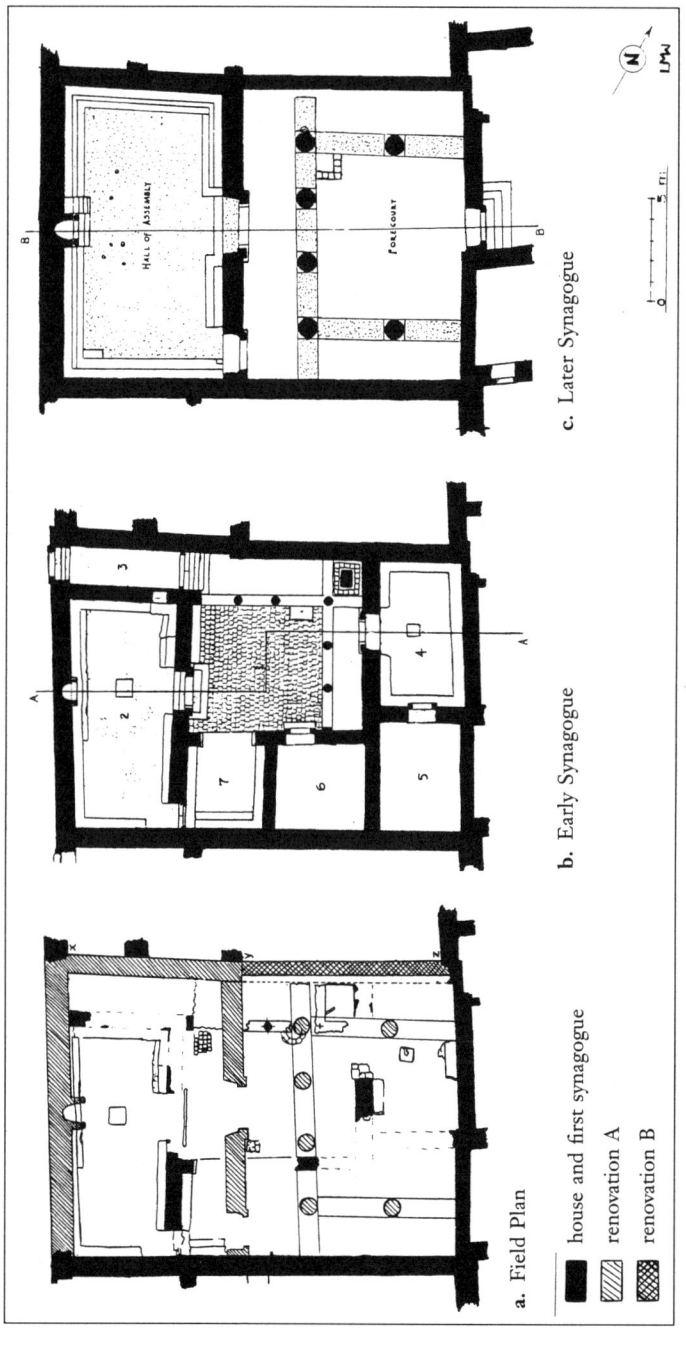

Fig. 15.
Plan restoration of the Early and Later Synagogue at Dura-Europos.

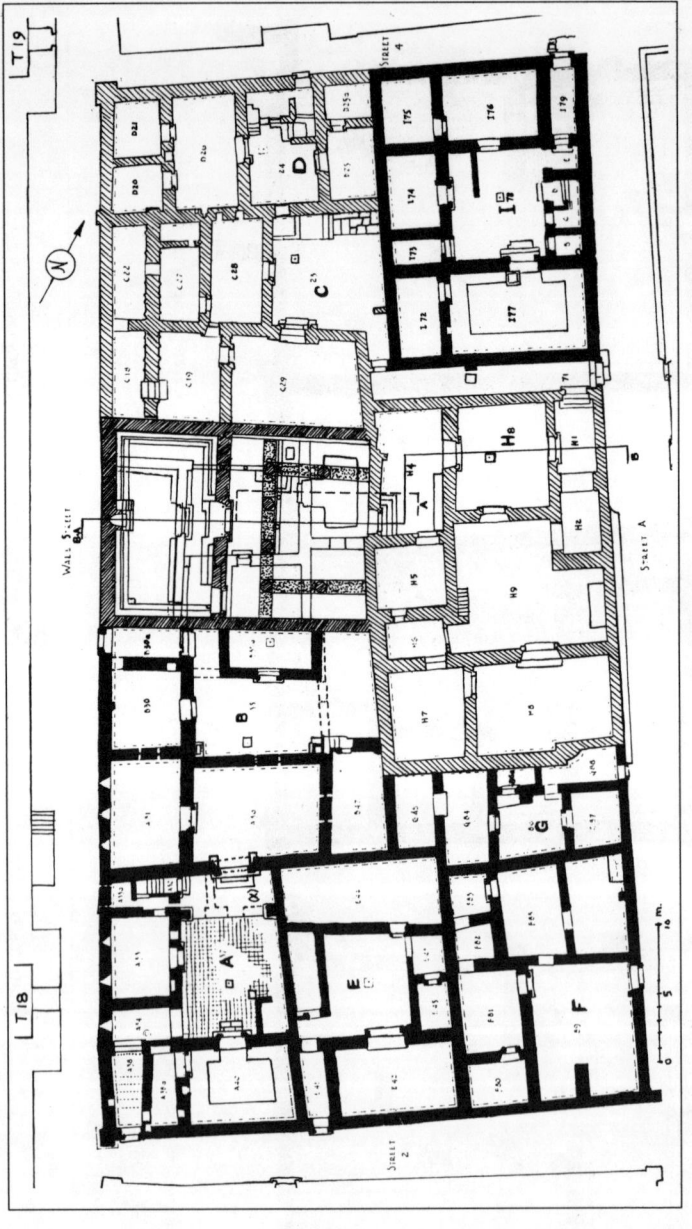

Fig. 16.
Plan restoration of Block L7 and the synagogue at Dura-Europos.

neighboring house was annexed to provide other rooms for community use. Still, some continuity with the first synagogue edifice can be observed, especially in the orientation of the hall of assembly around the placement of a Torah niche. The niche preserves the location of an earlier Torah shrine, from the first synagogue.

That the structural modifications of the Later Synagogue carry strong social implications can be seen in several factors. First, rebuilding the hall of assembly necessitated the total destruction (down to foundation level) of two exterior walls of the house, one that faced onto a main street, the other a party wall with a neighboring house (C) (see fig. 16). Thus, the architectural adaptation cannot have gone unnoticed by the populace.[32] Second, the entrance to the building was shifted entirely to the other side of the insula block through a suite of chambers in the annexed house (H). Thus, a practical physical alteration (calculated to provide more space for assembly) had an additional social impact: the entrance was moved to a nicer street. Third, the synagogue itself became considerably larger and more opulent, suggesting increased wealth and social standing for the Jewish community. In addition to the scale of construction and the acquisition of additional property, this fact is further indicated by the decoration of the hall of assembly with representational art. Not only are the paintings of professional quality, they also reflect an accommodation to popular temple decoration style found among pagan sanctuaries in Dura.[33] From inscriptions it is possible to correlate this renovation with a conscious community building program under the direction of several synagogue leaders, who also served as major donors.[34] At least one of these individuals, Samuel bar Yedaʿya (who is called elder, priest, and archon), might well have been the owner of the house in which the synagogue was established.[35]

The Role of Patrons: Social Factors in Adaptation

Because there was no set form for Diaspora synagogues it is impossible to evaluate the construction history in terms of architectural patterns alone. The more compelling insights come from the way architectural adaptation, especially in multiple stages, sheds light on Jewish social life in the Diaspora. By precise analysis of the construction history and the planning of renovation from existing buildings it is possible to see evidence of the social makeup and activities of individual Jewish communities in their local environment. There was great diversity in theology and internal community organization, determined in part by varying degrees of accommodation to local culture. Still, certain lines of continuity can be seen from time to time, as in the introduction in several later synagogues of a permanent Torah ark.[36] In terms of translocal patterns, one also begins to sense the importance of individual benefactors and patrons in construction and community leadership. Some were clearly wealthy and prominent Jews, both men and women, who by virtue of their generosity were accorded leadership roles and social status within the synagogue community. In other cases, however, benefactions by non-Jews resulted in similar grants of honor and status.[37] The permeation of this socioeconomic mechanism from the culture at large into the fabric of Jewish community life has further implications for understanding the diffusion of Judaism (and later Christianity).

No evidence exists regarding the acquisition of properties at Priene and Delos. Generally, one would expect that private donations were at work in order to make a domestic edifice available for community use. While Jewish communities are known from earlier times, the first evidence of synagogue activity in each case comes from the physical adaptation, however minimal, for religious use. Such donations came from (or at least through) the owner of the house, who first served as host to the community and then as its patron. In the third century (after the Mishnah had been codified back in the Homeland) this was still the case at Stobi.[38] Claudius Tiberius Polycharmos served as patron and benefactor of the community alongside the religious authority of a local patriarch. There was a Jewish community at Stobi in the mid-third century when Polycharmos made his bequest. Yet, there was no highly evolved synagogal organization, and the first archaeological evidence for this community comes with the adaptation of Polycharmos' house and the references in his donor inscription. It is likely that the Jews had met in his house previously, before he set aside a portion of it to be a holy place (*hagios topos*).[39] The rest of the house remained, at least for some time, in private domestic use by Polycharmos' family. His donation, then, constituted an act of private devotion for which he was granted special honors and status within the Jewish community. He is called, therefore, "father of the synagogue" (*patēr tēs synagogēs*), a title that is used in both the long honorific inscriptions and the painted floor decorations of the synagogue rooms. Polycharmos the "patron," for that is what *pater* connotes, was not at all shy about the social and economic implications of his gift.

The synagogue at Ostia probably benefitted from similar donations by the earlier property owner, Mindis Faustus, who, as he says, gave his own rooms for the construction of the building and the Torah ark.[40] Unfortunately, no information is given regarding the later rebuilding projects, and we do not know whether they resulted from individual bequests or from community projects. At Stobi and Ostia it is clear that the decision on the part of an individual to donate the space and allow for its adaptation had to be balanced by a conscious decision on the part of the religious community. Also, donation of private property would have been especially desirable in the earlier stages of the community's history for reasons of economic feasibility and public recognition.

The case of Delos points to the role of non-Jewish patrons among diverse Jewish groups in the second and first centuries B.C.E. Of the two "Jewish" communities known on the island, one worshipping *Theos Hypsistos*, the other honoring Mt. Gerizim, neither can be considered normative.[41] The Samaritan enclave seems to have been organized as a commercial agency with its prayer hall serving as the collegial as well as the worship center. It is significant, then, that this group received benefactions from Greeks who apparently were not of the Samaritan enclave. The inscriptions indicate that Menippos from Crete gave the funds for the construction of the Samaritans' hall. Later, another Cretan named Sarapion (perhaps of Egyptian descent) gave unspecified benefactions, probably for the renovation or decoration of the same building.[42] The Samaritan community responded in a manner befitting the conventions of Greek benefactions: the benefactors were honored with gold crowns and stelai decorated with laurel wreaths and inscriptions. The inscriptions proclaimed to all the acts of beneficence, and both the benefactors and the Samaritan community shared in the honor and public recognition. But other than the desire for honor that motivated much private benefaction, why would pagans from Crete choose to donate funds to the Samaritan enclave? Most likely the answer lies in the social relationships between members of the group and the benefactors, as they were probably engaged in trading activities together. It is possible, too, that a formal status of foreign residents "in Delos" was accorded to the Samaritan agency as a result of their trading activities and social contacts.[43] Other "Jewish" groups on the island did not have such status and had to live as legal aliens (*paroikoi*).[44] In the case of the Samaritan enclave, therefore, social accommodation and building patronage went hand in hand.

From Greece and Asia Minor in the early Principate there are records of building donations to Jewish communities by prominent men and women. According to later talmudic tradition one would not have expected women to hold leading positions in the synagogue; however, in the early synagogues of the Diaspora such restrictions on the status of women did not apply. Nor is there evidence (literary or archaeological) of a segregated place for women in synagogue architecture; the "women's gallery," known from several Galilean-type synagogues, seems to have been an exclusively Palestinian invention of the fourth and later centuries.[45] The honorific title "mother of the synagogue" (*matēr synagogēs*) is known from several inscriptions from Italy and should be taken as the equivalent to the honor and status accorded the benefactor Tiberius Polycharmos, *patēr synagogēs* at Stobi. At Mantineia in Greece it was Aurelios Elpidus, called "father of the community for life" (*patēr laou dia biou*) who donated the construction of a *pronaos* for an existing synagogue edifice.[46] At Smyrna, Irenopoios, called "elder and father of the society" (*pres(byteros) ke patēr tou stematos*), contributed decorations, mosaic for the hall, and chancel screens (*skamnokankelous*).[47] Unlike other offices in the synagogue, *patēr* and *matēr* seem to have been statuses earned chiefly through conspicuous acts of generosity. In many ways they are parallel to similar acts by more typical synagogue officials, such as the *archisynagogos* or *archon*,[48] suggesting that leadership roles in the synagogue, as in other religious associations, entailed benefactions.[49] The terms represented the leading member of the synagogue who displayed his or her devotion through acts of benefaction and patronage, chiefly financing the construction or renovation of the synagogue edifice itself.[50]

From Asia Minor come two especially noteworthy cases. At Phocaea, in Roman Lydia, a woman named Tation built the edifice and court and then gave it to the Jewish congregation.[51] The nature of the bequest and construction was very similar to that of the Samaritan edifice at Delos several centuries earlier.[52] Tation was also honored with a gold crown and a *proëdrion*, a front seat, in the synagogue hall. It is noteworthy that a woman should have such a prominent position in the synagogue organization, a place regularly reserved for the wealthy patrons and leaders of collegial associations.[53] In this case it appears that Tation was a member of the congregation, or at least a sympathizer, even though it is doubtful that her husband participated.[54]

At Acmonia in Roman Phrygia, Julia Severa also made a gift of a building to the local Jewish community.[55] In this case, however, it seems that the edifice was already standing, and her bequest simply made it the property of the Jewish congregation. Julia Severa was the wife of Lucius Servenius Capito, a decurion (municipal *archon*) at Acmonia under Nero. She is also known to have served as a priestess in the imperial cult.[56] It is highly unlikely that she was Jewish or even a pious gentile sympathizer within the Jewish community. Still, Julia was duly honored as a benefactor of the synagogue. Thus, it was left to the leaders of the congregation to undertake a renovation project to turn the edifice she had donated into a synagogue building. The same inscription honors three men, two *archisynagogoi* and an *archon*, for their efforts in this capacity.

This case is interesting in several ways. First, the honors accorded the three Jewish leaders suggest that they, not Julia Severa, were the ones who donated the funds for the actual renovation project. Second, it remains curious why Julia would have donated the property to the Jews to begin with. The explanation probably lies in social ties between Julia Severa and the Jewish leaders. The name of the first, Publius Tyrronios Clados, may well suggest that he was a freedman or client attached to the family of Julia Severa.[57] In this case, then, two related acts of patronage were at work: Julia's was directed toward her Jewish clients, the synagogue leaders; theirs, in turn, was directed toward the congregation. Both acts of patronage were duly celebrated by the Jewish congregation, using common honorific conventions from the local urban environment, suggesting that such Jewish freedmen or clients were thus able to solidify their social standing within that environment. The three leaders possessed a measure of wealth and status, at least relative to others in the Jewish community, although they in turn were dependent upon local aristocrats. The result was the acquisition of an existing edifice and its physical adaptation to serve as a synagogue through an intricate network of social and religious affiliations.

From a public perspective many of the synagogue communities were organized after the fashion of collegia, as merchant guilds or ethnic trading agencies. A typical and accepted feature of such organizations would have been their dedication to ancestral religion, hence an ethnic *thiasos*, and their reliance on patrons and private benefactions.[58] From Ptolemaic and early Roman Egypt there are records of donations made to synagogues under the direction of a president (*prostatēs*), a collegial officer.[59] Synagogues were often designated by common terms for collegial assembly, such as *synodos* or *koinos*.[60] There were also social subgroups or lesser associations attached to the larger Jewish community, such as a burial society (*koinos syntaphiastōn*) which met in the synagogue hall.[61] An extensive pyramidal social organization after the collegial model, more likely in Alexandria or Antioch at an earlier period, reflects the tacit, though at times grudging, social acceptance obtained by resident Jewish communities. From a legal perspective, too, collegial identity probably facilitated private benefactions by non-Jewish sympathizers. As at Acmonia, the gifts could be placed under the direction of the collegial officers, who saw to the specifics of use in renovation or decoration.

Major renovation projects, such as those at Sardis and Dura-Europos, certainly had the support of the entire congregation even though a few prominent individuals took the lead. Any decision on the part of a congregation to renovate reflects consciousness of the needs or circumstances that make such work feasible or necessary. That the bulk of known synagogue construction work was the result of individual donors attests to the currency of private benefaction.[62] In some cases, however, a major individual donation probably served as the occasion for a community project as well. It seems there was no hesitancy to renovate, rebuild, add on, or redecorate.[63] At Berenice in Cyrenaica the renovation of the synagogue proper was celebrated in an inscription as a group project, with individual contributions, large and small, duly noted.[64] Two earlier inscriptions from the same locale indicate benefactions and political favors from Roman officials.[65] However, the language of the honorific suggests that the list of eighteen contributors was only a fraction of the entire Jewish congregation. These eighteen fall neatly into three subgroups by amount contributed. The first eleven named gave 10 drachmae each, and of these eleven, nine bear the title *archon* and one *priest*. A second column lists four donations of 5 drachmae each, two from women. One name from this group appears to be another member (a younger son?) of the family of Dositheos, one of the *archons*. Altogether, Dositheos, his two older sons who were also *archons*, and their younger brother gave 35 drachmae out of the total 208. Finally, three larger contributions total another 78 drachmae; these, along with the contributions from the family of Dositheos, made up more than half of the project, while most of the rest came from various synagogue officers.

Because of the dominance of individual acts of patronage, even group renovation projects relied on leading donors. In the case of the Aegina synagogue, the *archisynagogos* Theodoros was accorded the honor of "building the synagogue from the foundations," when it is clear that a community treasury supplied some of the funds.[66] Yet, it is also clear that Theodoros was the "curator" or "overseer" (*phrontiasas*) of the building project precisely because he donated over half of the funds from his own resources, or as he says, "from the gifts of God."[67] It is further indication of the social standing of Theodoros and his family within the Aegina synagogue community that later his son (and namesake) also held the honorific title of "steward" or "curator" (*phrontistēs*) and completed the renovation project begun by his father with the decoration of the hall with a mosaic pavement, in which were rendered the honorifics for both father and son. In the same manner at Side (in Pamphylia), Isaac, who is called "curator of the most holy first synagogue" (*phrontistēs hagiot/[ēs] protēs synagogēs*), also supplied the marble decoration of the building.[68] Inducements for prominent individual donors were the display of their honors through inscriptions commissioned at their own expense. At Sardis, for example, in addition to the major structural renovations of the third and fourth stages, there was a need for elaborate decorations.[69] Competition for honors by both Jewish and non-Jewish donors resulted in the placement of the mosaic pavements in the hall and the forecourt. The larger sections of mosaic each reveal a central medallion bearing the name of the donor and the extent of the donation. Thus, in one bay we find the bequest of Aurelius Alexandros, a citizen and municipal councillor of Sardis.[70] Still, such individual acts of patronage supplemented a community project and continued a pattern of personal devotion existent since the first phase of synagogue activity in the building at Sardis.[71]

The major difference in the later Sardis synagogue renovations was in the number of prominent individuals who participated. It is really a sign of the wider cultural acceptance of the Sardis Jewish community that it no longer needed to rely on one or two leading patrons for its projects, and the scale and opulence of the building amply attest to this social success.[72] Private donations provided a vast array of decorations, embellishments, or paraphernalia. Inevitably, the donors' inscriptions attest to the gifts of paintings,[73] floor mosaics or pavements,[74] marble revetments,[75] fountains and basins,[76] lamps and *menoroth*,[77] and altars.[78] This practice of private donations of decorations eventually came to bear on the development of synagogues in the Homeland as well, attested equally in Greek-speaking communities of the coast, near-Syria, and in the Galilee.[79] The practice is also seen in Hebrew- or Aramaic-speaking communities, primarily from the Amoraic period.[80] By the fifth century, when both Jewish and Christian monumental architecture had achieved more formal qualities, the patterns continued in close proximity. At Maʿon, in the highly romanized coastal strip near Gaza, the floor mosaics of the synagogue and the nearby church seem to have come from the same workshop, and in each case the inscriptions of the private benefactors bear testimony to the donation.[81] Construction and decoration through the beneficence of donors ultimately yields insights into the developing organization and social location of synagogues in the Homeland as well. Patterns of patronage and adaptation pioneered in the Diaspora came home to Roman Palestina.

Adaptation, Development, and Accommodation

While the synagogue eventually became the central institution of Jewish worship and communal identity, it took several centuries for it to develop normative canons of architecture and organization, especially in the Diaspora. A crucial period of transition came in the first and second centuries C.E. with the destruction of the Temple and the reconstruction of Jewish worship life under the more univocal guidance of the Rabbis. It is not insignificant, then, that this is the same period during which the Christian movement emerged and became a separate entity, that is to say, when church and synagogue went their separate and sometimes inimical ways. Here the literary sources present complex problems for historical interpretation alongside the archaeological and epigraphic data. The primary literary references come from the Jewish historian Josephus and from the Christian gospel tradition, in particular Matthew and

Luke-Acts. These two bodies of writings are roughly contemporaneous, coming from the last decades of the first century C.E. In each case, caution is demanded since apologetic or polemical concerns are reflected in the manner in which pre-70 C.E. synagogue communities are depicted.[82]

Convergence between such literary sources and our archaeological remains is to be expected, of course, as in the edicts incorporated by Josephus concerning the Jewish communities of Sardis, Delos, and elsewhere.[83] Yet, it must be noted that very little in the way of historical detail is provided about organization and buildings. For example, in Luke 7.3–6 is the case of the Roman centurion who was benefactor for the building of a synagogue. The wording of this passage clearly has a ring of authenticity about it, as it incorporates the conventionalized honorific language commonly found in building inscriptions among both Jews and pagans.[84] Nonetheless, it would be difficult to make out of these uniquely Lucan additions a normative picture of Palestinian synagogue practice in Jesus' day. Instead, the use of the benefaction language more likely reflects the concerns of both Jews and Christians in Luke's own day, around the end of the first century C.E. Thus, in Luke-Acts one finds a thematic emphasis on benefaction by prominent pagans and Jews as a sign of the success of the Christian movement. One must guess that the tendency to use social conventions, such as patronage and benefaction, both in Josephus and Luke-Acts, stems from thematic projection across the great diversity of the Diaspora, and it should not be used to create an anachronistic sense of normative Judaism. In many cases, synagogues were still held in households or minimally renovated homes, especially prior to 70, or even 135 C.E. The common range of synagogue terms is also reflected in Luke-Acts, and the situation generally corresponds to some of the factors that have already been observed from archaeological data.[85] For example, the case of the *archisynagogos* Crispus and Titius Justus, whose house was "contiguous to the synagogue," makes much more sense in light of the archaeological evidence for renovated domestic quarters, as at Priene or Dura-Europos.[86] We should well expect that synagogue officers and leading patrons often lived adjacent since property ownership was a major factor in the development of individual buildings. Nonetheless, it must be noted by way of contrast to the prolific mention in Acts (especially in Paul's travels), that Paul, whose genuine letters come from before 70, never once referred to the synagogue, either as institution or edifice, even though he clearly knew Jewish communities or individuals in several localities in Greece and Asia Minor.[87] All too often the legal status and organization of the sizeable Jewish populations at Antioch and, especially, Alexandria have been wrongly assumed to apply equally to the many small, diverse Jewish communities throughout the Diaspora.[88] Thus, one must exercise caution in projecting the developments and tensions of the period after 70 onto the earlier situation. At the same time, the social setting and the development of Diaspora synagogue communities offered a broad, though by no means uniform, avenue for diffusion of new Jewish idioms into the Hellenistic-Roman environment. Among those new forms would have been the emergent Christian movement.

Before 70 the synagogue was not an institution in the later talmudic sense. It originated, rather, as a place of Jewish assembly, of ethnic and religious identity, especially in the alien environment of the Diaspora. Here the *proseuchē* as "house of prayer" served both as place of religious assembly and as social center to the congregation (*synagogē*).[89] Even in the Homeland this development exerted some influence alongside another, indigenous impulse, the Pharisaic fellowships (*haburoth*), which emerged into the rabbinic tradition of the *bet ha-midrash* ("house of study").[90] One of the few bits of archaeological evidence for synagogues from pre-70 Judea suggests a direct link with the Diaspora communities. The Ophel inscription, as it is known, represents the construction of a synagogue in Jerusalem by a certain Theodotos, a priest and *archisynagogos*.[91] The fact that the inscription makes specific provision for guest quarters (*xenōna*) for travelers (*xenēs*) points to a foundation by and for Diaspora Jews who would come to Jerusalem as pilgrims. It has been suggested that the name of Vettenos, Theodotos' father who is credited in part with the foundation, correlates with references to the synagogue of the Libertines at Jerusalem known from Acts.[92] This title comes from the Diaspora organization of synagogue communities after the pattern of collegia, but now transported back to the Homeland.[93]

The interplay of community building projects and leading individual patrons, both Jewish and non-Jewish, can also be seen in the recently discovered Jewish inscription from Aphrodisias in Caria. The inscribed stone probably stood at the entrance of a building; it honored the long list of donors named in three columns.[94] It might have come from the synagogue itself, or more likely from the building which is the subject of the dedication. The project is of some interest here, for it seems to have been a Jewish charitable agency, a kind of soup kitchen (*patella*). Moreover, it was instituted consciously to make contact with the community at large: "for the relief of suffering in the community" (*eis apenthēsian to plēthi*).[95] The difficulty comes in understanding the makeup of the list of donors and their relations to the synagogue membership. The honored group of donors is called a *dekany* under the "presidency"(*prostatēs*) of a certain Jael.[96] These designations suggest that the *dekany* was a collegial association with its own president, but somehow attached to the synagogue proper. The synagogue as a religious institution had its own identity, organization, and leadership under other named officials, such as the *presbyter* Samuel and the *archon* Joshua.[97]

The *dekany* roster of the Aphrodisian synagogue undertook establishment of the charitable institution. The names are listed in three columns, in such a way as to indicate some subtle social differentiation. The first includes a mix of clearly Semitic derivations plus several designated as either proselyte (*prosēlytos*) or god-fearer (*theosebēs*). The second and third columns give names and professions, ranging from menial laborers to city councillors and bureaucrats. Column three, following a break in the text, lists "the rest of the godfearers" (*hosoi theosebais*), and the first nine names are titled as "city councillors" (*bouleutēs*). The rest of the 52 names in the third column seem to be largely of Greek extraction and reflect a typical variety of urban occupations. Column two with its more explicitly Semitic names is set apart, like column three, though any official designation for this subgroup is now lost from the stone. Still the names and occupations of as many as 74 individuals reflect considerable diversity within the ethnic Jewish population of the city.[98] The organization of this building project at Aphrodisias therefore suggests social ties between Jewish residents and their non-Jewish neighbors in close cooperation through individual donations toward the common goal.

One avenue of social interaction would seem to be the constitution of a separate collegial association attached to the synagogue (and made up at least in part by Jewish leaders) which could foster social activities and contacts outside more restrictive religious or worship contexts. Two epithets are applied to the *dekany: "lovers-of-learning" (philomathōn)*, also called *"all-blessing" (panteulogōn)*. They represent the titles by which the collegial association was formally constituted, and they suggest an intentionally neutral public image.[99] Yet there was a degree of double entendre on the connotations of "study" (*mathōn*) and "blessing" (*eulogōn*) from a Jewish perspective.[100] In this sense "god-fearers" (*theoseboi*) also had both a neutral and intentionally ambiguous quality. It could be used by pagans of Jews, meaning pious members of the culture at large.[101] In turn designation by Jews of non-Jewish members of the collegial association as "god-fearers," however, would not have required them to be attracted actively toward Jewish worship, though some surely were. Nor would they necessarily have had diminished social status within or as part of the worshipping synagogue community.[102] The separate constitution of a collegial association, in fact, avoids the tensions that would result from imposing status distinctions (second-class membership) on prominent non-Jews, such as city councillors, who would normally expect the honors and status due to patrons. Other texts indicate that the parallel practice of benefactions was observed for the decoration and embellishment of the synagogue hall itself.[103] It is noteworthy in light of many of the earlier cases that no women appear in the membership list of the *dekany*. Thus, in the final analysis we must give proper attention to the social organization of the *dekany* under the publicly honored president, Jael, an

Aphrodisian Jew.[104] By the same token, it must be recognized that sharper boundary lines were being drawn between Jew and non-Jew, at least in the sense of ethnic identity and religious practice, if not in social aspects. Social contacts with a number of city councillors, listed among the *theoseboi*, clearly reflect a high degree of civic visibility and prominence. The building program was intended as a cooperative venture to serve the community at large, and honors to the *dekany* accrued to the social acceptance of the synagogue community as well. This case may give evidence of a subtle change in religious self-consciousness among local Jewish communities by the third or fourth century. It suggests the beginnings of a more restrictive definition of synagogue as religious institution as opposed to collegial or social association. It must be seen in contrast to earlier cases in which both women and non-Jews, whether or not religious sympathizers, were full participants in synagogal activities and honors. Still, the contemporary situation at nearby Sardis suggests further that the Aphrodisian solution to the matter was not translocal.

The collegial organization of Jewish communities in Egypt and Cyrenaica arising under the Hellenistic monarchies offered unique possibilities for social interaction which then continued under Roman rule. At Berenice, Cyrenaica, in the early Principate the Jewish *politeuma* seems to have convened its assembly (*synodos*) in its own amphitheater.[105] One inscription from this edifice records the private benefaction of Decimus Valerius Dionysius for plastering and painting the amphitheater.[106] Later, a Roman official, M. Tittius, granted favorable political concessions to the *politeuma*. In return for his act of patronage the *politeuma* pronounced public honors in the amphitheater on Jewish holy days.[107] In both cases such obvious acts of patronage by non-Jews through political favors and construction point to the social accommodation of the Jewish population. Especially noteworthy is the first example, since Valerius Dionysius was granted exemption from regular civil liturgies as a result of his beneficence toward the Jewish *politeuma*. Such exemptions were often granted (as recorded in numerous papyri) for meritorious service or benefaction toward the city. That in this case such civic honors should be merited by an act of private beneficence for the renovation of a Jewish establishment suggests a social context analogous to that of Numerius Celsinus' donation to the Isis temple at Pompeii.[108] The high social standing of the Jews recorded under M. Tittius a generation later must have continued from this same organizational accommodation. Still, the precise nature of the Jewish *politeuma* is difficult to surmise.

The *politeuma* at Berenice and elsewhere is often simply equated with the *gerousia* organization known from Alexandria and so hotly debated in the days of Philo. After a pogrom under the governor Flaccus the citizenship rights (*politeia*) of the entire Jewish population were at risk. A chief feature of these rights was the provision for self-governance parallel to the Greek citizenry. The term *gerousia*, derived from classical usage and meaning a council of elders, was applied by Philo to the governing council over the entire Jewish population at Alexandria. It has also been equated with the term *sanhedrin*, either as the council at Jerusalem or in talmudic usage as the great council of Rabbis. Hence, it is assumed to be equivalent to the "Great Synagogue" at Alexandria, which presumably governed all the various synagogue congregations in the city. It was headed by an *ethnarch* or *gerousiarch*, who represented Jewish interests before the city magistrates. At Alexandria, it is generally assumed, the *gerousia* was composed of leaders from the various synagogues as a kind of umbrella organization to provide for consistency and uniformity in Jewish social life and religious practice. While the case of Alexandria after the rescript of Claudius probably established certain precedents for other Jewish communities, nonetheless, the *gerousia* organization must be considered a local phenomenon.[109] It would be dangerous to assume that every large city with several synagogues (such as Rome) would have had a *gerousia* at this early stage. At Berenice the *politeuma* with its building seems to have been distinct from the synagogue community and its edifice, known from another inscription.[110] Yet both groups had a leadership using the title *archon*. This situation corresponds with that at Alexandria in that the *gerousia* seems to have been an umbrella organization distinct from, but probably representing, the individual synagogue communities. There was a similar organization at Antioch.¹¹¹

A collegial organization of segments of the Jewish population might also have used such terminology drawn from local magistracies or common collegial associations and would have facilitated the participation of non-Jews in the social life of the Jewish community, and vice versa. In many early Diaspora communities the boundaries between Jew and gentile were less rigid and allowed for access to the assembly and worship. At Sardis, it seems that such fluidity continued well into the fifth or sixth century and resulted directly in the architectural and social accommodation of the Jews. It may also have had some bearing on the fortunes of the early Christian community at Sardis.¹¹² Among the Jews at Aphrodisias, on the other hand, there may have been a growing tendency to separate the worshipping community from the collegial interaction with non-Jews. Each type of organization seems to have depended, therefore, on local circumstances relating to, among other things, the character and experiences of earlier synagogal groups and the social history surrounding their facilities. In other major cities, such as Rome, where multiple Jewish groups are known, similar organizational needs evolved over time.¹¹³

Certainly prior to 70, but continuing through the second century as well, the establishment of synagogue communities throughout the Diaspora must have generally followed the same steps as those followed at Delos, Priene, and Stobi. Private household gatherings gradually gave rise to formal establishments through a process of architectural adaptation sponsored in large measure by private benefactions. At Stobi the first edifice was nothing more than a portion of the house of the patron, Claudius Tiberius Polycharmos, set aside for the use of the Jewish community. The provisions of the bequest allowed for the remainder of the house to continue to be occupied by his family and heirs.¹¹⁴ The donation included remodeling the interior of the building to form a hall for assembly. The renovation and decoration were largely at Polycharmos' expense, though other private donations were also involved.¹¹⁵ Subsequently, catastrophic events necessitated a rebuilding of Polycharmos' synagogue quarters.[116] The renovation entailed much more substantial construction of interior and exterior. Only then did the synagogue take on more formal articulation as a religious edifice designed for assembly and worship. It must be assumed, then, that such extensive construction work would have attracted public attention and presupposed some measure of wealth and community stability, else a rebuilding could not have been considered.

Jewish Communities in the Adaptive Environment

The range of social factors that converge in and condition the adaptation of an edifice for synagogue use can best be seen in the cases of Dura-Europos and Sardis. In both cases there is longitudinal evidence, since each went through multiple stages of renovation. In both the evidence points to a Jewish presence since Hellenistic times, but an identifiable synagogue edifice emerged only in the Imperial period, around the end of the second century. In both the character of the synagogue architecture was determined by the adaptation of an existing edifice, wherein the precise features of renovation were dictated, in large measure, by local conditions and circumstances.

Dura-Europos

At Dura-Europos, the caravan city on the banks of the Euphrates, Jewish merchants and mercenaries were present since the second and first centuries B.C.E. Yet all that remain of their presence are signs of their economic activity, in the form of Hasmonean coinage.[117] There is no evidence of an established synagogal (or collegial) organization prior to renovation of the house in Block L7 in the late second century.[118] While a resident Jewish community was undoubtedly active, there is no clear indication of where they met prior to this event. Meetings, if they occurred, must have been held in the homes of individual Jews, which would have had no physical articulation for religious use. At a certain point the community decided to move toward articulation of a synagogue space by renovating a private house to accommodate an assembly function. We can only guess at these earliest stages of decision because evidence from the Early Synagogue is scant. Still, the remaining evidence points to local leaders in the Jewish community, whose names appear in that commonest form of self-proclaimed honors, graffiti.[119] The texts, in Aramaic with heavy Syrian and Palmyrene dialectical colorations, suggest the immigrant character and social location of these individuals. One name alone really stands out: *Minyamin* ("Benjamin"), who was a commissary (*apothekai*), presumably an overseer of stores or shops.[120]

More indicative of the community's social location is the form of the first synagogue building. At this stage, of primary concern was the acquisition and adaptation of an existing edifice to meet the needs of the Jewish community. The original house was fairly typical by Durene domestic standards, insula groupings of Hellenistic-oriental modifications of peristyle housing. The plan clusters several rooms around a central court entered from the street by a vestibule or passageway. In the adaptation of house to synagogue no external modifications were made and the plan was hardly changed from the domestic mode. All refurbishing was restricted to the interior.[121] The eastern portions of the house remained more private, domestic-style quarters. One room (Room 4; see fig. 15) observed the arrangement and accouterments of a diwan or dining room typical at Dura. Some internal structural modifications occurred on the west and south sides of the court, in Rooms 2 and 7. Here one large room (2), with an adjoining chamber (7), was created to serve as the hall of assembly. The functional articulation was achieved through remodeling at several significant points. The doorway from the court to Room 2 was enlarged and embellished. The doorway from the court to Room 7 was widened and arched, while a separate, smaller doorway was cut through the adjoining wall into Room 2. Interior work in Room 2 included raising the floor level and installing benches around the walls. Room 7 was also fitted with benches. Both rooms were then freshly decorated: the ceilings with coffers, the walls with geometric designs in fresco. Finally, perhaps even a bit later, a small, false aedicula was constructed on the bench of the west wall of Room 2 at a point directly opposite the main door from the court.[122]

SYNAGOGUES IN THE GRAECO-ROMAN DIASPORA

This process reflects a conscious plan of adaptation despite the fact that no major structural changes were made. Room 2 became a formal hall of assembly, albeit modest in size and decor. Room 7 probably served as an antechamber, a "sacristy" or *naiskos* of sorts for the Torah.[123] Presumably, then, the graffiti, if only a partial record, preserve the names of donors who contributed to the project; however, any record of ownership of the house, of the major donor, is lost.[124] It is possible that the owner, or a resident caretaker (*ḥazzan*), continued to use the domestic rooms on the eastern side of the court, but they would have served as well for community functions or hospitality.[125] The plan and outfitting of the assembly hall suggest that some formal notions of synagogue worship were beginning to emerge, though they were by no means normative. Most notable in this regard is the appearance of a fixed Torah shrine. Even though it was more decorative (and probably did not serve as the permanent repository), this case marks the earliest identifiable archaeological evidence of the Torah shrine as a physically articulated focal point in the architecture of assembly.[126]

Circumstances in Dura's Jewish community in the early third century made possible an extensive rebuilding project for this First Synagogue. Honorific inscriptions in both Aramaic and Greek celebrate the project and its donors, and place the date in the year 244/245 C.E.[127] The building program consisted of three major projects: first, renovation of the structure of the Early Synagogue; second, annexation of the contiguous house (H) to the east; and third, appointment and decoration of the enlarged hall of assembly (in two successive stages).[128]

The structural modifications of the Early Synagogue that were undertaken were enormous (see figs. 15 and 16). All of the interior walls were demolished along with the exterior west wall along the street, which had been the entrance to the building. Necessarily, the roof was also removed. In addition, the exterior wall on the north (which was a party wall with neighboring House C) was completely demolished, while the one on the east (the party wall with House H) was at least partially removed. The reconstruction began by raising thicker carrying walls: one on the west exterior; another parallel to it, across the middle of the space; and one on the north (the party wall with House C). These walls were consciously erected to carry a greater ceiling height over a broader expanse, and thus was created the new, more monumental hall of assembly. It occupied the same basic placement as that of the early hall (Room 2) but was expanded to the north and east. Moreover, the spatial arrangement of the room remained essentially the same, including the orientation of the main doorway, a smaller south entrance, and the central aedicula. The rest of the area of the earlier house now became an enlarged porticoed courtyard framing the main doorway to the hall. This new building was no longer a house, even though it remained within its previous property lines in the domestic insula.

It must be noted that the construction plans called for the former entry vestibule to be incorporated into the expanded assembly hall. Thus, a planned feature of the renovation involved a reorientation of the entry to the east side of the building through the court. The annexation of neighboring House H allowed for a new entrance to the court by cutting through the party wall (in Room H4), and with the arrangement of a suite of entry chambers (through Rooms H1, H3, and H4). The remaining rooms of House H seem to have continued their private, domestic form and function, with Room H8 serving as the diwan. It appears, however, that the acquisition, or at least the physical annexation, of House H came after the rebuilding of the hall and court of the synagogue proper. This is suggested by the unusually narrow party wall with House C in the area of the court, especially given its evident lack of fit with the structural components of the portico. Thus, the porticoed court was completed before the side wall section. It is entirely likely that, before gaining physical access through House H, entry to the synagogue court came temporarily through House C (Room C29).[129]

These features of the construction project are further suggestive of circumstances within the Dura Jewish community through the first half of the third century.[130] The renovation project was occasioned by growth in numbers, wealth, and status. The enlarged hall of assembly could accommodate more than double the capacity of the earlier one, not counting the expanded area of the court. With the annexation of House H the area of the synagogue complex was nearly two and one-half times its earlier size. The destruction of exterior and party walls and the monumentalization of the proportions created an edifice that stood out noticeably from its domestic surroundings. Likewise, the demolition of party walls must have had measurable impact on those living around, and it may suggest that other houses in the block (especially Houses C, B, and D) had passed into Jewish hands.[131] In particular, it seems likely that House C was owned by the priest and *presbyter*, Samuel, who is honored as the "builder," that is the leading patron, in the renovation of the Later Synagogue.[132] The inscriptions indicate that Samuel in effect headed a community building project assisted by other leading members of the congregation, including Silas (a proselyte), and by contributions from the congregation at large (a building fund).[133] The Jewish community had grown in numbers as the city itself had increased in population under the Roman buildup of the early third century. It may mean that other Jews had moved there, and the multilingual inscriptions attest a more cosmopolitan membership.[134] That one person prominent in the rebuilding is also called a proselyte may further suggest some lines of recruitment among the non-Jewish population as well.[135] Numerical growth and economic initiatives probably correlated with increased status or prominence for the Jewish community, or some of its members, within Durene society. The new synagogue was a recognizable, public, religious edifice, and there are signs of accommodation to norms of Durene temple style from pagan religious architecture.[136] Even the entrance to the building was moved from the dirty back street next to the city's west wall around to the other side of the block, a more auspicious location. Yet for all its opulence, expansion, and accommodation, it must be remembered that the later synagogue derived its basic spatial features from the earlier house synagogue and its patterns of worship.

Sardis

In some ways the synagogue at Sardis reflects what might have happened at Dura had the prevailing trends of growth and acculturation continued. While there is no precise analogy between the two sites, the massive Sardis synagogue presupposes several generations of active growth and social mobility by just such a local Jewish enclave. While more Jews may have arrived in Lydia in the second century B.C.E., it is clear from a Roman decree preserved by Josephus that there was a well-established community by the middle of the first century B.C.E.[137] The Roman decrees were responses to petitions by Sardian Jews to claim their legal and ancestral religion. Their request, like those of the Jewish communities in Ephesus, Pergamum, Halicarnassus, and Delos, was heard favorably by the Romans. One peculiar feature of the Sardis situation was the right claimed by the Jews to have their own place (*topos*) for assembly and governance of their affairs. Since the texts refer to worship, legal activities, and communal gatherings, an early collegial hall and synagogue complex is likely; however, it may yet have been some more private building, conceivably a renovated house. A substantial period elapsed before the Jewish community once again undertook building programs, after coming into possession of new property in the later second or early third century C.E.[138] The new hall was part of the monumental bath-gymnasium complex dating from the Antonine period. Its acquisition and renovation by the Jews must have depended upon municipal authorization, suggesting that there was already a thriving Jewish community with a well-established rapport with its environment. The municipal approval suggests a high status placement for the Jewish community, or some of its members, within Sardian society even before the acquisition. The earlier *topos* might have gone through several stages of embellishment, not unlike developments at Dura-Europos. Unfortunately, no archaeological evidence has been found to indicate either the plan or location of the earlier building. By the third century, however, the Jewish community had moved into its new building. There, through three phases of renovation and remodeling they adapted a public bath hall into a basilical synagogue hall, the largest and most opulent known from the later Roman empire.

The inscriptions of the Sardis synagogue bear witness to the favored social position of the Jewish community in civic life among leading citizens, who were sympathetic toward the worship of the one God. No doubt this favor accounts in large measure for the acquisition of the municipal property. Among the donors to the synagogue decoration and building projects, three men are identified as citizens (*Sardianos*), three as city councillors (*bouleutes*), and six more use both titles.[139] Twelve people, then, appear to be part of the local decurionate, although Jewish ancestry is not clear. A good number of these donors and others also bear the *gentilicium* Aurelius, indicating that they had received the grant of Roman citizenship through the *Constitutio antoniana* of Caracalla in the year 212 C.E.[140] Two other donors are identified as clerics (*boēthoi taboulariou*) in the provincial administration; another was a former procurator (*apo epitropon*); another was a count (*comēs*). Many of these inscriptions come from the last stages of renovation, when the synagogue had been firmly established as a social center in Sardian civic life. Most were the result of prolific donations both by members of the Jewish community and by non-Jewish sympathizers for outfitting and decoration of the basilical hall.[141] One inscription from the forecourt, a later addition, mentions renovation (*ananeōsis*) and corresponds to the multiple stages of architectural adaptation.[142] Earlier inscriptions refer to other leading members of the Jewish community who contributed to the building and decoration, such as the unnamed husband of Regina or the religious official, also unnamed, whose titles include priest (*hiereos*) and "teacher of wisdom" (*sophōdidaskalos*).[143] Thus, not only the size and opulence of the synagogue building but also the prosopographic evidence of the inscriptions attest to the numerical popularity, the economic strength, and the social influence of this Jewish community.

When the Jewish community of Sardis took possession of the municipal property it was, at best, a plain public hall.[144] At first, it appears, the Jews used the hall as it was, but before long, probably around 212 C.E., some renovations were undertaken to make it more suitable for their purposes.[145] These renovations included minimal structural changes and the first stages of decoration in the western, apsidal end of the hall, which seems to have served as the primary area of assembly at this stage (see fig. 14). Only in later stages was the rest of the hall renovated and incorporated into the assembly functions of the synagogue. Hence some growth is reflected in the architectural progression, until the synagogue achieved its final form in the renovation of the fourth century.[146] In this stage major structural modifications were introduced, most notably in the construction of a partition wall toward the east end to set off the area of the forecourt. This wall construction and the transformation to an atrium forecourt necessitated removing a portion of the ceiling and masonry work down to subfoundation levels in order to carry the high ceiling of the basilical hall. Meanwhile the atrium forecourt became an elaborate and highly decorated formal entrance to the building, leading to a tri-portal to the assembly hall proper. In the hall new decorations were introduced, such as the mosaic work of the apse, the lion statues, and the marble "Eagle Table."[147] At the east end, facing out from the newly erected crossing wall, two aediculae were constructed using Doric- and Corinthian-style building spoils. These steps reflect greater formalization in the liturgical adaptation of the synagogue hall. The introduction of fixed Torah shrines, here doubled to flank the central doorway symmetrically, marks a development in worship. At the same time, these renovations and additions indicate a complete reversal of the orientation of the hall from the western apse end to the eastern aediculae, at least for certain aspects of worship. This reorientation corresponds to a more formalized liturgy and was captured in the new decorative mosaics.[148] Thus, one sees a building that was decorated as a public showplace by a highly acculturated Jewish community, and yet was undergoing more formal liturgical development, which suggests stricter lines of worship.[149]

Whatever the meager beginnings of the Sardis Jewish community in the second century B.C.E., by the later Roman period it had been brought into the mainstream of public religious life in that city. One must be careful to account for the local circumstances of each synagogue community, especially since the evidence at two nearby cities, Priene and Aphrodisias, suggests still other interpretations. Social standing and private patronage must be considered when evaluating the acquisition and adaptation of property for religious use by these Jewish communities. A common thread for the diffusion of Jewish groups in the Diaspora, as with other foreign religious associations, was to move first into private quarters which over time were gradually adapted more to the peculiar needs of religious use in accordance with the social circumstances of the community.

5
From House Church to Church Building
Phases of Christian Growth and Adaptation

▲ ▲ ▲

To the Roman historian Tacitus, writing in the early second century, the Christians had begun to emerge as a separate and identifiable new religious group. As such they were liable to popular as well as official suspicion. They were seen as another among the numerous foreign superstitions that had flooded toward the capital as a result of the *Pax Romana*.[1] Still, it must be noted that while Tacitus was commenting on events in Nero's day, he was a contemporary of the Emperor Trajan. He was also a good friend and protege of the younger Pliny, whom he had visited while the latter was serving as imperial legate in Bithynia as a special favor to Trajan. In fact, Pliny's personal correspondence with the Emperor (Epp. X.96 and 97), written during this same period, constitutes the first official recognition on the part of Roman authorities of Christians as a religious group separate from Jews. Tacitus himself also served as proconsul of Asia in 112–113, about the time that Ignatius of Antioch passed through Ephesus and Smyrna on his way to martyrdom at Rome. Thus, Tacitus' histories may have projected onto the actions of Nero a cognizance of Christian group identity not possible in that earlier period. By the second century, however, Christians were becoming identifiable among the myriad travelers on the roads to and from the seats of Roman power. Missionaries, priests, charlatans, and shams come to the fore also in Apuleius and Lucian, and even moreso by the time of Celsus and Galen.[2] By way of contrast, the earliest form of the *Jesusbewegung* (or "Jesus movement"), as Gerd Theissen calls it, had no such self-consciousness.[3] As a sectarian apocalyptic movement within first-century Palestine, its identity was dominantly Jewish and millenarian. Within these groups, Jesus was remembered as saying, "Go only to the lost sheep of the house of Israel" and "You will not have gone through all the towns of Israel before the Son of Man comes" (Matt. 10.6, 23). The mission and message of the earliest Jesus sects were by and for Jews exclusively.[4]

The exclusively Jewish mission of the earliest Jesus movement apparently had little need for formal places of worship, especially prior to the destruction of the Jerusalem Temple. Other Jewish groups offered models of causal assembly for prayer and study as well.[5] The passage of time, the movement beyond the limited scope of the Jewish mission, and the experience of the broader Diaspora environment for private religious groups gradually prompted new needs for accommodation and adaptation.

The House Church

Like the early Pharisees, we may imagine the followers of Jesus and other teachers of the time gathering occasionally for fellowship, prayer, and study.[6] This practice is depicted both in the gospel narratives regarding Jesus and in the traditional picture of Acts. In Acts 2–5 the earliest disciples at Jerusalem reportedly met "from house to house" or just "at home," while also attending to traditional Jewish observance at the Temple.[7] Beyond this little more can be said. It would appear that there were relatively few, if any, settled communities, since the original leadership was vested in wandering charismatic teachers and prophets, including the original disciples.[8] There is evidence of more settled Christian groups after the mid-forties. This evidence comes mainly from the accounts of the Jerusalem council and may reflect only the circumstances of Jerusalem and Antioch. Of what was happening in other localities, such as the Galilee or nearer Syria, hardly anything is known. The dominant expectation remained for a speedy consummation of apocalyptic hopes, an imminent political eschaton, which might have militated against rapid institutionalization.[9] There is some evidence of an emerging tension between the ethos of itineracy held by wandering charismatics and the ethos of localized gatherings in the homes of individual leaders.[10] Still, we may suppose with the author of Luke-Acts that the earliest cells of the Jesus movement began to assemble with regularity in houses and that this practice spread with the initial expansion of the movement outside the exclusively Jewish Homeland. In the initial move to the Diaspora, the pattern of house synagogues could well have afforded the first lines of Christian organization. Even so, early questions and shifts over community practice and boundaries could have generated diverse responses from cell to cell.[11]

Whatever our speculation regarding the beginnings, the most explicit indicator of a move toward household location for the movement comes from Paul's Aegean mission. In these areas it became typical for Christians to meet in the home of an individual member who served as host and patron. The Pauline mission was largely an urban phenomenon in the romanized centers on major trade routes through western Asia Minor and Greece. Even in areas not founded directly on Paul's efforts, such as Rome or Cappadocia, similar patterns are indicated.[12] Thus, by the fifties and sixties there was a proliferation of settled house church cells as part of the process of expansion through the Roman world. It is possible that Pauline missionary practice grew out of his initial efforts at a gentile mission while in the region of Syria near Cilicia, before his ill-fated confrontation with conservative factions at Antioch.[13] It is significant to note that the way west, to the Aegean and on to Rome, was already well marked by the establishment of synagogue communities in major urban settings (as noted in the previous chapter). Still, one must exercise caution regarding the traditional picture, since many of these synagogue communities also began in homes or other private settings. Nor can we naively assume that Paul went to household meetings only after being forced out of the synagogue by Jewish opposition to his Christian message. Many Pauline house churches seem to have been drawn almost entirely from the non-Jewish population, and the pattern of organization had to have been recognizable and acceptable in their environment.[14]

By definition, these earliest Pauline house churches would have had no distinguishing features, since there was no move toward spatial articulation or architectural adaptation. For the most part private houses were used for casual assembly. Otherwise they remained in domestic use. Other kinds of private meeting places were also available, such as the "hall" (*scholē*) of Tyrannus at Ephesus (Acts 19.9). The apocryphal *Acts of Paul* depict a large crowded assembly of Christians in a warehouse (*horreum*) on the outskirts of Rome.[15] Still, by far the most common reference in the early literature, including the apocryphal Acts, focuses attention on the private domestic setting.[16]

The house church setting offers two important features for understanding the nature of the Pauline mission: first, in the social organization, and second, in the nature of assembly. In the first, then, when one looks carefully at any of Paul's letters, it becomes clear that each one presupposes an active interchange through travel and correspondence. His correspondence with the Christians at Philippi probably involved five exchanges (including a personal envoy from Philippi to Ephesus to bring Paul money) prior to the present Philippian letter of the New Testament.[17] Perhaps better known are the multiple letters and visits to and from Corinth. In addition to the several pieces preserved, there were at least two lost letters from Paul, three visits by Paul alone (not counting those by his helpers), and at least one official delegation from Corinth, carrying a letter to Paul in Ephesus.[18] In short, the mission must have been a beehive of activity as Paul, his co-workers, other Christians, and letters by all of them crisscrossed the Aegean. This enterprise depended upon the social organization of the house church communities.

In the major cities there were probably several such house church cells loosely tied together. There may have been six or more at Corinth during Paul's time. According to Acts 18, when Paul first arrived at Corinth he stayed and worked with Prisca (Priscilla) and Aquila. Later, however, it seems that Prisca and Aquila moved to Ephesus, where they also hosted a church in their house.[19] By the time Paul wrote to Rome, they had gone ahead to set up yet another house church there.[20] Back at Corinth, then, it is noted in Acts 18.7 that Paul also worked out of the house of Titius Justus, who lived adjacent to the synagogue.

We know, too, that the households of Stephanas, Crispus, and Chloe played a pivotal role.[21] Still another house church cell was located at Cenchreai (the eastern port at Corinth) under the patroness Phoebe, and another elsewhere in the house of Gaius.[22]

Group organization and travel depended upon the hospitality of these house church owners. A number of important social conventions developed around the practice of household hospitality, which came to apply equally well to groups as to individuals. Some of these social conventions can still be glimpsed in the letters in terms of "extending the right hand of fellowship" or "greeting with a holy kiss."[23] Letter-writing itself was part of this social fabric. We may notice especially the case of the house church patron Philemon, to whom Paul wrote requesting that a guest room (*xenia*) be readied.[24] Thus, Paul regularly lodged with the house church patron. Letter-writing served not only as a means of transmitting information, but also for securing hospitality for himself or a protegé. So widespread was this practice that a convention of letter-writing developed. The "letter of recommendation" had a virtually standardized form and technical language for the implicit social obligations of the household.[25] Typical phrases such as "receiving" and "sending on one's way," therefore, are recognizable literary clues to the social networks of hospitality and patronage in the house church organization.

Even the massive Roman letter carried, as one of its intentions, a request that hospitality be shown to its bearer, Phoebe, who was probably acting as Paul's personal envoy.[26] Thus, the same kindness and generosity that she had extended to Paul and the church at Cenchreai was now to be shown to her in a house church at Rome. It appears that Phoebe was directed first to the house of Paul's old friends Prisca and Aquila, by then at Rome, before addressing the several other house churches of the capital.[27] Paul's old house church network from the Aegean was now providing entry into the new house church networks at Rome, through the exercise of letter-writing and hospitality. In the same vein, it should be recognized that in sending Phoebe (with the letter as a kind of manifesto for himself) Paul was anticipating his own trip to Rome. Paul wanted not only to be received hospitably in their house churches, but also to be "sped on his way" by them in his intended mission to Spain.[28] In other words, using the conventions of hospitality, letter-writing, and patronage centered in the house church setting, Paul was requesting financial support for his mission in terms that the Roman Christians could hardly misunderstand.

If the house church setting was basic to the social fabric of Paul's mission, it was also the center of assembly and worship within the local group. Housing patterns, of course, varied considerably across the Empire. The Italian villa, the Greek peristyle, the Hellenistic-oriental multistoried insula, apartments, and others had their own local stylistic traditions. We must expect, then, that as with mithraea and synagogues there was considerable diversity from place to place depending on the local circumstances of each cell group.[29] In sharp contrast to the assumptions of older theories regarding Christian architecture, it is now believed that it was highly unlikely that Christians assembled in any regular fashion in the atrium of a large Campanian style villa.[30] For the cities of the Aegean coast a different type of house setting must be envisaged. It seems that assembly was regularly convened in the dining room of the house, which in some cases might open onto a peristyle or portico. Often the triclinium, or dining room, was the largest area in the house and the most suitable for a gathering of people. Greeks and Romans alike were well known for their dinner parties, and the larger houses came well equipped to accommodate the social functions.

In dealing with the circumstances of worship, Paul presupposes that the gathering was held around the common table. This is precisely the situation one must imagine to understand the setting and the problems in 1 Corinthians 11, which deals with the Lord's Supper, as well as in chapters 12–14. Many of the problems seem to come naturally from the social composition of the house church group. We should not assume, however, that all the Christians in a given city got together regularly for the eucharist or that the eucharist was functionally separate from the meal itself. Thus, dining in individual house church

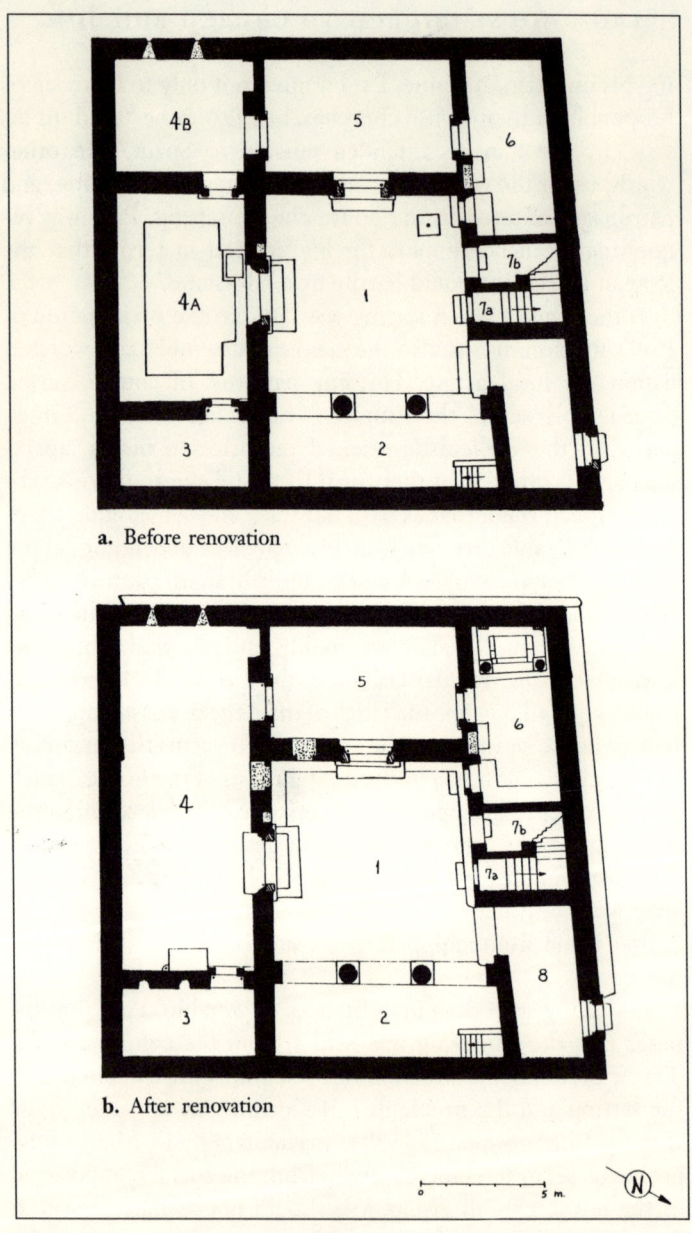

Fig. 17.
Plan reconstruction before and after the Christian Building at Dura-Europos was renovated into a domus ecclesiae.

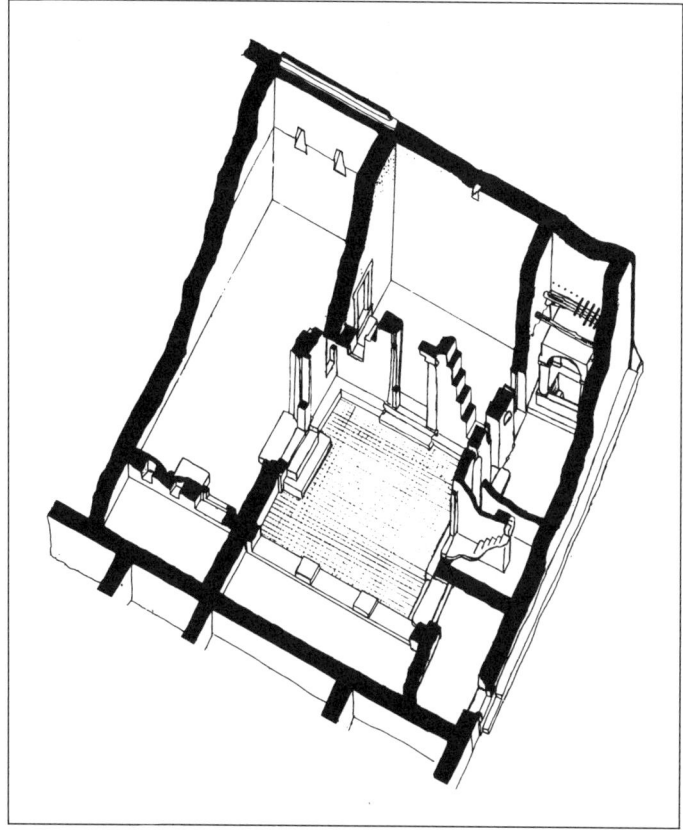

Fig. 18.
Isometric reconstruction of the Christian Building at Dura-Europos.

groups was fundamental.³¹ At Corinth, in the context of communal dining, a lack of discernment regarding the meal as a sign of fellowship among the members of the group was creating dissension.³² Still, the communal meal was the center of fellowship (*koinōnia*), as eating was a sign of social relations with others. The extension of hospitality through the meal setting was the central act that served to define the worshipping community, the church (*ekklēsia*) in household assembly.³³

How long this indistinct household setting continued to predominate in Christian practice is difficult to judge. The Johannine epistles still clearly reflect a localized house church setting under a patron in western Asia Minor by the early part of the second century.[34] This picture is consistent in the works of other contemporaneous Christian writers from the region, such as 1 Peter, the works of Ignatius, the works of Polycarp, and the Pastoral Epistles.[35] The earliest and clearest archaeological evidence of the development is, of course, the Dura-Europos Christian building (see figs. 17 and 18). Its renovation from a house into a church building can be securely dated to before the mid-third century;[36] however, given its somewhat isolated location, one would not think it the first to have undergone such architectural adaptation. Literary evidence suggests that household and other private meetings continued through the second century. The *Martyrdom of Justin* points to the situation at Rome at least until 165.[37] Justin had initially come to Rome in around 150 and had taught there in his own school. Upon his arrest, he was asked by the prefect Q. Junius Rusticus where the Christians customarily met. Justin shrugged off the notion of a single meeting place, but admitted of his own assembly in the same place where he also lived and taught, "above the baths of so-and-so." It is unfortunate that the text is corrupt at precisely that point where the baths or their owner were named, as it might have provided evidence of a concrete locality in Rome.[38] Nonetheless, it appears that private or domestic settings were still in use in the middle of the second century for at least some groups. In his own writings Justin indicates that baptism was still administered at a convenient spot "wherever there is water."[39] If these two texts of Justin can be tied together, then baptism might well have been performed downstairs at the baths. In any case, nothing in Justin's description of worship explicitly required physical renovation such as that at Dura-Europos. Given the allusion to a meeting place "above the baths," a large urban insula of the type typically found at Rome might be presupposed.[40]

FROM HOUSE CHURCH TO CHURCH BUILDING

The Domus Ecclesiae

To gain some sense of the development that occurred in Christian attitudes toward their buildings, we need only reflect momentarily on the situation of Justin's assembly compared with that at Dura-Europos less than a century later. For Justin the needs of communal assembly could still be met in the same location that he lived, while the liturgical functions of baptism required nothing more than access to water, even that in an otherwise typical bathing establishment. At Dura, however, such catch-as-catch-can arrangements were no longer adequate or desirable. The edifice itself, to be sure, was still just a house in external form, but one room had been set aside as an assembly hall, and the self-consciousness reflected in the adaptation for another room as a private and carefully laid-out baptistry is even more striking. It had become a "church building" of some sort.

Needless to say, these two cases are not precisely comparable in historical terms, since they are so distant from one another in time and geography. One expects intuitively that local circumstances and social factors would condition distinctive features of the setting for assembly between Rome in the second century and Syria in the third. As a heuristic device, these cases are indicative of courses of change and development in stages, as orders of magnitude rather than rigid categories of architecture. They reflect the beginnings of physical adaptation of an existing edifice to make it more suitable for the specialized religious and social functions of Christian assembly. Thus, since we have defined the unrenovated space of the Pauline period as the *house church*, we may call a specially adapted building the *house of the church*, hence a *domus ecclesiae*. It is natural to suppose that in some cases private homes where Christian groups had met were gradually given over more and more to specific church functions. In other cases it is possible that new buildings became available, as local Christian congregations grew and began to hold property. Often we can only guess the steps in this process for any given group or locality, since the recognizable church building from an archaeological perspective depends upon renovation to a domus ecclesiae. In the case of Dura-

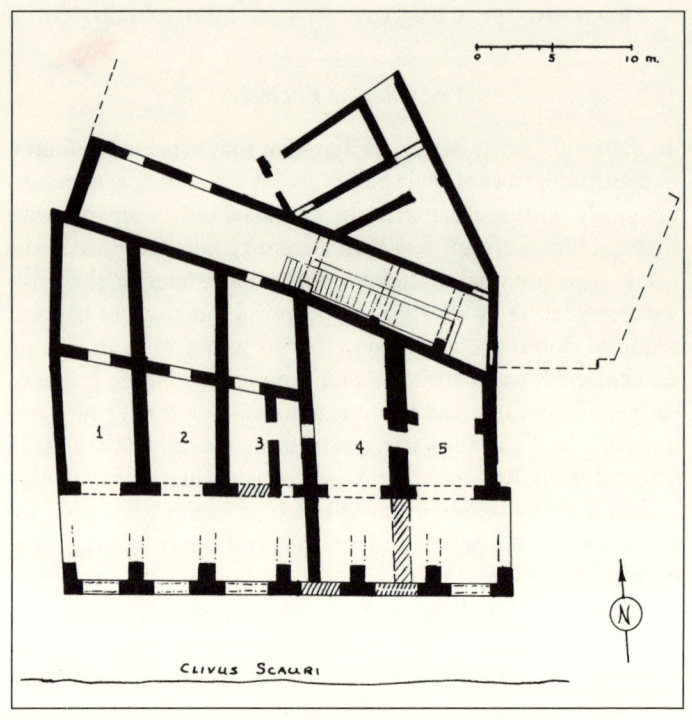

Fig. 19.
Plan restoration of renovated insula in *titulus Byzantis* at Rome.

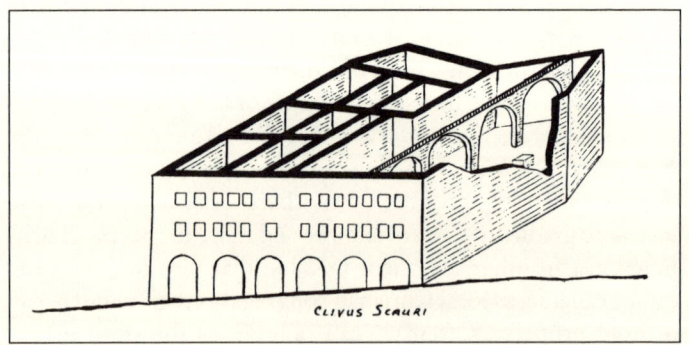

Fig. 20.
Isometric reconstruction of *titulus Byzantis* at Rome.

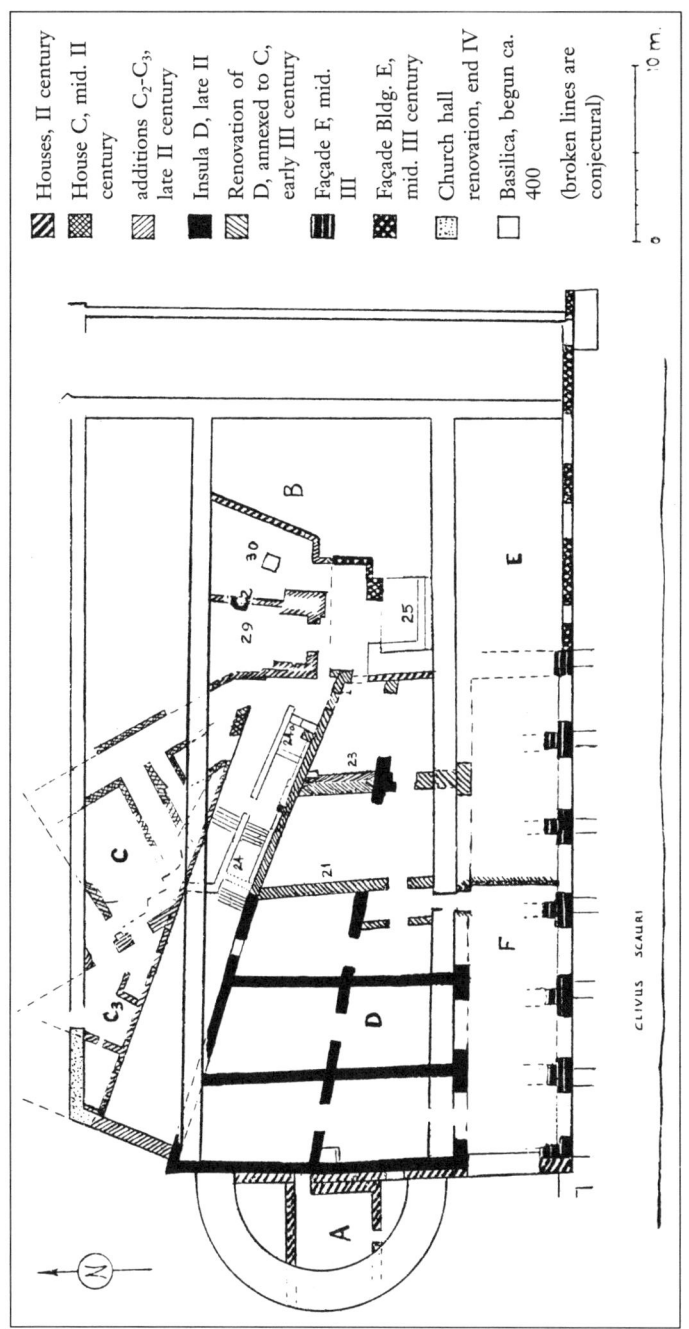

Fig. 21.
Plan restoration of the Basilica SS. Giovanni e Paolo at Rome.

Europos, it is not clear that the Christians met in that particular house prior to its renovation as a church building. Nonetheless, through its physical adaptation we may observe the activities of an existing local Christian group in the process of development.

In general, it appears that the first steps toward adaptation occurred in an edifice where the Christians were already accustomed to meeting. Renovation reflects a natural course of functional usage by designating areas spatially that had become associated with specific forms of religious actions or assembly. Partial or gradual renovation of an existing house church location is probably indicated by the third century for at least two of the roman *tituli*, later known as parish churches. The *titulus Clementis* (later the Basilica San Clemente) is linked by tradition to the renowned figure of Clement, a "bishop" and author of a letter to Corinth at the end of the first century.[41] While clear evidence of Christian usage is lacking in the private structures of the first-century levels, by the third century the edifice had been taken over and renovated in successive stages from a domus ecclesiae. It was finally converted to basilical form in the fifth century. In the case of the *titulus Byzantis* (later the Basilica SS. Giovanni e Paolo; see figs. 19, 20, and 21), Richard Krautheimer has suggested a continuum of Christian adaptation beginning by the late second or early third century.[42] It progressed from an insula complex, in which a small Christian cell met in a rear shop, to a renovated domus ecclesiae. Gradual adaptation continued until the entire insula had been taken over, well before the time it was converted to basilical form in the early fifth century. Not long thereafter (around 540) the future pope Gregory the Great was born in a house just across the street.

Partial renovation in many cases seems to have been the initial stage of architectural adaptation for Christians as for Jews and other groups in the Roman environment. Partial renovation is also indicated in archaeological remains for the earliest levels beneath the Basilica Euphrasiana at Parentium, Istria.[43] The site had originally been occupied by a large villa, in which one room appears to have been designated for Christian usage. Later, in the fourth century, the entire house was taken over and renovated more substantially, prior to its subsequent monu-

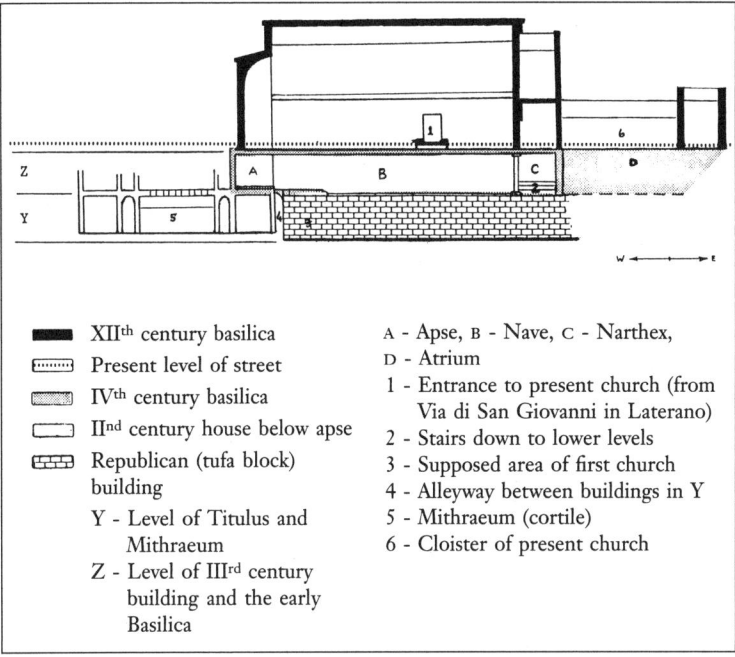

Fig. 22.
Schematic section of the Basilica San Clemente at Rome.

mentalization as a basilica in the fifth and again in the sixth centuries. Other sites that may provide archaeological support for intermediate stages of partial renovation from private domestic structures include the so-called Church of Julianos at Umm el-Jimal, Syria/Arabia, and the supposed villa and domus ecclesiae beneath the Church of Bishop Theodore at Aquileia, Istria.[44] We may surmise that in some ways these cases are analogous to the provisions made in the contemporary renovation of the house of Claudius Tiberius Polycharmos into a synagogue, or in a number of mithraea, where gradual growth and expansion is reflected in subsequent stages of renovation.[45]

It is difficult to glimpse the features of these intermediate stages of adaptation, since they were so often overlaid or destroyed in later rebuilding. At San Clemente (fig. 22), for

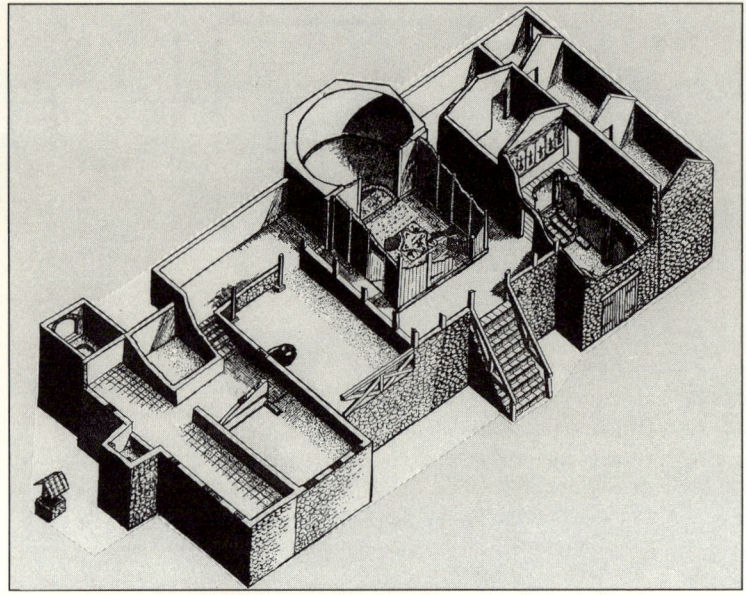

Fig. 23.
Isometric reconstruction of the Roman villa with Christian chapel at Lullingstone.

example, supports for the later basilica were built down to the level of the earlier buildings, thus removing some of the most significant archaeological remains. Dura-Europos is all the more significant, therefore, since it offers such evidence without later levels of usage. Another illuminating case comes from the Lullingstone villa in Roman Britannia.[46] Here, in the last half of the fourth century, one wing of a large estate home was given over to serve as a Christian "chapel" (see fig. 23). In the renovation the area was given a separate entrance and an antechamber to the "chapel" hall, while the rest of the villa continued in private domestic occupation. After a while the house was abandoned, but the chapel continued to be used by a local Christian group until the barbarian invasions when the entire complex was destroyed. The nature of these renovations suggests a concrete design on the part of the owners of the villa to articulate architecturally an assembly space. Their role can probably be seen in the decoration of the chapel room and antechamber, reflecting a kind of familial patronage over the Christian community. It is also possible to see a gradual segregation of the "chapel" wing from the rest of the house, accomplished finally by a physical alteration. The access hall to the rest of the house was walled off, and a new doorway was cut to the outside to allow entry without going through the house. Thus, a partial renovation gradually achieved a more autonomous function as a domus ecclesiae through continued adaptation. It was no longer just the house church of the owner/patron; it had become the church building of the local Christian community.

More often than not, we must guess, partial renovation of an existing edifice depended on its tacit designation by the local religious group as a permanent place of assembly. Naturally, such a designation depended not only on the habits and self-consciousness of the community, but also on the auspices of the owner, especially in the case of a house. Among the factors that gave rise to partial adaptation was a focus on assembly as the central area of concern. Articulation of an assembly space began most likely as a modest and utilitarian design, with other functional adaptation or decorative treatments coming later. Often, the initial adaptation of an assembly space might entail little more than a minor physical alteration or an artistic flourish to demarcate the space for worship. So, at Parentium the first adaptation in the villa's tablinum (living room) seems to have been a mosaic floor with cryptic Christian symbols. Other Christian floor treatments are seen in the Roman house at Hinton St. Mary's near Dorset, England, where there is otherwise little indication of a place for worship.[47] In most cases such minimal adaptations have been obscured by later layers of Christian rebuilding and monumentalization.

Exactly when Christians first began to renovate houses or other private structures into church buildings is hard to say with certainty. One would not expect the transformation to have taken place overnight, and a different pace was likely from region to region within the Empire.[48] Dura-Europos was hardly the first. The earliest clear reference to an identifiable Christian edifice comes from the Syriac *Edessene Chronicle*.[49] Ostensibly a court history, the *Chronicle* records a flood that swept through the city in the year 201 C.E. Numerous buildings, including the palace, were damaged or destroyed. In the listing of damages is "the temple [*haikla*] of the church of the Christians." The passage is debated, some taking it more or less at face value, others questioning it as a later historiographical projection from Catholic orthodoxy.[50] The problem lies in interpreting the redundant phrase "temple of the church," at a time when orthodox basilical church architecture did not exist. In fact, the seeming redundancy of the phrase is similar to usage found in some synagogue inscriptions that refer to the holy place (*hagios topos*) or prayer hall (*proseuchē*) of the Jewish congregation (*synagogē*).[51] Far from evincing an early instance of monumental church architecture, the passage probably reflects a building that had become publicly identifiable to locals as the regular meeting place of the Christians. Hence, reading "the holy place of the congregation of the Christians" would suggest a renovated domus ecclesiae.[52] This reading may be supported by another entry from the *Edessene Chronicle* for the year 313. It records the building of the "church" at Edessa, which was begun under the famous bishop Kûne (ca. 284–313) and completed under his successor, bishop Saʿad (313–324).[53] With Walter Bauer, I take this passage to refer to the erection of the first monumental church building by the orthodox, in some measure as a replacement for the buildings of earlier times used by divergent Christian groups.[54]

There are perhaps other indications of architectural change around the beginning of the third century, or at about the same time as the earlier entry from the *Edessene Chronicle*. Between the time of Justin (ca. 165) and the year 212, with the universal grant of citizenship under the *Constitutio Antoniana*, there was an emergence of a more distinctively Christian material culture. Graydon Snyder, for one, sees the years from 180 and 200 as the period during which Christian art, funerary symbolism, and building began to achieve their own cultural definition.[55] In terms of the development of the domus ecclesiae this period

FROM HOUSE CHURCH TO CHURCH BUILDING

seems to correspond with the emerging needs within the Christian community for specially articulated places of worship. These needs can be seen in some measure as a direct, functional development of the kind of assembly that had obtained in the house church setting.

In Paul's day and into the second century the primary setting for assembly had been the communal meal in the dining room of the house. Paul's own version of the Last Supper tradition stressed the meal setting by having the eucharistic elements of bread and wine literally bracket the meal proper.[56] The problem addressed by Paul at Corinth was the distortion of the meal as a result of social stratification within the community, so that its communal intentions had been destroyed.[57] Given the problem and Paul's corrective, we may see that the eucharist, as later understood, had not yet become an act of worship separate from the communal meal, sometimes called the agapē or love feast.[58] The main arena of worship assembly, including both the eucharist and other acts of instruction and exhortation, was the communal context of the dining table in the house church.[59] Nor should we assume that in Paul's day all the various house church cells in a given locality ever got together regularly for a larger eucharistic assembly.[60]

Two interrelated factors may have created the need for a different articulation of worship space. The first is numerical growth of the house church community, which would make a meal gathering within the confines of typical domestic architecture impractical. The second, then, is the gradual separation of the eucharist from the agapē meal.[61] Together these two factors would contribute to lines of architectural definition in individual communities. There is no direct evidence for a separate eucharist prior to the middle of the second century; agapē and eucharistic assembly still appear to have been interchangeable.[62] Even within the liturgical instruction of the *Didache* there is no clear separation of setting.[63] As the meal became less practical, however, it was possible to stylize the meal elements into symbolic forms, resulting in the liturgical pattern seen in Justin and Tertullian in the latter half of the second century.[64] Ritual forms then came to replace the casual elements of house church dining though they attempted to preserve it through symbolism. As the actual amount of dining diminished less food was needed and the voluntary offering for the common table was reduced. The offertory developed as a symbolization of individual contributions to the meal, a ritualization of common meal actions, even though the actual practice was changing.[65] These shifts were by no means uniform or unilateral; however, they resulted in a gradual separation of the stylized eucharistic liturgy from the older casual form of communal dining. The earliest direct evidence for this separation comes from the beginning of the third century, seen then as more or less a fait accompli. Clement of Alexandria reflects this sharper division in his references to the agapē meal practice.[66] The clearest regulation of private agapē meal practice apart from public assembly for eucharist appears in the *Apostolic Tradition* of Hippolytus.[67] This separation of eucharist from agapē, whether for pragmatic or theological reasons, had a correlative impact on the arrangements and setting for assembly. As the eucharistic assembly was no longer confined to the domestic dining area, it became possible, or necessary, to adapt the assembly space to another kind of arrangement. At this point the archaeological evidence points to the emergence of a hall arrangement for assembly, much as in the formalization of the synagogue. Both cases are in evidence from Dura-Europos.

The Dura Christian building represents a thorough transformation from house to domus ecclesiae through architectural adaptation. Since there is no evidence of partial adaptation at an earlier stage, it is not possible to claim that the Christians had been accustomed to meeting there as a house church prior to its renovation.[68] The renovation project dates to around 240–241, at which time the house was entirely devoted to religious functions and all domestic activities ceased. How the property was acquired by the Christians is uncertain; however, an outright purchase or individual donation is likely. Indications of personal acts of patronage may be evidenced in the inscriptions of the baptistry room.[69] In any case the legal principles of ownership remain a clouded issue for many religious sanctuaries in this period. Functionally, at least, the Dura building had become a

FROM HOUSE CHURCH TO CHURCH BUILDING

"church," a domus ecclesiae, donated to and property of the local Christian community. The manner in which the Dura building was renovated also illuminates the process of adaptation. On the exterior no major structural modifications were undertaken to change the essential domestic character of the edifice. On the interior no basic changes were made in the arrangement of rooms around the central court. Even though the building was devoted entirely to Christian religious functions, and all habitation ceased, the adaptation is closer to the structural level of the earlier rather than the later synagogue at Dura.

The major adaptation for assembly came with the enlargement of the diwan or dining room (triclinium) by knocking out the partition wall to create the elongated hall, Room 4 (see fig. 17). The process suggests a well-defined plan to accommodate assembly and liturgy. The orientation of the room toward a dais (probably used as a pulpitum or bema) at one end created a more formal order to the assembly than that expected in the dinner setting.[70] The other major area of adaptation occurred internally in Room 6, transforming it into the baptistry. The changes included construction of a low ceiling and the font edifice, and decoration of the walls. These measures were designed consciously to make the set liturgical function of baptism spatially distinct from other acts of assembly.[71] Other modifications were also implemented in the renovation of the Dura building to accommodate communal religious functions both in and out of strictly cultic or liturgical contexts. Benches were installed around the courtyard, and shuttered windows were made to communicate between the court and the Assembly Hall (as well as Room 5). These measures suggest conscious adaptation for specific patterns of ritual, movement, and communication in and between the various areas of the domus ecclesiae.[72] Thus, liturgical as well as socioeconomic factors are seen in the conscious plan of adaptation of the Dura building. Through this process the house was transformed into a domus ecclesiae and redefined through architectural articulation into a church building. Its identity was not in any way secretive. Even though there were no major exterior alterations to public religious architecture, the fact that it was now a place of gathering rather than a domicile was not likely to go unnoticed in the neighborhood social life of a small town.

Other sites where a house was completely taken over and renovated as a domus ecclesiae are relatively rare in archaeological remains, partly because many are buried beneath later levels of ecclesiastical architecture.[73] The literary sources provide more widespread corroboration of the process although the detailed steps of architectural adaptation cannot be seen as readily. An official record, dated 19 May 303 (during the great persecution), details a search made of a church edifice at Cirta, Numidia.[74] From the record the church was apparently a renovated house in which various areas of the domestic plan had been turned to specific functions. It contained a library (*bibliotheca*) equipped with cupboards and barrels as well as a dining room (*triclinium*) containing four large jars and six barrels. In other rooms a quantity of gold, silver, and bronze implements were stored, apparently for use in the building. Also in storage were numerous items of men's and women's apparel, recorded in detail in the inventory. Too numerous to constitute a private wardrobe, these clothing items probably represent the charitable store of the Christian community.[75] In this case, then, some formal lines of adaptation seem likely; however, the precise degree of formality remains uncertain. No reference is made to larger areas specifically designed for assembly or other cultic functions. It should be noted here, in contrast to Dura, that the domus ecclesiae still preserved the dining area and function of the domestic edifice. Yet the building was clearly known as the church edifice to the local authorities.

Similar observations are available from several documentary papyri from Egypt around the end of the third century. At Pannopolis in the Thebaid a municipal street survey provided a list of buildings that included a church edifice (*ekklēsia*).[76] The survey was conducted street by street with the buildings listed sequentially by owner's name or functional public designation, or both. On one street, which consisted almost entirely of private houses, the recorder entered on the ledger without a second thought, "the house which is the such-and-such of the church" (*oikia ētoi ekklēsias s[. . .]*). Unfortunately the document is damaged just at the crucial point that might have given more information regarding the form or use of the building. The formula *oikia ētoi* was used by the recorder in other instances to indicate that the building so designated was a house of typical domestic plan, known publicly to be used for other purposes. In this case the house seems to have been the property of the local Christian community. Whether it was the actual church building, a renovated domus ecclesiae, or some other dependency, cannot be determined with more certainty.[77]

At Oxyrhynchus in Arcadia a municipal survey of street wardens for around 295 listed two streets known as North-Church Street and South-Church Street.[78] Since the streets on the list are usually identified by a prominent building or landmark, it seems that in these two sections of town a church edifice had become physically identifiable. In both cases the street had become associated with its major building, the *ekklēsia*, as a toponymic landmark. The progress of Christianity in Oxyrhynchus had been established publicly by means of the two buildings. Less than a decade later, even in the nearby Coptic village of Chysis, which fell under Oxyrhynchite jurisdiction, a Christian church building was readily identifiable. In the year 304 under the Diocletianic edicts the building was confiscated. The papyrus records preserve the inventory of the search and seizure, which took place much in the same manner as the one at Cirta, Numidia.[79] In this case, however, an even more modest domus ecclesiae seems to be indicated, as it contained "neither gold nor silver, nor money nor clothes, nor beasts nor slaves, nor lands nor property," except some bronze implements that were sent to Alexandria.

Beyond the Domus Ecclesiae

By the third century, then, Christian buildings in many areas of the Empire were becoming recognizable landmarks even though they had not yet begun to achieve monumental architectural definition. Such recognition must have depended upon at least a minimal degree of physical adaptation to a domus ecclesiae as a formal setting for assembly. Other references in the literary sources may point to these developments. Although the physical arrangements are seldom discussed in detail in Christian writings, some general lines of development may be seen. In Cyprian's letters, for example, passing reference is made occasionally to accouterments of the assembly. The fact that they are taken for granted indicates the degree to which the adaptation had progressed as a natural course. In reference to the act of ordaining the confessor Celerinus to the office of reader in the year 250, Cyprian speaks of placing him "upon the pulpitum, that is upon the tribunal of the church," which was "propped up in the place of highest elevation and conspicuous to the entire congregation."[80] In Cyprian's church, then, the act of ordination had become defined in terms of the physical arrangement of the assembly hall. To "ascend the platform" (*ad pulpitum venire*) became part of the technical vocabulary of clergy and ordination.[81] We cannot ascertain the general plan or size of Cyprian's church, even though these clues suggest continued growth and adaptation. Still, by the years 250–252 it can be determined that the area physically defined for assembly was sufficiently large to accommodate a segregated area for the clergy and a raised platform, called the pulpit or tribunal. In a letter of 252 to bishop Cornelius of Rome, Cyprian alludes to this area as "the sacred and venerated congestum of the clergy."[82] What is probably reflected here is the forerunner of the chancel and synthronon as articulated spatial features of the assembly hall.

Similarly, at Syrian Antioch, records indicate that the tribunal was being introduced into the assembly setting just after the middle of the third century. There, however, in contrast to the unassailed acceptance under Cyprian, these developments were viewed as dangerous novelties, since they were associated with the innovations of the infamous schismatic Paul of Samosata (bishop from 261–270).[83] Of course, some allowances must be made for the rhetoric in our sources, since they are documents preserved by Eusebius from the group that ousted Paul from the episcopate. Once again, references to the physical arrangements of the church building arise in passing, as the tribunal

FROM HOUSE CHURCH TO CHURCH BUILDING

had become a symbol of Paul's arrogance. Thus, in keeping with his faulty theology, the synodal letter charges, Paul manifested his irreverence and self-aggrandizement by installing a throne and secretum on the bema of the assembly area. These were features directly associated with the tribunal of a public magistrate.[84] It is perhaps more indicative of the degree to which adaptation had progressed that when Paul was removed forcibly from the Church, with the aid of an imperial decree, the bema edifice seems to have remained.[85]

In major urban centers such as Antioch, Carthage, or Rome the process of architectural adaptation seems to have been far ahead of the lesser, remote cities. The domus ecclesiae at Dura-Europos was precisely contemporary with Cyprian; however, the scale of adaptation seems to have been quite different. To be sure, some common lines of assembly pattern were emerging, as both moved toward a longitudinal hall with a platform at the end. Yet, the Dura Christian building cannot be thought comparable in scale to that at Carthage, or even at the much nearer Antioch. There were still further possibilities for adaptation and renovation beyond the initial developments of the domus ecclesiae. Factors such as population and constituency, the size, wealth, and social standing of the Christian community account for both the nature and the pace of architectural adaptations. Such factors were operative from locality to locality for Christians just as for Jews or Mithraists.

Some church buildings were pushed ahead through renovation and adaptation, others lagged behind. At Lullingstone (see fig. 23) a much simpler type of domus ecclesiae, only partially renovated, continued in use through the fourth century. The pattern of local adaptation through the private auspices of a patron's house was still a viable starting point. The reasons may lie in the relative isolation of the Lullingstone villa, a rural estate in a faraway province. Similar suggestions have been made regarding the archaeological evidence from other areas of the Empire, as in Tripolitania.[86] In most cases, however, there is evidence of an awareness of fourth-century trends back at Rome, so they cannot be dismissed as throwbacks to a more primitive time.[87] The pervasiveness of architectural adaptation from private buildings was a widely accepted process, for pagans, Jews, and Christians alike.

It should not be a surprise, then, that in the year 303 the church edifice at Cirta was still very much a house in plan. Perhaps it also served as the bishop's residence, or maybe it had been his own house before. It is uncertain, but it may be significant to the development of North African Christianity in general that Augustine's church at Hippo Regius is now thought to have grown from what was originally an adjacent peristyle house and then served as an episcopal residence.[88] Nearly two years later (4 March 305) a synod convened at Cirta in the house of Urbanus Donatus to elect new bishops.[89] Still later, Optatus, bishop in around 400 at nearby Mileve, suggests that the synod met in a private home "because the Churches had not been rebuilt" after the edict of destruction in 303.[90] This view is partially substantiated by a hagiographical record of martyrs from another Numidian village, Abitina, from 12 February 304.[91] For them assembly was easily managed in the homes of private individuals, either Octavius Felix or the lector Emeritus.[92] It is likely that many of the church buildings, having become publicly recognizable through architectural adaptation, were confiscated. However, the move back to the private household setting was not a big step. In times of duress, it was not difficult to return to simpler forms.[93] Donatist conventicles in North Africa continued to preserve these simpler church buildings in opposition to the more elaborate church buildings of the Catholics at Carthage.[94] For a variety of reasons—persecution, controversy, geography, social status, wealth, and patronage— the adaptation of church buildings progressed at an uneven pace. The earliest instances of partial adaptation commenced in the second century, but the practice continued through the fourth. On the whole, however, the domus ecclesiae as a building devoted to Christian usage and defined through physical renovation had become fairly typical by the third century. The process continued as subsequent renovations were introduced to accommodate new needs.

FROM HOUSE CHURCH TO CHURCH BUILDING

The Aula Ecclesiae

Subsequent stages of adaptation eventually produced even larger and more formal types of church buildings. Cyprian takes for granted a setting for assembly in a hall of some size. The letter of Malchion of Antioch states that the church of bishop Paul had become a showplace for the surrounding region. We should not expect that these buildings were as yet on the grand scale of the monumental basilicas of the next century; still, they had progressed well beyond the domestic dining room of Paul's house churches at Corinth. By the third century there was a growing need for a more regularized hall of assembly among both Jewish and Christian congregations.[95] These changes can be seen in comparable ways in the renovations of the Christian building and the Jewish synagogue at Dura-Europos and elsewhere.

The Christian historian Eusebius, writing during the violent years of the great persecution, refers to a building "boom" in the last half of the third century. Chronologically, Eusebius was describing the period from Cyprian's death in 258 to the first edict of Diocletian in 303. In book VII of his *Church History* Eusebius deals with the upheavals within the church precipitated by the likes of Paul of Samosata. In book VIII, he turns to the period of persecution and what he viewed as the eventual triumph of the Christian church. It is significant, therefore, that Eusebius regularly refers to the persecution as "the destruction of the churches," a reflection of a new perspective on the development of church buildings emerging in the early part of the fourth century. Thus, at the beginning of book VIII, Eusebius describes the situation on the eve of persecution:

> How could anyone describe those assemblies with numberless crowds and the great throngs gathered in every city as well as the remarkable concourses in the houses of prayer? On account of these things, no longer being satisfied with their old buildings, they erected from the foundations churches of spacious dimensions in every city.[96]

Reading the historiographical interpretations of Eusebius is sometimes difficult. In older studies of Christian architecture this passage and others were taken to represent the inception of the basilica as monumental church architecture prior to the beginning of the fourth century.[97] But since we have seen that the basilica was not introduced until after Constantine, we must attempt to understand Eusebius's reference in a different light. To be sure, his reliability has to be tested; however, in this case the pattern does seem to reflect the ongoing process of adaptation and renovation from existing domus ecclesiae.[98] Although it is, from what we have seen elsewhere, a vast overgeneralization, it must have been the case for some localities. The language used, in fact, is precisely that found often in building inscriptions. In particular we should note the phrase "erected from the foundations" (*ek themeliōn anistōn*), also prominent in a number of mithraic and synagogue inscriptions where it usually refers to the rebuilding of an existing edifice.[99] It is possible, then, that Eusebius knew such inscriptions from Christian buildings as well. It is also worth noting that Eusebius does not predicate renovation on architectural style, but rather on issues of numerical growth and social status.

Well before Constantine introduced the basilica to Church architecture, the Christians had begun to move toward larger, more regular halls of assembly. It is for this stage of the development that the term *aula ecclesiae* ("hall of the church") has been chosen.[100] The term is intended to connote a direct continuity with the domus ecclesiae, from which it evolved through a continued, natural course of adaptation. Archaeologically, this continuity can be seen in two cases from the early fourth century. At this time the villa at Parentium that had been renovated at least partially into a domus ecclesiae was more thoroughly rebuilt into a tripartite hall structure.[101] Despite the tripartite configuration, the building was not a true basilica, as each hall was physically separate. Instead, the plan and configuration of the halls depended upon the liturgical use of the same areas in the earlier villa. The middle hall served for the assembly, while the smaller flanking halls served as a baptistry and martyrium respectively. A funerary inscription from the martyrium seems to verify that the tripartite hall-church was renovated from the earlier church edifice (probably the villa as domus ecclesiae) of the bishop Maurus, who was honored as martyr or confessor.[102] A comparable case is known from an inscription at Laodicea Combusta in Lycaonia. There the epitaph of the bishop Marcus Julius Eugenius attests that he personally rebuilt the church "from its foundations" during or just after the persecutions of 303–313.[103]

At Qirkbize in Coele-Syria a different process of construction was followed, but with similar results. There the church edifice was built as an entirely new construction in the first third of the fourth century.[104] Since the village was just being developed it had no existing structures from which to be rebuilt. It is interesting, then, that the church was built as a modest aula ecclesiae, though the exterior plan was clearly modeled after the house next door, which was owned by the founder and patron of the church. Externally, the church complex resembled domestic architecture. Internally, however, all the space, both floor plan and elevation, was designed as a single hall of assembly. Originally, it was nothing more than a plain rectangular hall with no internal divisions or specially marked areas save a raised platform on one end. Only later, through five stages of renovation covering two centuries, did this simple aula ecclesiae come to have the trappings of typical eastern basilical architecture.

By the end of the third century, some church buildings had become more prominent public edifices. This is confirmed by pagan observers as well, one offhand barb in particular from a pagan detractor. Porphyry, a student of the philosopher Plotinus at Rome in around 262–263, was a contemporary of Paul of Samosata. In his view the Christians were inconsistent and irrational since they deprecated pagan worship but, he says, they "erected great buildings" of their own, "imitating the construction of temples."[105] It should be noted that the case of Paul of Samosata attracted the attention of the emperor in matters pertaining to the disposition of Christian buildings. Thus, Eusebius reports that the case was appealed to the emperor Aurelian (ca. 270–272), with the result that the church building (*oikos ekklēsias*) was declared the property of the "orthodox" group.[106] Still earlier, under Severus Alexander (222–235) it is reported (in the *Historia Augusta*) that a dispute over a piece of property was similarly decided by imperial fiat in favor of the Christians.[107] In this case the dispute was with a group of cooks who wanted the property; the imperial decree expressly favored its use for religious purposes instead, even though the property must not have been a public sanctuary. Even allowing for the historiographical excesses of the *Historia Augusta* and Eusebius' *Church History*, it seems that public notice had ratified the presence of Christian buildings of growing proportions and social prominence.

At the beginning of the fourth century the public position of church buildings in the city of Nicomedia, Bithynia (Diocletian's eastern capital) was described by the Christian writer Lactantius. He reports that as the first official act of persecution in 303 Diocletian ordered this church building destroyed while he looked on from the palace.[108] Apparently the church building was an eyesore because it symbolized the recalcitrance of the Christians. Moreover, it rose up to greet his view, as it was "situated on a high spot visible from the palace," in the midst of a number of large houses. Lactantius calls it a "lofty temple" (*fanum editissimum*). The description indeed suggests a larger renovated aula ecclesiae, though clearly not a monumental building, since it was razed in a matter of a few hours. More significant, perhaps, was its location in a wealthy residential quarter and the fact that it was well known to the general populace as the Christians' church building. In the same year the smaller domus ecclesiae at Cirta (Numidia) and Chysis (Egypt) were similarly well known to local authorities who carried out Diocletian's edict of search and seizure.[109]

If these church buildings were not yet monumental public basilicas with a peculiarly Christian architectural form, what made them so clearly recognizable to local authorities? The evidence points to the process of renovation and construction as an accepted part of daily life for religious groups of all sorts. Tearing down exterior walls in order to erect new ones "from the foundations" must have drawn attention to the project. The more elaborate the rebuilding, the more local contractors and workmen would have been involved. For example, it is possible, given features of design and decoration, that the font edifice in the baptistry room of the Dura Christian building was built by the same workshop that produced the Torah shrine in the synagogue and the altar canopy in the mithraeum at Dura. The remodeling of the house into a religious building was not self-consciously secretive, even if the rites performed there after completion were.

If the more limited interior remodeling of the Dura Christian building was tacitly public, the remodeling of the later synagogue at Dura was an overtly and self-consciously public statement on the part of the Jewish community. By analogy, the later Dura synagogue corresponds to the phase of development we are describing as the aula ecclesiae, since the former reflects a subsequent renovation with a conscious plan to redesign the entire edifice for religious functions. Walls were torn down to create an elevation above the other houses in the block, while the entrance was moved to the other side of the block on a nicer street. The central focus of the plan was the enlarged hall of assembly and its entrance through the formal courtyard. Within the hall itself the spatial and visual focal point of the room centered on the Torah niche, around which the artistic decoration, seating, and acts of worship were coordinated.

Similar factors can also be seen in the move from domus ecclesiae to aula ecclesiae on the Christian side. Had not Dura been destroyed, the Christian building would probably have undergone comparable renovation, assuming that the community continued to grow and develop apace. Each locality tended to follow its own course, according to local styles, conventions, and circumstances. Elsewhere on the Christian side the general process can be seen in the renovation of the *titulus Byzantis* at Rome in the later third century. Whereas the earliest Christian cells met in the rear shops of the ground floor, later the entire mezzanine level (*piano nobile*) was taken over and converted into a large open hall. This conversion was marked by substantial construction work (including knocking out the interior partitions, perhaps through two levels) on the upper floor, as well as annexing and integrating the rooms from the street-side facade.

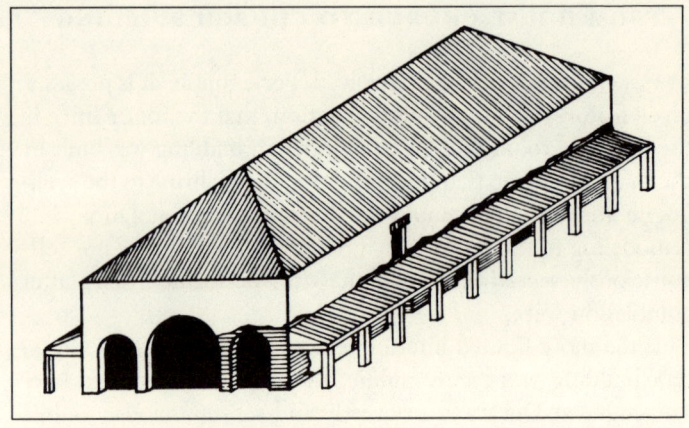

Fig. 24.
Isometric reconstruction of the First Church (aula ecclesiae) below San Crisogono at Rome.

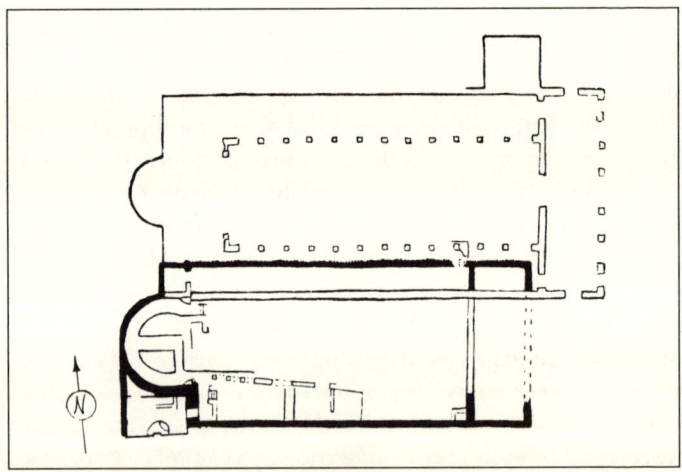

Fig. 25.
Siting plan of the fourth- to sixth-century church beneath the medieval basilica of San Crisogono at Rome.

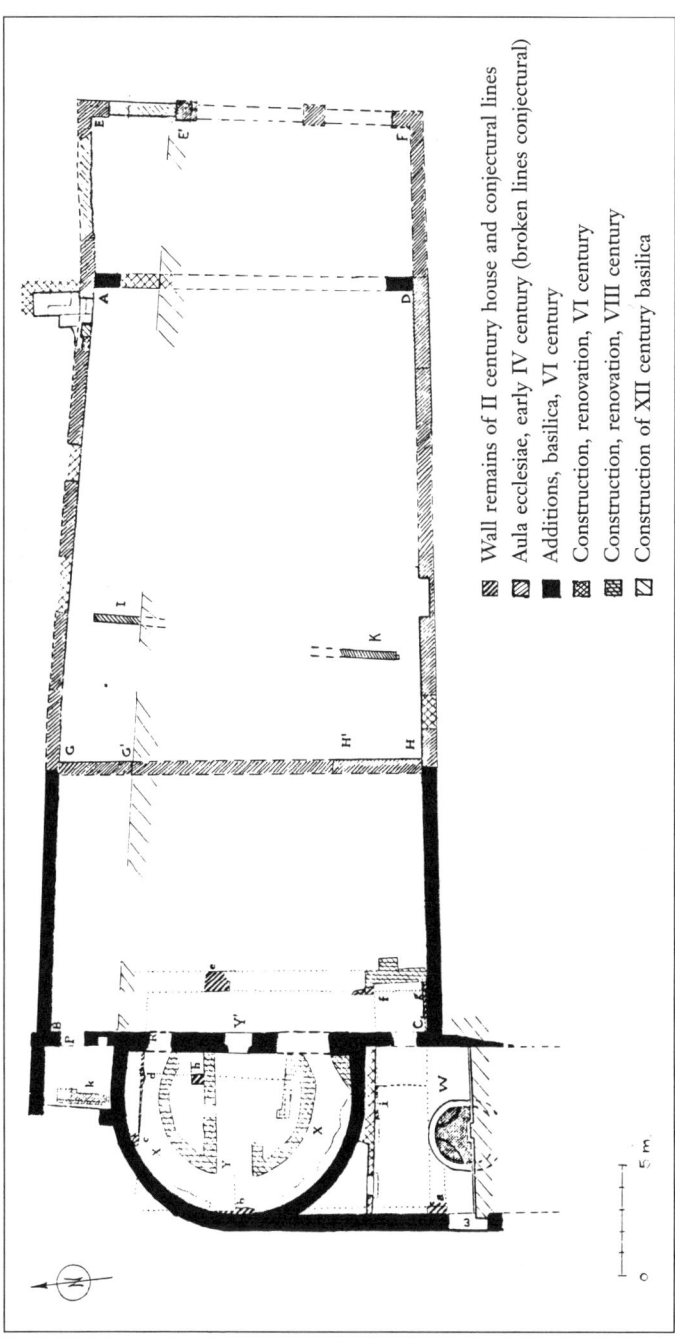

Fig. 26.
Plan restoration of San Crisogono and aula ecclesiae at Rome.

Also, massive load-bearing walls were added in the ground-level shop area to carry the open elevation of the upper floors by means of pillars in place of partition walls.[110] In all likelihood the other known titular churches at Rome that can be dated to the late third century, San Clemente and San Martino ai Monti, are also examples of the construction of halls for assembly out of previously existing buildings. In both cases, however, these halls seem to have been subsumed when the churches were later rebuilt in basilical form at the beginning of the fifth century.[111]

There are other cases at the beginning of the fourth century in which hall churches were being built de novo. In the case of Qirkbize (noted above) the hall followed domestic planning on the exterior. The best example of the new dimensions of the aula ecclesiae can be seen in San Crisogono at Rome.[112] This church was built in the Trastevere, sometime around 310 (see fig. 24). Originally, it was nothing more than a large rectangular hall with no interior aisles or partitions. Still, it was obviously not a house; more like a warehouse in plan, but with exterior porticoes. Thus, it was made to conform to a large public concourse in style and function. Only later would it, like other churches at Rome, be remodeled to basilical church form by adding on an apse and crypt, and by partitioning off the entrance area to form a narthex (see figs. 25 and 26). Such hall structures in public buildings, as San Crisogono, probably provided assembly space that could then be accommodated to the new aesthetic of an emerging Christian architecture.

It is likely, however, that the first phase of building or rebuilding of churches after the persecution continued the lines of domus ecclesiae and aula ecclesiae, as in the so-called "basilica" of Paul at Philippi, which was built by Bishop Porphyrius in about 334 (see fig. 27). Most of the edicts of toleration contained some provision for the restoration of confiscated church properties.[113] Despite the rhetoric of Eusebius, it appears that the majority of Christian buildings were merely confiscated and closed rather than destroyed. Thus, there were many localities that could resume the use of older church buildings, although the new sense of freedom and triumph might well have been stimulus to renovation. In other cases rebuilding was indeed

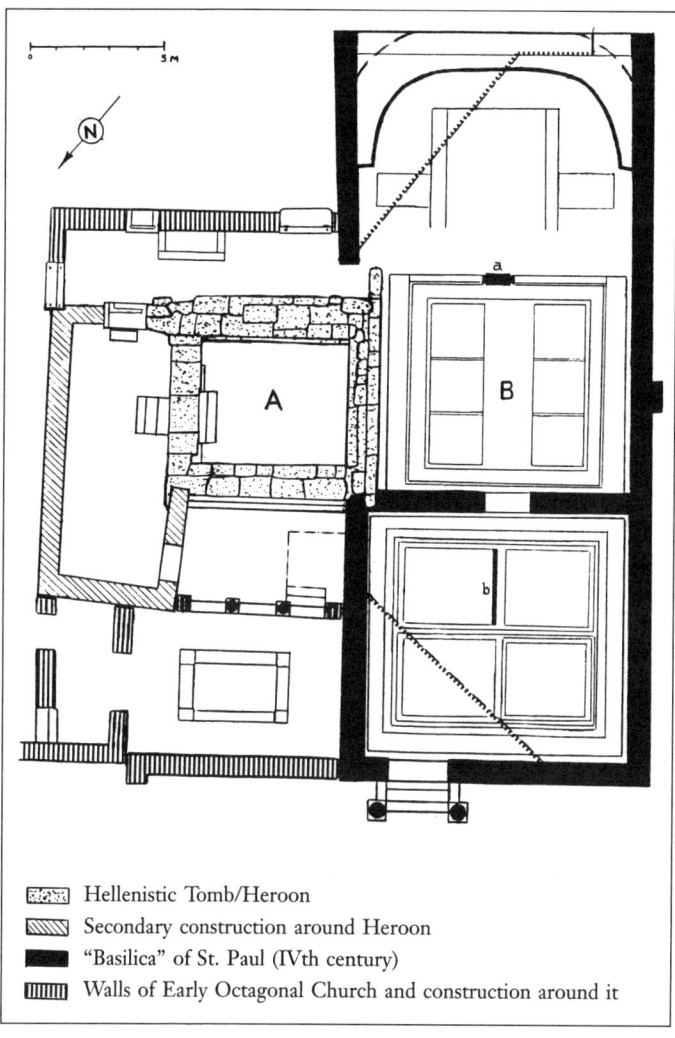

Fig. 27.
Plan restoration of the fourth-century hall church and heroon beneath the Octagonal church complex at Philippi.

notable and monumental. But, as in the case of the church of bishop Theodore at Aquileia begun in around 314, many were just more elaborate local or personal expressions of the hall model, only later to witness the superimposition of basilical form.[114] The epitaph of the bishop Marcus Julius Eugenius at Laodicea Combusta also reflects the rebuilding of churches after the cessation of persecution. His account suggests that the existing church edifice was used in the rebuilding, enlarged or elaborated according to local needs and his own sense of triumph and benefaction.[115] This case, known only from the epigraphic record, is similar on many levels to the better known account of the rebuilding of the church at Tyre after the persecution.

The church at Tyre was rebuilt by the young, aristocratic bishop Paulinus and was dedicated in 317. The nature of the rebuilding is not known from archaeological remains, but is renowned from the elaborate panegyric delivered at the dedication by none other than Eusebius himself.[116] Generally, it has been assumed that the new church was a basilica, since it was built after the Constantinian triumph and since Eusebius regularly refers to the edifice as a temple, comparing its rebuilding to the "glory" of the Second Temple in the days of Zerubbabel.[117] Despite the decor and more monumental scale of the rebuilt church of Paulinus, it was probably not a basilica, but an elaborated aula ecclesiae in form.[118] Many of the features of Eusebius's description, indeed, suggest affinities for, or perhaps developments toward, what would become Constantinian basilical form. For example, there was an atrium forecourt with tetrastoa opening onto a triportal main entrance (HE X.4.39, 42). There were other annexes or dependencies that served for specialized functions, such as a baptistry (par. 45). Still, there is no mention of an apse or synthronon, only a raised platform on one end for bishop and clergy (par. 44), not unlike that at Antioch or Carthage a generation earlier. Nor does it seem that there was an internal colonnade in the nave, as has sometimes been supposed, but rather an external portico along the long sides of the building similar to that suggested by Krautheimer for San Crisogono at Rome.[119]

FROM HOUSE CHURCH TO CHURCH BUILDING

What is architecturally significant about the continuity of the aula ecclesiae is a tendency to standardize the rectangular hall plan for assembly and cluster ancillary rooms, annexes, or dependencies around it. Existing edifices could be modified to suit this need. A good example is the so-called Church of Julianos at Umm el-Jimal.[120] Dating to the fourth or fifth century, the church is a modest basilical plan containing an apse but no aisles. The peculiarity of the structure lies in the fact that the apse end of the hall protrudes from an otherwise typical housing complex. There is evidence also that features of the hall itself, including the tri-portal entry, were already in use prior to construction of the basilical extension. In other words, it appears that the housing complex might have already been converted to a hall structure (perhaps a Christian aula ecclesiae) in the late third or fourth century, prior to full-scale conversion to the basilical hall plan.

There is also an increased possibility for new design and construction, either of an independent sort or in conjunction with existing structures already in use. The period during which such transitions occurred ranges from the middle of the third century, especially in larger urban centers, through the end of the fourth century. The domus ecclesiae-aula ecclesiae patterns for adaptation and growth continued well into the period when Constantinian influence began to reshape Christian architecture into the basilica. At this time synagogue architecture, even in the Homeland, was beginning to develop its own pattern of regularized hall forms in freestanding edifices.[121] Most of the active synagogues known from the Diaspora at this time were also going through multiple stages of adaptation to elaborated hall forms. Thus, despite the fact that they were still very much conditioned by local customs and circumstances and by the constraints of existing architecture, there were additional features of architectural articulation and orientation. They, too, may reflect the influence of the emerging normative synagogue worship of the mishnaic and talmudic periods.[122]

In the diverse developments of the Christian aula ecclesiae interior arrangements tended to become more defined and gradually standardized as liturgy, clerical orders, and congregational seating became oriented in terms of the longitudinal axis of the hall plan. More formal segregation of the clergy in a designated area at the front of the hall had already taken place in Carthage in the mid-third century. By the time of San Crisogono and Theodore's church at Aquileia, the focal point of the hall was the area set aside for altar, clergy, and bishop.[123] Several other features of liturgical development are probably correlated with this development. It certainly presupposes a separate eucharistic liturgy with its focal point in the front of the hall. Also, such strict clerical ordering might have been an initial stimulus toward processional patterns of entry and exit.[124] The shift from the dining arrangement for assembly to a hall plan also resulted in a move to more formal seating arrangements for the congregation in assembly. We may take special note of instructions from the late third century (ca. 270) Syrian church order known as the *Didascalia Apostolorum*.[125] This document presupposes some separation of clergy from laity, as the presbyters were to be seated in "the eastern part of the house" with the bishop "in their midst." Behind them were first, the adult men, seated from east to west, then the women, apart in a separate area also seated from east to west, and finally the mothers with babies and all the rest of the children, sitting or standing on the sides (presumably at the rear of the hall).[126] While the hall itself does not seem to have been more than a plain edifice, conceivably even a renovated domus ecclesiae like that at Dura, there was already a rigid sense of order in the articulation of assembly space. This rigidity and formality is also attested by the fact that one of the deacons, probably the one who was assigned to stand at the door while the people entered, was charged with making sure that all assumed their proper places.[127] Such formality, combined with the articulation of space seen at Carthage and elsewhere, might lead quite naturally to further provisions for the chancel and the bishop's cathedra well before the advent of basilical form.[128] Likewise, developments in the catechumenate and in penitential practice were probably made more formal in spatial definition as the church edifice grew into the formal hall pattern.[129]

Seen from this perspective it may be suggested that the gradual adaptation toward the aula ecclesiae had already achieved accommodation of Christian assembly and worship. The Constantinian innovation of basilical architecture, therefore, seems less abrupt. Although it surely represents a radically new imposition of scale and style on the architecture and aesthetic, it still depended on some continuity with earlier church buildings. The basilica may be seen as a further adaptation, monumentalization, and ultimately a standardization of diverse pre-Constantinian patterns of development. It is noteworthy, too, that with Constantine some of the same social and economic factors in patronage and adaptation were at work as in the earlier periods.[130]

6

Conclusions

Christian Adaptation and the Social Environment

▲ ▲ ▲

In buying houses, maintaining extended household relations, or adapting houses for communal assembly Christians were fully in touch with the world around them. One is reminded of the apologia for the Christians' social life given by the unknown writer to Diognetus:

> For the distinction between Christians and other folk is neither in country nor language nor customs. For they do not dwell elsewhere in cities of their own, nor do they use some strange deviation of dialect, nor do they practice a conspicuous manner of life. . . . Yet while living in Greek and barbarian cities, as each one has been allotted, and following the local customs, both in clothing and food and in the rest of life, they show forth the wonderful and admittedly strange character of their citizenship. They dwell in their native lands, but as if sojourners. . . . They pass their time upon the earth, but they have their citizenship in heaven.[1]

Christians lived and operated within the bounds of society at large. Though they originated as a sect in outback Palestine, nowhere were they more at home in the Roman world than in the house church. They were "in the world, but not of the world," the apologist to Diognetus might say. Yet this firsthand observation points to the social circumstances behind the practices of housing and especially of adapting houses to religious use.

All too often it has been assumed that the early Christians' adoption of the domestic setting for their worship necessarily implied an antisocial attitude on the part of a movement of the

CONCLUSIONS

dispossessed. Indeed, some statements by the Christians themselves seem to imply this.[2] Yet other comments, even in the second century, reflect the movement at the other end of the social spectrum, as there were occasionally Christians among the ranks of the local elite.[3] By the third century both pagan and Christian observers were referring to the lofty "temples" of the Christians.[4] Prior to Constantine, then, there were signs of the growth and social appeal of the Christian movement. One of the most important of these signs of social growth was the landmark position of Christian buildings. Owning and renovating property was a sign of status.[5]

Ever since Ernest Renan began to visit Greece (in 1867) during archaeological work on the Pauline cities, interest has been sparked in the social setting of the New Testament. Among other things, Renan was the first to note an epigraphic parallel between the Pauline formula, "the church in the house of so-and-so," and "the collegium in the house of Sergia Paullina" at Rome.[6] It has long been noted that the house church in Paul and Acts significantly colors our understanding of the pregnant theological term *ecclesia*.[7] Concerned with social expansion, Adolf Harnack recognized the house church as a factor in the growth and triumph of the Christian movement.[8] He also attempted to correlate development from the earliest house meetings (the simplistic and natural) with social and theological factors in the emergence of church buildings. In particular he saw the rise of a specifically Christian architecture, the basilica, as a product of "the church's great expansion" during the early third century.[9]

As we have seen, however, Harnack's model of development, expansion, and triumph must now be reconsidered in the light of new archaeological and historical evidence.[10] In particular, the house church and its gradual adaptation into more specifically Christian forms raises different issues and offers new insights. Early on Floyd Filson called for a fuller study of the house church in order to assess the social background of the New Testament.[11] Among the issues that he suggested would be enhanced were the separation from Judaism, the stress on family relationships, the propensity toward divisiveness, and the social status of householders. While not all of his conclusions can be maintained, Filson's basic sense of the issues has proved to be right on target. In our examination the adaptation from house church to church buildings points to two primary social aspects of the Christian movement: the social location or status of the Christian movement and models from the environment for communal organization.

The proletarian or lower class origins of the Christian movement have been a longstanding scholarly assumption. Direct references were drawn from the New Testament itself, supported by the comments of pagan detractors and later Christian apologists.[12] The notion was given its fullest expression by Adolf Deissmann but was also the hallmark of Marxist historiography.[13] Far too often the origins of the house church were seen solely from this perspective. The primitive nature of Christian household assembly was assumed to be a product of poverty and low social standing. In addition, persecution and the Christians' disdain of pagan idolatry was believed to have forced them into the shadows of private household gatherings.[14] The archaeological and social evidence paints a different picture. The Hellenistic and Roman environment was quite open to the many groups that used and adapted private buildings for communal and cultic activity. Especially in the larger cities, the adaptation of private buildings was a common sight that would have brought even the more exclusive religious groups, Mithraists, Jews, and then Christians, to public notice. Renovation of existing buildings was hardly a secret affair, and required the acquisition of property as well as some expendable treasury. Somehow, then, the Christians also had access to higher socioeconomic strata.

In more recent New Testament scholarship the traditional view of proletarian origins has been modified, and the house church and its development are central to this understanding. An insightful observation by E. A. Judge concerning the situation in 1 Corinthians launched this reconsideration of social status. Judge argued:

CONCLUSIONS

Far from being a socially depressed group, then, if the Corinthians are at all typical, the Christians were dominated by a socially pretentious section of the population of the big cities. Beyond that they seem to have drawn on a broad constituency, probably representing the household dependents of leading members.[15]

Judge's comment focuses attention not only on the social prominence of leading members but also on the constituency of the community that was based in the household.[16] A central social position, then, is recognized for the house church and its patrons. In attempting to identify Christians of higher social status in the prosopography of Pauline congregations, Gerd Theissen considered ownership of the houses in which the church met a primary indicator.[17] Despite reservations concerning the sectarian origins of the Christian movement in rural Palestine,[18] these observations have contributed to the understanding of the social makeup and problems of early urban Christianity.[19] They provide the backdrop for discussions on hospitality, ethics,[20] and role and status of women,[21] and the nature of communal life and organization.[22]

The house church organization also points to models from the Roman environment in which the early Christian movement spread.[23] In this wider social context Christians would have appeared similar to a number of other kinds of groups familiar to the urban environment. These include collegial associations, philosophical schools, the synagogue, and the household itself.[24] Such groups offered patterns for the social ordering of foreign groups in larger cities.[25] Considerable attention has focused on the nature of the extended household in Greek and Roman society.[26] It may be inappropriate to consider these "models from the environment" as mutually exclusive categories, since a number of overlaps may be observed. For example, synagogues could be organized as collegia and still use private houses for meetings. Likewise household cults are known of, and may help to explain the emergence of women in leadership roles.[27] Adaptation of the domestic setting for social and religious functions was not peculiar to the Christians.

At Dura-Europos, it must be remembered, both the Mithraists and the Jews assembled in renovated houses located just down the street from the Christian building. In both cases the sanctuary originated in only one or two rooms set aside for cultic functions, while the rest of the house remained a domicile in every respect. Gradually, each house was further adapted to the peculiar needs of its worshipping community. In the case of the mithraeum, there were two subsequent stages of renovation; in the synagogue, one more. Yet in its final form each building was given over wholly to religious functions and identity. Through physical adaptation they were fully transformed from domestic edifices to cult buildings recognizable to the culture at large.[28] The detailed features of adaptation suggest factors in the life of each religious group that made possible the process of change and renovation. There was substantial growth in numbers and wealth, seen in both the enlargement and decoration of the buildings. These changes can be correlated with the social composition and circumstances in the city. Through inscriptions the renovation projects can be linked to patronage by leading members. For the mithraeum it was a military commander; for the synagogue, Samuel the elder and priest.[29] The evidence suggests, moreover, that similar social factors were at work in other Mithraic and Jewish communities throughout the empire.[30] At Dura Mithraists, Jews, and Christians had invested themselves both socially and economically in the adaptive environment.

The economic implications of property ownership were part and parcel of the verticality of the social pyramid in the Roman order.[31] Ramsay MacMullen estimates that the percentage of people in the top categories of wealth distribution was miniscule, only the very pinnacle of the pyramid.[32] Housing and property were a mirror of this social structure, as senators maintained several palatial estates in and around Rome. The younger Pliny owned six houses in Italy, and, by his own admission, was far from the wealthiest.[33] The more lavish homes at Rome, which took up to 33 percent of the residential space, housed only a small portion of the total population of the city; probably no more than 3 percent, and that includes extended families and

CONCLUSIONS

household slaves.[34] The rest of the population was crowded into the huge insulae or tenements.[35] There, even the meager rent could be oppressive, and real property ownership was out of the question for the masses.[36]

In general the semiprivate collegial societies and cults did not purchase property outright in the manner of investors. Instead they obtained it through gifts, donations, and dedications, either in property itself or in trust backed by property.[37] Even the major temples and cult centers accumulated substantial fortunes in this manner, the chief social mechanism being the exercise of personal benefaction and patronage.[38] Such patronage was encouraged and expected of the wealthy to support the social structure, and the display of one's wealth through benefaction was a sign of status.[39] In the Roman period, the public honors of benefactors were rivaled in the private clubs and cults as well, a sign of the proliferation and privatization of the culture. The quest for status and honor through the display of one's wealth on a dedicatory plaque penetrated even the secret chambers of the mithraeum, and in the synagogues both Jewish and non-Jewish patrons were honored for their benefactions. More often than not, such patronage earned not only public recognition of honorifics but also a position of rank and status within the social organization of the group.[40]

The role of patrons can be seen in the Christian house church from the days of Paul.[41] The nature of the extended family, with slaves, freedmen, and other clients attached to the household, also meant that the loyalties of the house church might be determined in large measure from the top down by the patron. Such factors can still be seen in the second century in the second and third Johannine epistles.[42] It should be noted, too, that the situation in 3 John presupposes that the Christians are still meeting in the home of Diotrophes, the leading member and patron. Yet subtle changes were already in the works, as entrance into the house church was a tacit equation with membership in the cultic fellowship.[43] In other words, the house church under the authority of its owner and patron was on its way to becoming physically identified as the church building. We must guess that the next logical step was to mark off some part of the house, if not the entire edifice, as a special place of Christian assembly and worship. And so patronage in the house church setting grew naturally into the development of the domus ecclesiae.

Unfortunately we do not know who owned the Dura Christian house prior to its renovation. A leading figure such as the Proclus honored in the major inscription of the baptistry seems a likely candidate, much like Samuel in the case of the Dura synagogue.[44] In both cases it must be recognized that the property was of considerable value. Renovation and decoration represented the auspices of leading patrons as well as the social standing and numerical growth of the religious community. Patronage can be seen as a significant factor in a number of the apocryphal Acts as well,[45] while the heresy of Marcion at Rome proved a difficult case precisely because he made a benefaction of some 200,000 sesterces to the church.[46] Later still, bishops such as Cyprian and Paul of Samosata exercised patronal wealth and authority over larger areas and in larger, renovated church buildings.[47] Of course one of the best known cases is the tradition of Clement of Rome behind the *titulus Clementis*.[48]

Access to property through patronage and donation was perhaps the sine qua non for the architectural development from house church to domus ecclesiae. There is no more striking evidence of the economic implications of Christian adaptation than the case of the *titulus Byzantis* (SS. Giovanni e Paolo) at Rome, which was converted from an insula complex.[49] If Krautheimer's reconstruction of the building history is correct, the renovation of the third-century hall for Christian use would have necessitated acquisition of almost the entire multistoried property and sufficient funds to undertake a major construction project. The rental value alone of such a property in Rome might have easily been in the neighborhood of HS 70,000 per year; therefore, the actual mortgage value of the property would have been substantially more, perhaps on the order of HS 750,000–1,000,000.[50] In addition to the property value and the cost of the renovation, we must account for the social impact of the renovation, as it would have meant displacement of both the commercial and domestic residents of the insula. Even if the

CONCLUSIONS

Christians had gradually begun to take over more and more of the property, the economic impact of the renovation project would have been enormous within the neighborhood life of third-century Rome. Perhaps this case will also throw into sharper relief the social and economic impact of the patron-bishops in the early fourth century, such as Paulinus at Tyre, M. Julius Eugenius at Laodicea Combusta, Theodore at Aquileia, Porphyrius at Philippi, Maximus at Alexandria, and many others. Their benefactions for the building of larger and more elaborate church buildings, along with those of the emperor Constantine, helped to seal the social triumph of Christianity after the great persecution.[51] Patronage, therefore, established a network of social relations whereby Christianity, like Mithraism and Judaism, found its way into the mainstream of Roman culture.[52]

These gross analogies on the cultic use of private architecture suggest a social-history approach to assessing archaeological and historical data on the development from house church to domus ecclesiae. The key issue is the process of adaptation, when one can begin to account for physical alterations in terms of attendant social factors. This requires painstaking archaeological data from which to pose historical and social observations. These observations are especially provocative when seen in incremental stages of renovation over time. In case after case, like those at Dura-Europos, evidence gained through observing adaptation can then be measured against other information from the immediate context and ever-widening circles of the environment. Not only does this constitute a type of longitudinal data often lacking in ancient history, it also allows for correlation with economic and prosopographic data garnered from documentary sources.

Architectural adaptation was a dynamic process geared to both the social and physical needs of the community. Throughout the first three centuries the changing status and composition of Christian groups necessitated ongoing adaptation seen architecturally in the process of development from house church to domus ecclesiae and to aula ecclesiae. The Constantinian revolution, with its own architectural transformation, also reflects substantial social changes in the status and composition of Christianity. By looking at the stages and methods of architectural adaptation in the context of the larger environment we see a barometer of the historical and social circumstances of development.

Notes

▲ ▲ ▲

1. Introduction

1. Edward Gibbon, *The Decline and Fall of the Roman Empire* (1776) chap. 71; cited from the abridged edition by D. M. Low (London 1960) 897. Gibbon says in his own concluding postscript that the same ruins of Rome that prompted Petrarch's comment were the setting and inspiration for his first reflections on the decline and fall (Low ed., 903).
2. Suetonius, *The Divine Augustus* XXVIII.3.
3. Martial (40–104 C.E.), *Epigrams* VIII.36: addressed to Domitian on the completion (in 92 C.E.) of his Palatine palace, the Domus Flavia.
4. Opening line from Shelley's "Hellas" (1821); cf. his "Ozymandias" (1817) and Keats "On Seeing the Elgin Marbles" (1817) and "Ode on a Grecian Urn" (1819).
5. Delivered as the Haskell Lectures at Oberlin College for 1919 and published under the title *Landmarks in the History of Early Christianity* (London 1920), the quotation is from p. 1.
6. In Acts 1.13 the term is *hyperōon* while in Luke 22.12 (parallel, Mark 14.15) it is *anagaion* (literally "upper floor"). On the issue of historiographical impulses in Luke-Acts see the discussion in Joseph Fitzmyer, *The Gospel according to Luke* (Anchor Bible, 2 vols., Garden City, NY, 1981, 1985) I: 3–21, 171–91, and bibliography cited there (I: 259ff.). See esp. Henry J. Cadbury, *The Making of Luke-Acts* (2nd ed., London 1958) 299ff. and *The Book of Acts in History* (London 1955) passim; L. E. Keck and J. L. Martyn (eds.), *Studies in Luke-Acts, Essays in Honor of Paul Schubert* (Philadelphia 1966); and most recently the attempt to reclaim Acts as a historical source by Martin Hengel, *Acts and the History of Earliest Christianity* (Philadelphia 1980) 35ff., but see also Jacob Jervell, *The Unknown Paul: Essays on Luke-Acts and Early Christian History* (Minneapolis 1984) 13–29. It would seem that Luke-Acts is likely to remain, using Van Unnik's term, "a storm-center in contemporary scholarship."
7. 1 Cor. 16.19; Rom. 16.3–5; Philem. 1–2; Col. 4.15.
8. Edwin A. Judge, *The Social Organization of Christian Groups in the First Century* (London 1960) 58ff.; Abraham J. Malherbe, *Social Aspects*

of Early Christianity (2nd ed., Philadelphia 1983) 71ff.; Wayne A. Meeks, *The First Urban Christians: The Social World of the Apostle Paul* (New Haven, CT, 1982) 9ff., 72ff.; Hans-Josef Klauck, *Hausgemeinde und Hauskirche im frühen Christentum* (Stuttgarter Bibelstudien 103; Stuttgart 1981) passim.

9. L. Voelkl, "Die konstantinischen Kirchenbauten nach Eusebius," RDAC 39 (1953) 60–64; Gregory Armstrong, "Imperial Church Building and Church-State Relations, A.D. 313–363," *Church History* 37 (1967) 3–17; Deno Genakoplos, "Church Building and 'Caesaropapism,' A.D. 312–365," *Greek, Roman and Byzantine Studies* 7 (1966) 168ff.; A. H. M. Jones, *Constantine and the Conversion of Europe* (New York 1948) 88, 176ff.; Ramsay MacMullen, *Christianizing the Roman Empire* (New Haven, CT, 1984) 43–58. The major establishments included St. John Lateran and St. Peter's at Rome, the Church of the Holy Sepulchre at Jerusalem, and the Church of the Nativity at Bethlehem. Others were founded at Nicomedia, Antioch, and the new capital Constantinople (including the Church of the Holy Apostles, Hagia Irene, and the original Hagia Sophia). The major texts for the Constantinian policy come from Eusebius (but include letters from Constantine), cf. HE X.4.37ff.; *Vita Const.* II.45, III.48ff., IV.58; *Laus Const.* IX.12, XI.2, XVIII.

10. Eusebius, *Vita Const.* I.42: *nai mēn kai tais ekklēsiais tou theou plousias tas par' eautou pareichen epikourias, epauxōn men kai eis hypsos airōn tous euktērious oikous, pleistos d' anathēmasi ta semna tōn tēs ekklēsias kathēgiasmenōn phaidrynōn* [ed. I. A. Heikel, Die griechischen christlichen Schriftsteller der ersten drei Jahrhunderte (Leipzig 1902), 27]. Cf. *Vita Const.* II.45; HE X.2.1.

11. In addition to works cited above in n. 4, cf. A. Alföldi, *Constantine and the Conversion of Rome* (New York 1941) 49ff., 96f.; J. Vogt, "Pagans and Christians in the Family of Constantine the Great," in *The Conflict between Paganism and Christianity in the Fourth Century*, ed. A. Momigliano (Oxford 1963) 38ff.

12. F. Deichmann, "Basilika," *Reallexikon für Antike und Christentum*, ed. T. Klauser, vol. I (Leipzig-Stuttgart 1941) 1225–59.

13. See Graydon F. Snyder, *ANTE PACEM: Archaeological Evidence of Church Life before Constantine* (Macon, GA, 1985) 4f.

14. Ibid., 7ff.

15. Cf. his *Mission and Expansion of Christianity in the First Three Centuries*, trans. J. Moffatt (2nd ed., 2 vols., London 1908) II:88; and my article, "Adolf Harnack and the 'Expansion' of Early Christianity: A Reappraisal of Social History," TSC 5 (1985/86) 97–127.

16. Discussed in White, *The Christian Domus Ecclesiae and its Environment: A Collection of Texts and Monuments*, Harvard Theological Studies 36 in association with the American Schools of Oriental Research (Minneapolis: Augsburg Fortress, 1990) (hereafter CDEE), Appendix A, no. 1.

17. Much of the nineteenth-century work was reviewed by J. P. Kirsch, *Die römische Titelkirchen im Altertum* (Paderborn 1918), and may have provided an impetus for Krautheimer's early work, as reflected in his article "The Beginnings of Early Christian Architecture," *RER* 3 (1939) 144ff., which outlines the task carried forward in his monumental work *Corpus Basilicarum Christianarum Romae*, 5 vols. (abbreviated CBCR hereafter; Vatican City 1939–1965).

18. On the excavations see Clark Hopkins, *The Discovery of Dura-Europos* (New Haven, CT, 1983) passim; cf. M. I. Rostovtzeff, *Dura-Europos and its Art* (Oxford 1943) 58ff.; Ann M. Perkins, *The Art of Dura-Europos* (Oxford 1973) 1ff.

19. DEF VIII.2, 3ff.; 228ff. See CDEE, no. 36.

20. Cf. collection of essays edited by J. Gutmann, *The Dura-Europos Synagogue, A Re-evaluation, 1932–1972* (Missoula, MT, 1973) passim. See CDEE, no. 60.

21. "The Relevance of Non-Literary Sources," in E. M. Meyers and J. F. Strange, *Archaeology, the Rabbis, and Early Christianity* (Nashville, TN, 1981) 19–30.

22. See note 16, above.

2. The Beginnings of Christian Architecture

1. For discussion of early architectural theories see the survey of E. H. Swift, *Roman Sources of Christian Art* (New York 1951) 12–30; F. Deichmann, "Basilika," *Reallexikon für Antike und Christentum*, ed. T. Klauser, vol. I (Leipzig-Stuttgart 1941) 1225–59.

2. The persistence of these theories can still be seen in some popular treatments and a few church histories, e.g., J. Lebreton and J. Zeiller, *Histoire de l'Église Primitive*; English trans., *A History of the Early Church: Volume II, The Emergence of the Church in the Roman World* (New York 1962) 226. There is neither literary nor archaeological evidence of underground meetings to escape persecution. Archaeologically, the so-called underground basilicas have been shown to be of later date, after the persecutions had ceased. In any case it would be hard to project such practice outside of Rome itself. Cf. Richard Krautheimer, *Early Christian and Byzantine Architecture*, 3rd ed. (New York 1979) 32.

3. K. von Lange, *Haus und Halle* (Leipzig 1885) 270–336.

4. See H. Kohl and C. Watzinger, *Antike Synagogen in Galilaea* (Leipzig 1916) passim.

5. Michael Avi-Yonah, "Ancient Synagogues," *Ariel, a Quarterly Review of Arts and Letters in Israel* 32 (1973) 29–43, repr. in *The Synagogue: Studies in Origins, Archaeology, and Architecture*, ed. J. Gutmann (New York 1975) 95–109. For implications in discussions of synagogue architecture, especially in the Diaspora, see below chap. 4 and L. M. White, "The Delos Synagogue Revisited: Recent Fieldwork in the Graeco-Roman Diaspora," HTR 80 (1987) 133–60.

6. In sharp contrast to the traditional views of synagogue influences stands the recent evidence of the basilical structure at Sardis. See A. T. Kraabel, "Impact of the Discovery of the Sardis Synagogue," in *Sardis from Prehistoric to Roman Times: Results of the Archaeological Exploration of Sardis 1958–1975,* ed. G. M. A. Hanfmann (Cambridge, MA, 1983) 178–90.

7. A. C. Zestermann, *Die antike und christlichen Basiliken* (Leipzig 1847) 158ff. proposed an eclectic theory in which both house and synagogue provided models for certain features of the basilica. G. Dehio, *Die Genesis der christlichen Basilika* (Sitzungsbericht der k. bayerischen Akademie der Wissenschaften, phil.-historische Klasse XII, Munich 1882) 301f.

8. Some of this early Italian work can be seen in A. Mau, *Pompeii: Its Life and Art,* English trans., F. Kelsey (New York 1899); E. Brizio, "Relazione degli scavi eseguiti a Marzabotto presso Bologna," *Monumenta antichi* 1891, 249–442.

9. One of the earliest to posit a more complex development in Roman housing was G. Patroni in *Rendiconti dell' Accademia dei Lincei* 1902, 467–507, who argued for the tablinum as the center of family life, over earlier views of the atrium. See also L. Crema, *L'Architettura romana* (*Encyclopedia Classica* III, vol. 12, Turin 1959) 105ff.; J. W. Graham, "The Greek and the Roman House," *Phoenix* 20 (1966) 3–31.

10. M. V. Schultze, *Archäologie der altchristlichen Kunst* (Munich 1895) 37ff.

11. R. Lemaire, *L'Origine de la basilique Latine* (Brussels 1911) 62–82.

12. S. Lang, "A Few Suggestions toward the Solution of the Origin of the Early Christian Basilica," RDAC 30 (1954) 189; R. Krautheimer, ECBA, 482 n. 24.

13. Walter Lowrie, *Monuments of the Early Church* (New York 1901) 94–101. Other proponents include: Henri Leclercq, "Basilique," *Dictionnaire d'archéologie chrétienne et la liturgie,* vol. II (Paris 1921) 1:526ff.; Heinrich Holtzinger, *Die altchristliche Architektur in systematischer Darstellung* (Stuttgart 1899); G. Dehio and G. Von Betzold, *Die kirchliche Baukunst des Abendlandes,* 2 vols. and 5 folios (Stuttgart 1887–1901); O. Marucchi, *Éléments d'archéologie chrétienne,* 3 vols. (Paris 1899–1903). Lowrie especially followed the work of Joseph Wilpert, cf. his *Roma Sotterranea: Die Malereien der Katakomben Roms,* 2 vols. (Freiburg im Breisgau 1903).

14. *Art in the Early Church,* rev. ed. (New York 1947) 105–28.

15. Ibid., 110–11. Lowrie here shifts from his earlier emphasis on the atrium and suggests diverse lines of influence, but he continues to favor the house form as the direct line to the basilica through what he calls a *Kunstwollen* ("will-to-form") deriving from the household lit-

urgy. For Lowrie the archaeological proof for the existence of basilical churches before the middle of the third century is adduced from the church at Emmaus, which is dated erroneously to ca. 220. Cf. CDEE, Appendix A, no. 1.

16. L. Duchesne, *Les origines du culte chrétien*, 3rd ed. (Paris 1903); English trans., *Christian Worship: Its Origin and Evolution*, by M. L. McClure (London 1903) 11ff.; Gregory Dix, *The Shape of the Liturgy*, 2nd ed. (London 1945) 19–35.

17. Ibid., 19, 21, cf. 35.

18. Ibid., 22. Dix cites Ignatius (*Mag.* 7.1; *Philad.* 4.1; and esp. *Smyrn.* 8.1); however, his description of the details is more in keeping with Hippolytus, *Apost. Trad.* XXVI.1–12.

19. Ibid., 23, cf. 28, 34. On his assumption that the agapē was always separate from the eucharist proper, cf. 96f.

20. Ibid., 160. Cf. n. 18 above.

21. Ibid., 26f., 32. For Dix, Dura-Europos proves that basilicas did evolve directly from private house churches.

22. See for example J. Jungmann, *The Early Liturgy* (Notre Dame, IN, 1959) 14f.; J. Murphy-O'Connor, *St. Paul's Corinth: Texts and Archaeology* (Wilmington, DE, 1983) 156f.

23. Cf. Dennis E. Smith, "Social Obligation in the Context of Communal Meals: A Study of the Christian Meal in 1 Corinthians in Comparison with Graeco-Roman Meals" (Ph.D. Dissertation, Harvard University, 1980); G. Bornkamm, *Early Christian Experience* (New York 1969) 123ff.; Wayne A. Meeks, *The First Urban Christians: The Social World of the Apostle Paul* (New Haven, CT, 1983) 68.

24. R. Krautheimer, ECBA, 482 n. 24.

25. The point is made explicit in Lowrie (cf. *Art in the Early Church*, 110 and pl. 34) but is implicit in Dix.

26. A. G. McKay, *Houses, Villas, and Palaces in the Roman World* (London 1975) 30ff.; cf. John Percival, *The Roman Villa: A Historical Introduction* (London 1976).

27. R. Krautheimer, RER 3 (1939) 144f.; cf. ECBA, 40f.; J. B. Ward-Perkins, "Constantine and the Origins of the Christian Basilica," PBSR 22 (1954) 69–90.

28. S. Lang, RDAC 30 (1954) 189ff. Lang, along with J. B. Ward-Perkins and L. Voelkl, "Die konstantinischen Kirchenbauten nach Eusebius," RDAC 29 (1953) 60–64, makes much of the term *basilica* due to its use by Eusebius and its "royal" etymology. The term did not have a technical architectural definition in antiquity. On the hypostyle see G. Leroux, *Les Origines de l'édifice hypostyle en Grèce, en Orient, et chez les Romains* (Paris 1913), which was used by V. Müller, "The Roman Basilica," AJA 41 (1937) 250–61; R. Bernheimer, "An Ancient Oriental Source of Christian Sacred Architecture," AJA 43 (1939) 647–68; cf. J. B. Ward-Perkins, PBSR 22 (1954) 71f.

29. ECBA, 42f.; RER 3 (1939) 145f.; Ward-Perkins, PBSR 22 (1954) 87.
30. PBSR 22 (1954) 85. The date of the beginning of construction in the Lateran basilica is not certain; it was probably completed by 319/320.
31. Cf. William MacDonald, *Early Christian and Byzantine Architecture* (New York 1977) 1ff. The first to make the distinction sharply was Krautheimer, RER 3 (1939) 144f.
32. CBCR, 5 vols. (Vatican City 1939-1956). The planned scope of the project is as yet incomplete.
33. The nineteenth-century work is summarized by J. P. Kirsch, *Die römische Titelkirchen im Altertum* (Paderborn 1918) passim. That some of the so-called pre-Constantinian *tituli* appear in my collection (CDEE) in Appendix A reflects Krautheimer's critical judgments on the claims for Christian use of earlier buildings. The stress on the distinct character of pre-Constantinian architecture has led Krautheimer to posit two different lines of architectural development which begin to merge after Constantine. These are the church buildings proper (architecture of assembly) and funerary structures (memorial architecture). Cf. ECBA, 28-38.
34. ECBA, 24f. The date 200 is taken from the reference in Tertullian, *Apol.* 39.15 (usually dated ca. 197), but it may also derive from Harnack. More recently Graydon Snyder, *ANTE PACEM: Archaeological Evidence of Church Life before Constantine* (Macon, GA, 1985) 164f. adopts a similar periodization, but with different implications.
35. ECBA, 26.
36. Ibid., 27. Here Krautheimer discusses Dura-Europos as a prime example along with the evidence from two sites at Rome (SS. Giovanni e Paolo and San Clemente). The term *domus ecclesiae* is taken over from Adolf Harnack, *The Mission and Expansion of Christianity in the First Three Centuries*, English trans. from 2nd German ed. by J. Moffatt, 2 vols. (London 1908) II:86f. (cf. II:610-18 in the 4th German ed.; Leipzig 1924).
37. ECBA, 37f.; 482 n. 22; Cf. CDEE, no. 55.
38. Ibid., 39, 46; cf. Ward-Perkins, PBSR 22 (1954) 81.
39. So also DEF VIII.2, 129.
40. Michael Gough, *The Early Christians* (New York 1961) 59; Kraeling, DEF VIII.2, 139f.
41. Cf. J. G. Davies, *The Secular Use of Church Buildings* (New York 1968) 1-3; ECBA, 24, 26.
42. Cf. Michael Gough, *The Early Christians* 61; cf. J. B. Ward-Perkins, PBSR 22 (1954) 81.
43. Cf. P. Testini, *Archeologia Christiana: Nosioni generali delle origini all fine del sec. VI* (Rome 1958) 559f.; Gough, *The Early Christians*, 62f.
44. Thus, note Gerd Theissen's erroneous use of Dura-Europos as

an example of the earliest type of Pauline "house church" in *The Social Setting of Pauline Christianity: Essays on Corinth* (Philadelphia 1982) 114 n. 45.

45. See CDEE, nos. 50, 57.
46. See CDEE, nos. 39, 41.
47. See CDEE, Appendix A, nos. 4, 8. See also Chapter 5, pg. 134, and Figure 27, below.
48. See CDEE, nos. 50, 52, 53, and perhaps no. 54.
49. The term *aula ecclesiae* is used here with some caution and reservation. In ancient sources *aula* (like *aedes* or *oikos*) could be used of almost any type of building, and had no explicitly technical architectural connotation. Cf. L. Voelkl, RDAC 29 (1953) 50f. The term is coined here for two reasons: to describe the hall-type rooms found in a number of prebasilical churches, and to retain a sense of continuity with the term *domus ecclesiae*, as would seem appropriate in the case of Dura-Europos. Thus, C. H. Kraeling (DEF VIII.2, 133f.) adopts the phrase "hall-like structure," while A. Harnack uses the term *Saalkirchen* (*Mission und Ausbreitung*, 4th ed., II:615f.). Our term *aula ecclesiae*, however, is not meant to connote any of the technical features of the basilica, save the rectangular plan. It does not suggest a direct line of evolution from house to basilica as suggested by Heinz Kähler, *Die spätantiken Bauten unter dem Dom von Aquileia und ihre Stellung innerhalb der Geschichte des frühchristlichen Kirchenbaues* (Saarbrücken 1957) 42ff.
50. Jean Lassus, *Sanctuaires chrétiennes de Syrie* (Paris 1947) 22f.; ibid., "Syrie," *Dictionnaire d'archéologie chrétienne et la liturgie*, vol. XI (Paris 1951) 1855ff.
51. Jean Lassus, "Les édifices du culte autour de la basilique," CIAC VI, 581–610, esp. 588. See also H. I. Marrou, "La basilique chrétienne d'Hippo d'après le résultat des derniers fouilles," *Revue des Études Augustiniennes* 6 (1960) 109ff.
52. Cf. S. L. Greenslade, "Christian Topography,"; W. H. C. Frend, "The Early Christian Church in Carthage," in *Excavations at Carthage 1976, Conducted by the University of Michigan, III*, ed. J. H. Humphrey (Ann Arbor, MI, 1977) 21–40.
53. See CDEE, no. 39, and Georges Tchalenko, *Villages antiques de la Syria du Nord*, 3 vols. (Paris 1953–1958)) I:332f.
54. CBCR I:146–64. See CDEE, no. 55. Cf. ECBA, 38 and 482 n. 22.
55. CBCR I:267–303. (See CDEE, no. 52); CBCR I:117f. (See CDEE, no. 53).
56. J. B. Ward-Perkins, "Recent Work and Problems in Libya," CIAC VIII, 219, 232, 236. He cites as a possible example of such a domus ecclesiae an atypical fourth-century church building from el Msufiin (Henschir Taglissi) in the Western gebel. Cf. J. B. Ward-

Perkins and R. G. Goodchild, "The Christian Antiquities of Tripolitania," *Archaeologica* 95 (1953) 39–41 and fig. 19. See CDEE, Appendix A, no. 11 for discussion and the text of a pertinent inscription.

57. Recent work on the progress of Christianity in rural Hispania in the fifth century has prompted Pedro de Palol to suggest an architectural development beginning in large estate villas which then gave rise to basilicas. Pedro de Palol, "Los monumentos de Hispania en la arqueología paleocristiana," CIAC VIII, 167–85. See CDEE, Appendix A, no. 13 for additional sites and references.

In Roman Britannia the few extant buildings from before the barbarian invasions (late fourth century) are generally small nonbasilical halls (as at Silchester, dated ca. 360) or chapels in houses (as at Hinton St. Mary's). Cf. K. S. Painter, "Villas and Christianity in Roman Britain," CIAC VIII, 149–66; and "Christianity in Roman Britain, Recent Finds: 1962–1969," CIAC VIII 373f. For discussion of the sites see CDEE, Appendix A, no. 12. Cf. P. Salway, *Roman Britain* (Oxford 1981) 380ff.; A. L. F. Rivet, ed., *The Roman Villa in Britain* (London 1969); C. Thomas, *Christianity in Roman Britain* (London 1976).

58. ECBA, 26, 28; cf. M. Gough, *The Early Christians*, 68f.
59. ECBA, 27, 28–30.
60. DEF VIII.2, 139–40.

3. "Private" Cults in a Constructive Context

1. Ramsay MacMullen, *Paganism in the Roman Empire* (New Haven, CT, 1981) 34–48. Further on the expense of maintenance see M. I. Rostovtzeff, *A Social and Economic History of the Roman Empire*, 2nd ed. P. M. Fraser, 2 vols. (Oxford 1957) I:147–48.

2. Despite the well-known complaints of authors such as Pliny, *Ep.* X.96.10. See also Ramsay MacMullen, *Christianizing the Roman Empire, A.D. 100–400* (New Haven, CT, 1984) 86–101; R. P. C. Hanson, "On the Transformation of Pagan Temples into Churches in the Early Christian Centuries," *Journal of Semitic Studies* 23 (1978) 257–67; J. C. Nassivera, "Ancient Temples to Pagan Goddesses and Early Churches to the Virgin in the City of Rome," *Echos du monde classique* 20 (1976) 41–54.

3. Cassius Dio, *History of Rome* LXVI.24.1–3, trans. E. Cary, LCL (London 1925), translation adapted.

4. Suetonius, *The Deified Titus* VIII.4, trans. J. C. Rolfe, LCL (London 1914), translation adapted.

5. Suetonius, *The Deified Vespasian* VIII.5–IX.1.

6. Thus, for Nero see Sulpicius Severus, *Chronicle* II.29: "But the opinion of all cast the odium of causing the fire upon the Emperor, and he was believed in this way to have sought for the glory of building a new city." Cf. Tacitus, *Ann.* XV.44; Suetonius, *Nero* XVI. On the re-

building program, according to Gaius, *Institutes* I.33, after the fire Nero offered citizenship as an inducement to Italian decurions who would build houses in Rome worth at least 100,000 sesterces (hereafter, HS).

    7. Martial, *De spectaculis* II, quoted from J. J. Pollitt, *The Art of Rome, c. 753 B.C.–A.D. 337: Sources and Documents* (Cambridge, England, 1983) 158.

    8. On cranes and machines see Martial's comment (n. 7 above) as well as Cassius Dio, *Hist.* LVII.21.5; Suetonius, *Vesp.* XVIII. Also, on the impact of heavy construction in the city see the edict of Julius Caesar (CIL I², 593, lines 56–67) restricting cart traffic within the urbs of Rome from sunup to sundown except for construction vehicles. Cf. Jerome Carcopino, *Daily Life in Ancient Rome* (New Haven, CT, 1959) 47–51.

    9. ILS 5506; cf. Ramsay MacMullen, *Roman Social Relations* (New Haven, CT, 1974) 145.

    10. Juvenal, *Satires* XI.12–13; III.223–25. Cf. Tacitus, *Annals* XV.46; Pliny, *Nat. Hist.* XXXVI.24.106; 54.126; Martial, *Epigrams* 117.7f.

    11. Juvenal, *Satires* III.193–202, trans. G. G. Ramsay, LCL (London 1918), adapted.

    12. Strabo, *Geography* V.3.7, trans. H. L. Jones, LCL (London 1923), adapted.

    13. Carcopino, *Daily Life in Ancient Rome*, 28–51.

    14. See Richard Duncan-Jones, *The Economy of the Roman Empire: Quantitative Studies* (Cambridge, England, 1974) 75–78, 124–26; Mac-Mullen, *Roman Social Relations*, 142–45. What is lacking at present is the same sort of study for construction costs (both primary work and renovation/repair) and housing rates (both purchase and rental) from the private sector in order to determine comparative scales.

    15. *Ep.* VII.18.2f.; ILS 2927; cf. *Epp.* X.8.2, IV.1, III.4.2; Duncan-Jones, *Economy*, 26–32.

    16. Duncan-Jones, *Economy*, 27 and n. 5.

    17. Ibid., 28; Pliny, *Epp.* X.8.2–4; IV.1.4.

    18. CIL X.846 (= ILS 6367):

*N[umerius] Popidius N[umerii] f[ilius] Celsinus
aedem Isidis terrae motu conlapsam
a fundamento p[ecunia] s[ua] restituit. Hunc decuriones ob liberalitem
cum esset annorum sex ordini suo gratis ad legerunt.*

On the role of freedmen in the diffusion of foreign religions and on the progress of freedmen in local society see Susan Treggiari, *Roman Freedmen during the Late Republic* (Oxford 1969) 204–5; 229–35, though it must be noted that the elder Numerius, *libertus Popidii*, must have gained freedom nearer the beginning of Principate. For other benefactions by members of the *gens Popidii* and other aspiring freedmen and slaves of prominent citizens at Pompeii see CIL X.187 (ILS 6384); CIL X.908; CIL X.794 (ILS 5538). Cf. John H. D'Arms, *Commerce and Social Standing in Ancient Rome* (Cambridge 1981) 121–48; *Romans on the Bay of Naples* (Cambridge 1970) passim.

19. Arthur Darby Nock, *Conversion: The Old and the New in Religion from Alexander the Great to Augustine of Hippo* (Oxford 1933) 50–53, 66–68.

20. W. Dittenberger, OGIS no. 594 (= IGRR I, 420).

21. W. Dittenberger, OGIS no. 595 (= IGRR I, 420). Cf. R. M. Grant, "Temple, Churches, and Endowments," in *Early Christianity and Society* (New York 1977) 147. For the honors to the emperor compare the collegium of Alexandrian shippers at Puteoli noted in Suetonius, *Augustus* 98. The rented property was probably the collegial hall, and would have included a room set aside for a sanctuary for the ancestral gods. Compare the similar situation on Delos (which was a model for the free port organization of Puteoli) of the Tyrian Herakleiasts and the Poseidoniasts of Berytus, Phoenician trading associations whose ancestral Ba'al had taken on hellenized identity. The Poseidoniasts' building, which contained a small court and sanctuary off the main hall, is described by C. Picard, *L'Établissement des Poseidoniastes de Berytos*, Exploration archéologique de Délos VI (Paris 1921) esp. 21ff. (cf. below n. 49). The term *statiōnos* ("agency") could be applied both to the merchants' association itself and to the rented hall. See also J. D'Arms, *Commerce and Social Standing*, 35, 121–48.

22. T. A. Brady, *The Reception of the Egyptian Cults by the Greeks (330–30 B.C.)*. University of Missouri Studies X.1 (Columbia, MO, 1935) passim; John Stambaugh, *Sarapis under the Ptolemies* (EPRO 25; Leiden 1972) passim. Regina Salditt-Trappmann, *Tempel der ägyptischen Götter in Griechenland und an der Westküste Kleinasiens* (EPRO 15; Leiden 1970) passim.

23. IG XI.4, 1299. Critical text with commentary by Helmut Englemann, *The Delian Aretalogy of Sarapis* (EPRO 44; Leiden 1975), and trans. in F. W. Danker, *Benefactor: Epigraphic Study of a Graeco-Roman and New Testament Semantic Field* (St. Louis, MO, 1982) 186–87. The following discussion summarizes the more detailed analysis of the inscription in light of more recent archaeological work, as presented in my article, "An Architectural and Social History of Delos Sarapeion A" (forthcoming).

24. IG XI.4, 1299, line 43, refers to worshippers (*therapes*) who were pleased with Demetrius' priestly service. Other inscriptions from the environs of Sarapeion A refer to several different sodalities connected with the sanctuary, again probably suggesting gradual growth in membership over time.

25. Pierre Roussel, *Les Cultes égyptiens à Délos* (Annales de l'Est III.6; Nancy 1916); Philippe Bruneau, *Recherches sur les cults de Délos*

(Écoles Français d'Athènes 217; Paris 1970) 457–62; Marie-Françoise Baslez, *Recherches sur les conditions de pénétration et de diffusion des religions orientales à Délos* (Paris 1977) 35–65.

26. A. D. Nock, *Conversion*, 53.

27. F. W. Danker (in *Benefactor*, 190 n. 68—which seems to depend directly on the argument of Engelmann, *Delian Aretalogy*, 45–47, 52) suggests two distinct charges: introducing a foreign cult, and building outside of his assigned plot. I see no evidence for the introduction of a foreign cult, either from the inscription itself or from the wider historical evidence from Delos in the late Hellenistic period. On the legal aspects of establishing a temple in Roman times see John Stambaugh, "The Social Functions of Roman Temples," ANRW II.16.1 (New York 1978) 558–63.

28. P. Bruneau, "Le Quartier de L'inopos à Délos et la Fondation du Sarapeion A," in *Études Déliennes* (BCH Supplement I; Athens/Paris 1973) 111–36.

29. The original field survey was conducted by P. Roussel (n. 25 above) and is assumed as the standard by H. Englemann (n. 23 above) and in the official publications of the École Français, *Guide de Délos*, by P. Bruneau and J. Ducat (Paris 1965) 133–35. (All references to Delos employ this offical numbering system, cited by the abbreviation GD.) It must be noted, however, that Roussel never attempted a construction history of the site in relation to the immediate archaeological context, essential in forming a complete picture.

30. The masonry of the north wall (fig. 2) shows a clear break in composition beginning at the stairs and running east. Especially indicative of the change is the high concentration of tan *poros* in this section and continuing around the east perimeter of the temenos through the bonded corner in Room D. To the west of the stairs the wall is unbroken and homogeneous through Room E and continuing to its termination at the west stair of Insula 91. Thus, the north wall of Room E was in place prior to construction of the Temple by Apollonius II.

31. The irregular west partition wall of Room E seems to have been erected in several phases, as indicated by the masonry composition and the fit of the unbonded corners with Insula 91. The sequence of construction, therefore, corresponds to the adaptation of Insula 91 during the extension of the Temple. The building sequence goes as follows (cf. fig. 2): (1) wall ϕ part of the original construction of Insula 91; (2) wall χ, clearly indicated by its distinctive masonry style (and which, earlier, may have had an aperture into Room E); and (3) wall ψ, which was constructed during the building of the Temple (it was used to close off Room II of Insula 91, and introduced a secondary overlap to the aperture in Room III, wall χ, which then became a niche). Finally, it should be noted that the corner of Room E at area J/IV, which forms the south termination of Room E, antedates the building of partition wall χ, and

thus also the construction of the Temple. Thus, there was a conscious physical alteration of Insula 91 through the erection of partition walls in Room E that served to segregate the Temple precincts from the rest of the existing structure. Room E was incorporated into the temple, while the rest of the temenos was constructed de novo.

32. Small naos A lies askew of the main axis of the temenos, but almost precisely on the line of the preexisting insula wall in Room E at area J (see n. 31 above). This area was a depression created by the drain line from the Inopos reservoir. During construction of the naos a crypt (A') was created beneath it and was tied into the reservoir using the existing drain canal. The main drain from the reservoir was thus diverted to the south of the temple under Room C and down the valley toward the House of Hermes (GD 89). The axis of the naos and crypt, therefore, was determined consciously to adapt the original drain line from the reservoir toward Insula 91.

33. IG XI.4, 1299 (lines 64–65) describes consecration of the dining hall by a "divine summons to a banquet." Line 90 of the inscription also refers to the *laos*, probably the cultic community referred to variously in other inscriptions from Sarapeion A as *therapes* (line 48), *therapeuontes* (IG XI.4, 1217), and *therapeuontai* (IG XI.4, 1215); cf. H. Englemann, *Delian Aretalogy*, 56.

34. "Le Quartier de L'Inopos," 121–23, which follows the topographical and architectural survey of René Vallois, *L'architecture hellénique et hellénistique à Délos jusqu'à l'éviction des Déliens (166 av. J.-C.)*, 2 vols. (Paris 1944, 1960) I:202ff.

35. See Robert A. Wild, *Water in the Cultic Worship of Isis and Sarapis* (EPRO 87; Leiden 1981) esp. 34–39; R. E. Witt, *Isis in the Graeco-Roman World* (Ithaca, NY, 1971) 67–68.

36. On temple foundation see Stambaugh, "Social Functions of Roman Temples," in ANRW II.16.1 (1978) 559ff. For texts compare the papyrus letter of Zoilus to Apollonius (ca. 258 B.C.E.) in F. C. Grant, *Hellenistic Religions* (New York 1953) 144 and compare the Mithraic inscription CIMRM I, 423 (= CDEE, no. 88).

37. The aretalogy specifies (line 67) "two windy indictments," and it refers to Apollonius' opposition as "allies" (line 87), facts that seem to have gone largely unnoticed in most discussions of the lawsuit. We may suggest, then, that the two charges (that were aired in the temple itself) had the effect of cancelling one another, since one claimed that Apollonius had defiled sacred ground (the spring) while the other claimed that he had sacralized common ground (the insula). Thus, mirabile dictu, was Apollonius delivered from his enemies by divine intervention to silence the accusers (lines 86–90).

38. A key comes from the wording of the second account of the events, the hymn or aretalogy proper (lines 29–94) composed by the priest Maiistas. In this section the original rented quarters (*en mis-*

thōtois) of the elder Apollonius (line 15f.) are designated as the "hall" (*melathron*, line 39) where the god was housed and worshipped. Later, the same term (*melathron*) is used to designate the dining hall (hence Room E) at the time of the consecration of the temple. It should also be noticed that (in sharp contrast to the rest of the description) there is no construction mentioned in connection with the dining hall, only outfitting and decoration. The crucial portion of the text reads as follows (lines 62–65): *sethen th' ama boulomenoio rēidiōs kai neios aexeto kai thyoentes bōmoi kai temenos, tetelesto de panta melathrōi edrana te klismoi te theoklētous epi daitas* ("In accordance with your will the sanctuary was built easily along with the altars of sacrifice and a sacred precinct; all the seats and the couches of the hall were consecrated with a divine summons to the banquet").

39. In line 65 (text given in n. 38 above), Sarapis himself issues the dinner invitation to the dedicatory banquet in Room E. Compare P. Köln 2555 (ed. L. Koenen), *Zeitschrift für Papyrologie und Epigraphik* I (1967) 121–26 with discussion; cf. H. Engelmann, *Delian Aretalogy*, 43, and G. H. Horseley in *New Documents Illustrating Early Christianity*, vol. I (North Ryda, Australia, 1976) nos. 51ff.

40. Awareness of these circumstances would have heightened the ironic tone of the aretalogy, and for the worshippers would have further strengthened the symbolism of incorporating the original rented quarters into the dining hall of the new temple.

41. Two vols. (Berkeley 1984) esp. I:9–10.

42. Ibid., I:54–55. Thus, the egalitarian force of personal *philia* in Greek sources often came to designate social stratification in the Latin *amicitia*, though it could also be used to blur status distinctions, when this served a purpose. Cf. J. D'Arms, *Commerce and Social Standing*, 165–66.

43. Gruen, *Hellenistic World and Coming of Rome*, I:158–200. Cf. Richard P. Saller, *Personal Patronage under the Early Empire* (Cambridge, England, 1982) 7–40; Erik Wistrand, *Caesar and Contemporary Roman Society* (Göteborg 1978) passim.

44. Cf. M. I. Rostovtzeff, *The Social and Economic History of the Roman Empire*, ed. P. M. Fraser, vol. I (2nd ed. Oxford 1957), 149–51; vol. II, 601, n. 13; P. Graindor, *Un Milliardaire antique: Herode Atticus et sa famille* (Paris 1930) 32, 72.

45. GD 100. Cf. P. Bruneau, *Cults de Délos*, 460–61; *Guide de Délos*, 137.

46. P. Roussel, *Cults égyptiens*, 47. See esp. ID 2610, a list of the priests of Sarapeion C appointed from Athens. For other dealings see ID 2614–15. Sarapeion C (despite the name) was in reality a more pan-Egyptian cult, with separate sanctuaries for Isis, Sarapis, and Anubis. It was the center for the Egyptian vogue on Delos during the later Hellenistic and early Roman periods and was heavily accommodated to

Athenian tendencies. Thus, there probably would have been theological as well as social differences with the older cult of Sarapeion A. One indication of the possible differences might lie in the absence of a Nileometer in Sarapeion C, while Sarapeion A was very closely associated to such water rituals. R. A. Wild, in *Water in the Cultic Worship of Isis and Sarapis*, 34, discusses the absence and later (65–67) discusses some shifts in usage in the Roman period.

47. ID 1510 (= Roussel 92, inscr. no. 14). Cf. T. A. Brady, *Reception of Egyptian Cults*, 42; R. E. Witt, *Isis*, 65. The *senatus consultum* was inscribed and set up in Sarapeion A as a perpetual charter.

48. ID 1510, lines 30–37: *peri toutou tou pragmatos houtos edoxen: kathōs to proteron etherapeuen heneken hēmōn therapeuein exestin, tou mē ti hypenantion tōi tēs sygkletou dogmati ginētai. edoxen.*

49. P. Bruneau, *Cults de Délos*, 622f; C. Picard, *L'Établissement des Poseidoniastes de Berytos*. The inscription from the architrave of the peristyle (ID 1774) reads: *to koinon Berytiōn Poseidoniastōn emporōn kai naukleron kai egdocheon/ ton oikon kai ten stoan kai ta chrēsteria theois patriois anethēken.* Also known through inscriptions is a similar merchants association designated as the "Herakleiasts of Tyre." The group is variously called (ID 1519) *sunodos* and *koinon*, yet also clearly considered itself a religious association, i.e., the *thiasitai* of *emporoi kai naukleroi* who were dedicated to Herakles-Melkart. Cf. P. Bruneau, *Cults de Délos*, 622.

50. Dennis E. Smith, "The Egyptian Cults at Corinth," HTR 70 (1977) 201–31 (esp. 212–14).

51. P. Kavvadias, *Fouilles d'Épidaure* (Athens 1891).

52. At Gortyn, Crete, Roman remains yield a rectangular cella and some annexed buildings for the Egyptian cult, construction dedicated by Flavia Philyra and her sons. Inscr. Cret. IV, 249: *Eisidi kai Sarapidi kai theois sunnaois Phlabia Philyra meta tōn / teknōn G. Metrōniou Maxi-[mou] kai Philyras kai Lyskias ton oikon ek themeliōn / kataskeuasas[a] ka[thidry]sen euchēn kai charistēion.* Text from Ladislaus Vidman, *Sylloge inscriptionum religionis Isiacae et Sarapiacae* (Religionsgeschichtliche Versuche und Vorarbeiten 28; Berlin 1969) no. 170. For the buildings see P. Roussel in REG ns 1 (1919) 91.

53. Cf. H. Engelmann, *Delian Aretalogy*, 43; Dennis E. Smith, "Social Obligation in the Context of Communal Meals: (Th.D. Thesis, Harvard University 1980) 18ff.; R. MacMullen, *Paganism in the Roman World*, 37–48.

54. Mikhail Rostovtzeff, *Dura-Europos and Its Art* (Oxford 1938) 20–42; Ann Perkins, *The Art of Dura-Europos* (Oxford 1973) 17, figs. 3, 4 and pl. 5. Also on localized variations in Roman period temples see Martin Henig, *Religion in Roman Britain* (London 1984) 36–67; G. Antier, "La galerie du fanum galloromain," *Information d'histoire de l'Art* 20 (1975) 210–14, which suggests the development of a complex temple

plan including multiple cellae, porticoes, and galleries. In part he attributes such variations to local ritual patterns.

55. DEP VII–VIII, 135f. and fig. 42. Datable epigraphic remains range from ca. 150–175 C.E.
56. DEP VII–VIII, 168f.: Inscr. no. 871 (for Chapel 38, dated 153 C.E.) and no. 873 (Chapel 5, 175 C.E.).
57. Ibid., 181f. and fig. 48.
58. Ibid., 190f., 213f.: Inscr. nos. 886, 888. In the latter (dated ca. 120/121 C.E.) Seleucus Theomnestus of Antioch, a citizen of Dura, is said to have "erected for the God Zeus Theos the temple and the outer doors [of an antechamber?]" (*anegeiren Dii theōi/ ton naon kai ta thurōmata*).
59. Ibid., 222f. and fig. 53.
60. Ibid., 226 and fig. 54.
61. Ibid., 230–31.
62. Ibid., 234–38.
63. Ibid., 278–80: Inscr. nos. 907 and 908. Most of the inscriptions are in Palmyrene and record votives to the "Gad of Palmyra."
64. Ibid., 257–58 and n. 31. The acquisition of the property is not discussed. It is possible that House A, which is quite large by standards of Durene domestic architecture, was built by the family of Nasor and Hairan, who figure prominently in the activity of the cult and the Palmyrene merchant enclave.
65. The House of the Scribes was built (early third century C.E.) by adaptation of two contiguous houses (A and B) in Block L7 (the same insula as the Synagogue). Part of House B remained in private domestic use, while the rest was renovated and annexed to House A to serve as the main hall for the guild of scribes. Cf. DEP VI, 226, 274 and pls VII, XI. Also for physical affinities to the house that was renovated to form the Synagogue see DEF VIII.1, 26–27.
66. DEP VII–VIII, 128–31: Inscr. nos. 867–869. The latter two inscriptions date from 116 and 118 C.E. respectively, and the last was reused in the construction of the altar table of the middle mithraeum, ca. 209–11 C.E. (cf. CDEE, no. 58b). The texts are as follows:

Inscription no. 868:
Ἔτους ηκυ'. ['Αν-]
ακαινίσας Ἀλέ-
ξανδρος Ἐπινί-
κου τὸν ναὸν τοῦτ-
5 {τ}ο ὃ οἰκοδομήσας
αὐτῷ ἀπὸ πάλαι Ἐπι-
νίκος ὁ πατήρ μου
καὶ προθησάμην ἐν
αὐτῷ πήχεις πέντε,

10 τὰ δὲ θυρώματα ἀρχαῖα
 λημφθέντα ὑπὸ τῶν Ῥω-
 μαίων, μετὰ δὲ τὴν αὐτῶν
 ἔνθεν ἀποχώρησιν ἐν δευ-
 τέρου ἐποιησάμην ἐπ' ἐ-
15 μαυτοῦ ἄλλα θυρώ[μα-]
 τα τῷ αὐτῷ ναῷ καὶ
 ἐξωτέρας. μνησ[θῇ]
 Ἀμμαῖος ὁ αὐτὸς Ἀ[λέ-]
 ξανδρος ἱερὺς [τοῦ]
20 θεοῦ καὶ κῆρυξ τῆ[ς πόλε-]
 ως πρὸς τὸν αὐ[τὸν θεόν].

Inscription no. 869:
 Ἀγαθῇ Τυχῃ.
 Ἔτους λυ'.
 Ἀνήγειρεν
 Ἀλέξανδρος
5 Ἐπινίκου τὸν
 οἶκον τοῦτο καὶ
 τὸ ἐξώτερον
 θεῷ κατ' εὐχήν,
 χωρὶς τοίχου ἐξω-
10 τέρου [— — —]η
 σ[— — — —]
 πα[— — — —]α

67. I concur with the view of the excavators (DEP VII–VIII, 183) that the references to naos and *oikos* do not indicate a formal temple complex. I disagree, however, with their view that there is no relation between the sanctuary of Epinicus and Alexander and the mithraeum building. I find it hard to account for the preservation of the Alexander inscription (no. 869) in the construction of the middle mithraeum (ca. 209–211) if there were not some physical preservation from the time of the first mithraeum (ca. 167–170), that was only minimally adapted from the earlier form of the edifice.

68. T. Wiegand and H. Schrader, *Priene: Ergebnisse der Ausgrabungen und Untersuchungen in den Jahren 1895–1898* (Berlin 1904) 172–78 and Anschn. XXI (CDEE, no. 69 and fig. 30).

69. Achille Vogliano, "La grande iscrizione Bacchia del Metropolitan Museum: I," AJA 2nd ser. 37 (1933) 215–31; Franz Cumont, "La grande inscription bacchique du Metropolitan Museum: II," AJA 2nd ser. 37 (1933) 232–63. Cf. H. Lietzmann, *An die Römer*, 4th ed. (Tübingen 1933) 134; Wayne A. Meeks, *The First Urban Christians: The Social World of the Apostle Paul* (New Haven, CT, 1983) 31 and 205 n. 143.

70. W. Dittenberger, *Sylloge Inscriptionum Graecorum* vol. III (3rd ed., Leipzig 1920) 113–19, no. 985; Grant, *Hellenistic Religions*, 28–30; O. Weinreich, "Stiftung und Kultsatzungen eines Privätheiligtums in Philadelpeia," *Sitzungsbericht der Heidelberger Akademie der Wissenschaften* 16 (1919) 1–68. Cf. Nock, *Conversion*, 217 and Wayne A. Meeks, "The Image of the Androgyne: Some uses of symbol in Earliest Christianity," *History of Religions* 13 (1974) 169. My suggestion that the inscription represents a household cult under Dionysius differs from the traditional reading (since Weinreich) that the text represents a private temple and cultic community.

71. Other cases that reflect the dilemma of understanding relations between private household cults and outsiders where the house also shows signs of renovation for religious use are two examples well known for their artwork. The first is the Villa Item at Pompeii, with its Dionysiac paintings. Cf. V. Maccioro, *From Orpheus to Paul* (New York 1930) 258; R. Herbig, *Neue Beobachtungen am Fries der Mysterienvilla in Pompeii* (Deutschen Beiträge zur Altertumswissenschaft; Berlin 1958); A. M. G. Little, *Roman Bridal Drama at the Villa of the Mysteries* (New York 1972) passim. The second is the House of the Mysteries at Antioch-on-the-Orontes, which contains scenes of an Isiac initiation ritual. Cf. Doro Levi, *Antioch Mosaic Pavements* (Princeton, NJ, 1947) II:19–55; R. E. Witt, *Isis in the Graeco-Roman World*, 161–62. Though both cases seem to portray initiation rituals, there is no physical evidence for actual assembly or cultic activities of a larger group.

72. IG IV.1, 659 (= CCCA II, 146 no. 469). Cf. Giulia Sfameni-Gasparro, *Soteriology and Mystic Aspects in the Cult of Cybele and Attis* (EPRO 103; Leiden 1985) 21. The date is uncertain.

73. H. Chadwick, "An Attis from a Domestic Shrine," *Journal of Theological Studies* 3 (1952) 90–92; cf. CCCA VII, 38 no. 132.

74. CCCA III, 47–61 nos. 225–45. M. J. Vermaseren, *Cybele and Attis: The Myth and the Cult* (London 1977) 45–47; Filippo Coarelli, "I Monumenti dei culti orientali in Roma: Questioni topografiche e chronologiche," in *La Soteriologia dei culti orientali nell' Impero Romano*, ed. U. Bianchi and M. J. Vermaseren (EPRO 92; Leiden 1982) 33–67; Margherita Guarducci, "L'Interruzione dei culti nel Phrygianum del Vaticano durante il IV secolo d.Cr.," in ibid., 109–22.

75. F. Coarelli, "Monumenti dei culti orientali in Roma," 42–43.

76. CIL VI, 494.

77. CIL VI, 641; CCA III, 40–43 nos. 207–13; M. J. Vermaseren, *Cybele and Attis*, 43–44; Coarelli, "Monumenti dei culti orientali in Roma," 34.

78. CIL VI, 30973.

79. So M. J. Vermaseren, *Cybele and Attis*, 43 and n. 233.

80. Compare Sarapeion B on Delos, P. Bruneau, *Cults de Délos*, 425. For corporations and collegia as religious associations see R. Meiggs,

Roman Ostia, 2nd ed. (Oxford 1971) 178ff.; S. Treggiari, *Freedmen during the Late Republic*, 194–207. In many cases even collegia were housed in more private quarters and the collegial hall could be called by various terms: a *domus* with *triclinium* (CIL XI, 5749, Sentinum); *schola* and *curia* (CIL VI, 541); *locus* (CIL III, 4038; VI, 10350); and *basilica* (CIL VI, 10295; III, 4779). See J.-P. Waltzing, *Étude historique sur les Corporations Professionelles chez les Romains depuis les origines jusqu'à la chute de l'Empire d'Occident*, 4 vols. (Louvain 1895–1900) I:223, 521. By the same token there are cases of extended households that were organized (similar to the household cults) as formal collegia. See CIL II, 3229 (from Laminium): *Alliae M. f. Candidae, collec[ium] anensem . . . clientes et liberti patronae posuerunt*; CIL XIII, 1747 (from Lugdunum): *collegium Larum in dom(o) Julian(a)*. Cf. J. P. Waltzing, *Corporations*, IV:167–76, 178–80.

81. Cf. CIL VI, 9149, 10260–64 (= J.-P. Waltzing, *Corporations*, IV, nos. 203–9.

82. M. Sordi and M. L. Cavigiolo, "Un'antica 'chiesa domestica' di Rome? (*Il Collegium quod est in domo Sergiae L. F. Paullinae*)," *Rivista di Storia della Chiesa in Italia* 25 (1971) 369–74. The suggestion is based on another inscription of the same family from Anatolia. Thus, Sordi (372) takes the phrase *[col]lecium m[ajorum] et mino[rum qui] sunt in [domo]* found in CIL VI, 10264 to mean "presbyters and laymen" in the house church. This reading seems anachronistic based on later ecclesiastical vocabulary. In fact, *majores et minores* were often used in the household to designate standard familial relationships implying status distinctions, such as *liberti* vs. slaves. Cf. Cicero, *De Domo sua* 77; *Pro Caecina* 96–100. The further prosopographic suggestions made by Sordi (*The Christians and the Roman Empire* [Norman, OK, 1986] 185–86), while intriguing, are based on very scanty evidence drawn from Acts.

83. A good example of the separation between public acts of worship and the more private communal activities of a religious association is found in the *acta* of the Arval Brotherhood from ca. 240 C.E. (ILS 9522; cf. F. C. Grant, *Ancient Roman Religion* [New York 1957] 236). The *acta* specify locations and movements especially connected with the communal fellowship of the group. On the social makeup see also John Sheid, *Les Frères Arvales: Recruitement et origine sociale sous les empereurs julio-claudiens* (Paris 1975) esp. 289–327; Ronald Syme, *Some Arval Brethren* (Oxford 1980) 70–78.

84. MacMullen, *Paganism in the Roman Empire*, 118–19.

85. Plutarch, *Pompey* 24.

86. M. J. Vermaseren, *Mithras the Secret God* (London 1963) 37–42. The notion of a "typical" plan is generally assumed since the work of Cumont, especially in his treatment of the mithraic liturgy as "sacraments." See Franz Cumont, *Les Mystères de Mithra*, 3rd ed. (Brussels

1913); English trans. (from the 2nd French ed.) *The Mysteries of Mithra* (New York 1956) 160–61.

87. The primary text is from Porphyry, *De antro nympharum* 5–6, which specifies a natural cave (*spelaion*, Lat. *antrum*) near running water as the proper place for Mithraic worship. Though a few natural cave sanctuaries are known (largely from rural areas in western provinces), they are rare. While some form of subterranean location was sought by many, the vast majority of mithraea used aesthetic means on the interior of the sanctuary to symbolize a cave. In many cases the walls or ceilings of the hall were treated with tufa, pumice, or stucco to give the effect of a grotto. (Cf. CDEE, no. 89a.) Cf. M. J. Vermaseren, *The Secret God*, 37–42. More recent work on the typicality of Mithraic planning comes from Ostia's 14 sites; cf. David Groh, "The Ostian Mithraeum," in *Mithraism in Ostia*, ed. S. Laeuchli (Evanston, IL, 1967) 10–17. See also W. Lentz, "Some peculiarities not hitherto fully understood of 'Roman' Mithraic sanctuaries and representations," in *Mithraic Studies*, ed. J. Hinnels, 2 vols. (Manchester 1975) II:358–77.

88. R. MacMullen, *Paganism*, 125. The "canopy of the heavens" iconography is articulated with painted or jeweled stars or with representations of celestial deities on the ceiling, as in the mithraeum at S. Maria Capua Vetere (CIMRM I, 179); cf. M. J. Vermaseren, *Mithraica* I (Leiden 1971) 50–54. On Mithraic iconography see also Leroy Campbell, *Mithraic Iconography and Ideology* (Leiden 1968) passim.

89. It is arguable, I think, that this spatial integration of sacrifice with communal dining, unique among the major pagan cults, in some measure prompted Franz Cumont's thesis that the Mithraic banquet was a "sacramental" meal. Cf. *Mysteries of Mithra*, 158–60; however, Cumont's Iranian thesis regarding the sacraments received its most explicit treatment in the 3rd French ed. (1913) 165, and M. J. Vermaseren has basically followed this view (*Secret God*, 102–3). For both Cumont and Vermaseren the sacramental meal, as communion with Mithras, was restricted to the initiation ritual, understood as the final reception of "salvation." In recent years, however, this thoroughgoing sacramentalism has been challenged; cf. J. P. Kane, "The Mithraic Cult Meal and its Greek and Roman Environment," in *Mithraic Studies* II:313–51, which denies both the limitation to initiation and the sacramentalism.

90. Samuel Laeuchli (*Mithaism in Ostia*, 91) appropriately coopted the term *Mithraic house church*. The largest mithraeum known from archaeological remains is at Sarmizegetusa, Romania (Roman Dacia); its sanctuary proper measured ca. 26 m in length and 12 m in width (CIMRM II, 2027). Another mithraeum from Königshoffen (Roman Germania) measured 31 m overall in its final form (including the pronaos), but the sanctuary proper was of more typical dimensions (length: 16.50 m; width: 8.50 m, CIMRM II, 1335). The smallest known mith-

raea are single rooms, such as the Esquiline at Rome (length: 3.30 m; width: 2.43 m, CIMRM I, 356) and the Mithraeum of Callinicus (Casa di Diana) at Ostia (length: 6.70 m; width: 5.18–6.10 m, CIMRM I, 216 = CDEE, no. 79).

91. The following data are based on the standard catalogue of mithraic remains by M. J. Vermaseren, CIMRM, 2 vols. (The Hague 1956, 1960). This collection is somewhat out of date (listing only 53 partially excavated sites); therefore, new finds and more complete excavation reports are taken into account wherever possible.

92. Britannia: CIMRM 814, 829, 844, 852(?); Gallia: CIMRM 909; Germania: CIMRM 1082, 1108, 1117, 1209, 1246.

93. CIMRM 716, which employed a natural cave in a hillside.

94. Warehouses at Ostia: CIMRM 238 (Porta Romana), 287 (mitreo delle setti porte), 299 (mitreo dei Felicissimus). Insulae at Ostia: CIMRM 216 (Casa di Diana), 224 (Lucretius Menander), 294 (mitreo dei serpenti).

95. Baths: CIMRM 229 (Ostia, Therms of Trajan); 457 (Rome, Caracalla Therms).

96. Cryptoportici: CIMRM 226 (Ostia, Fructuosus: *favissae* in cryptoporticus of collegial temple), 476 (Rome, Aventine: attached to large urban domus), 180 (S. Maria Capua Vetere).

97. Storage chambers: Cf. E. Lissi-Caronna, *Il Mitreo dei Castra Peregrinorum (S. Stefano Rotondo)* (EPRO 104; Leiden 1986) and compare Caesarea Maretima.

98. Private homes: CIMRM 34 (Dura-Europos), 250 (Ostia, Palazzo imperiale), 264 (Ostia, pareti dipinti), 272 (Ostia, planta pedis), 338 (Rome, San Clemente), 356 (Rome, Esquiline).

99. CIMRM 216 (Reg.III, Is.iii.3) = CDEE, no. 79.

100. G. Becatti, *Scavi di Ostia*, II: *I mitrei* (Rome 1954) 15.

101. Callinicus: CIMRM 220 (= CIL XIV, 4310); names of household members from a graffito (so Vermaseren, following Becatti), CIMRM 218.

102. CIMRM 222–23 (= CIL XIV, 4311–13). See also CIL XIV, 4569 which identifies Caerellius Hieronimus as a member of the prominent *collegium fabrum tignuariorum* at Ostia, whose collegial hall was located on the Decumanus Maximus (Reg.I, Is.xii.1) near the Casa di Diana insula; cf. Meiggs, *Roman Ostia*[2], 462.

103. Reg.IV, Is.iv.11; CIMRM 282 (= CIL XIV, 70). The reuse of an earlier mithraic monument in another sanctuary is also seen elsewhere at Ostia, the Palazzo imperiale mithraeum, dated ca. 203 C.E. (Reg.III, Is.xviii), CIMRM 250, 255. The latter is an earlier dedication (dated ca. 168 C.E., in the consulship of Q. Junius Rusticus) by the priest C. Caelius Ermeros, who is known to have made other dedications while serving as priest in the mitreo delle pareti dipinti at Ostia (CIMRM 269, cf. CDEE, no. 81, and n. 105 below).

104. Reg.III, Is.i.6; CIMRM 264 (= CDEE, no. 81) dated late second century. The suggestion of a second stage, to enlarge the sanctuary, is based on the author's recent fieldwork on the site, focusing especially on the masonry of the original house and the walls used to set off the mithraic hall. In the initial stage one room (A) was adapted to a typical mithraic layout; however, the unusual angle of the walls necessitated a unique construction for the cult niche in order to bring it into proper alignment with the main axis of the hall. An outer room (B, probably a pronaos at first) was created off one aisle of the peristyle (at the same time that the peristyle was walled in to created a cortile). In the second stage the area of the pronaos was integrated into the plan of the sanctuary and the benches of the main hall (A) were extended.

105. CIMRM 269 (see above n. 103). Caelius Ermeros is also known to have served as *antistes* and donor for the construction of the mitreo dei Palazzo imperiale, which dates to ca. 193–203 C.E. (Reg.III, Is.xviii; CIMRM 255). A number of monuments at Palazzo imperiale date to ca. 162 C.E., and these were probably reused from another mithraeum, CIMRM 250 (cf. G. Becatti, *Mitrei Ostia*, 53–56). It is possible, then, that the earlier sanctuary was itself relocated to new (more auspicious) quarters under new leadership, patronage, or both. Transfer of the older monuments was anticipated in the construction and physical planning of the Palazzo imperiale sanctuary. This suggests a conscious plan of relocation and renovation on the part of the Mithraic cell. That Caelius Ermeros shows up at Palazzo imperiale in such a capacity also suggests competition (or at least shifting memberships) among the Ostian Mithraic cells. The date for Caelius Ermeros (and hence the Pareti dipinti mithraeum) is based on the consular notation in CIMRM 255.

106. CIMRM 476 (= CDEE, no. 89 and figs. 41–42). The detailed excavation report is by M. J. Vermaseren and C. C. Van Essen, *Excavations in the Mithraeum of the Church of Santa Prisca* (Leiden 1965). The original edifice was a large urban domus (dating from Trajanic period), which apparently was acquired and renovated by the Severan family (ca. 193). In this renovation the house was subdivided and a new wing added, construction that apparently made the existing basement-level cryptoporticus less accessible for normal domestic use. At this juncture part of the basement area came into the hands of the Mithraists, and the adaptation to create the sanctuary was undertaken. While the circumstances suggest a measure of good fortune in that the basement area became available for other than domestic use, they also suggest benefaction on the part of someone in the household, perhaps even a member of the imperial family.

107. The constituency of the Aventine Mithraeum remains unclear. The names preserved in inscriptions and dipinti suggest a large number of individuals of eastern origin (so M. J. Vermaseren, *Secret*

God, 45), which would seem likely in the extensive retinue of the imperial family. On the other hand, Vermaseren (*Secret God*, 51) wanted to read the processional scenes from the walls of the sanctuary as indicating an "official state mithraeum," since he interpreted the scenes as reflecting the *suovetaurilia* (a public sacrifice, rather than a Mithraic ritual). This view has not been generally accepted, particularly since other Mithraic processional scenes have come to light (cf. Vermaseren, *Mithraica* I, 50–53). Thus, it seems more likely that Mithraeum I was founded by a core of members of eastern origin from the extended family (freedmen, slaves, or clients) with some nominal support from the family itself and from other members. However in stage II a broader constituency, reaching into higher social circles perhaps, is indicated by the growth in size and opulence of the mithraeum. Expansion of the mithraeum to accommodate numerical growth seems to have followed natural patterns of adaptation, such as incorporating the pronaos into the sanctuary proper by extending the *podia* (especially if the pronaos was on the axis of the main hall). As in the Pareti dipinti mithraeum at Ostia, such expansion could be accomplished with minimal structural modification. At the Aventine the only changes required to lengthen the hall involved widening the existing doorway between the two rooms and installing benches. Thus, I would disagree with Laeuchli and company (*Mithraism in Ostia*, 19) that there was a "liturgical" reason for the change, i.e., a desire to segregate lower grades of initiates. In view of the fact that partitions were rare in the sanctuary proper (and were never specially constructed), the more likely explanation is that this process reflects a natural and accepted course of adaptation among mithraists, given their proclivity for using existing buildings. Further on possible liturgical factors in the adaptation of the three side rooms of Mithraeum II, see Vermaseren-Van Essen, *Santa Prisca Mithraeum*, 142–44, 232–38. The processional scenes, representing movement of masked *mystae* toward an enthroned *heliodromos/pater*, probably reflect an actual mithraic ritual corresponding to the movements through the rooms of the sanctuary (rather than a symbolic portrayal of the afterlife, as once suggested by Cumont). Cf. Kane, "The Mithraic Cult Meal," 344–50; and for the hymnic dipinti see H. D. Betz, "The Mithras Inscriptions of Santa Prisca and the New Testament," *Novum Testamentum* 10 (1968) 62–80. Further on the proliferation of Mithraism at Rome and Ostia see Filippo Coarelli, "Topografica Mitriaca di Roma (et Ostia)," in *Mysteria Mithrae: Atti del Seminario Internazionale su "La specificità storico-religiosa dei Misteri Mithra, con particolare riferimento alle fonti documentarie di Roma e Ostia," Roma e Ostia, 28–31 Marzo, 1978*, ed. U. Bianchi (EPRO 80; Leiden 1979) 69–83.

108. DEP VII–VIII, 80–136 (= CDEE, no. 58). On the prosopography see E. D. Francis, "Mithraic Graffiti from Dura-Europos," in

Mithraic Studies, II:424–45. From the first mithraeum there is indication of a mixed group, as both Semitic (Palmyrene) and Greek are used in the inscriptions (CIMRM 41). Note esp. the designation of Ethpeni, one of the founders, as *istratēga* in the Greek text; the term reflects a semitized variation of *stratēgos* ("commander") paralleled in the Palmyrene text (CIMRM 39). It is likely, then, that the founders Ethpeni and Zenobios were native officers of a Palmyrene *numerus* attached to the II Ulpian mounted cohort, which saw action on the Euphrates frontier during the campaign of Lucius Verus. Apparently they were garrisoned at Dura soon thereafter, at which time they founded the Mithras cell in an existing house. Also on the military records see DEF V.1, 24ff.

109. The precise terms of the acquisition are unknown, but an outright purchase or grant of the existing property seems likely. The name Zenobios appears in two other graffiti from a house (D) near the Roman baths (Block C3, cf. IM Dur. 121) and suggests further acquisition of domestic property. Cf. Francis, "Mithraic Graffiti from Dura-Europos," 436.

110. DEP VII–VIII, 85 (Inscr. no. 847 = CDEE, no. 59, correcting CIMRM 53).

111. On Valentinus see Francis, "Mithraic Graffiti," 428. The inscription was on a *tabula ansata* set prominently on the entry wall of the pronaos. In the reinforcement the garrison was expanded, and the mithraeum was then located in the military quadrant of the city. Other temples in this area, such as the Temple of Bel (or Temple of the Palmyrene Gods) also show signs of increased Roman administrative and military activity during this period and continuing to the destruction of the city; notice the well known painting of Julius Terentius from the Temple of Bel, cf. R. MacMullen, *Paganism*, 80 (fig. II), 111 and n. 70. In 209 Valentinus would have held the same relative position in the garrison and city administration that Julius Terentius (military tribune and *dux ripae*) held later, when the XXth Palmyrene Cohort was stationed there.

112. Francis, "Mithraic Graffiti," 434–36. Many of the names are Greek or Latin, given with the military affiliation and the donation to the mithraeum. Rostovtzeff had argued earlier that the growth of the middle mithraeum represented a radical shift in constituency, from predominantly oriental to more Roman military personnel (cf. DEP VII–VIII, 88; *Dura-Europos and Its Art*, 50). Francis concludes, however, that there were Roman administrative officials as well as oriental recruits across all ranks that swelled the size of the mithraeum in the later periods as the constituency of the garrison itself shifted ("Mithraic Graffiti," 437). Thus, the success of the Mithraic community is indicated by its ability to attract adherents or new recruits under the changing circumstances of the garrison. At the same time, this success

eventuated in the changes to the mithraeum itself through adaptation.

113. Once again the expansion corresponded to a reinforcement of the garrison, as the eastern *limes* were buttressed against increasing threats from the Sassanians in the years leading up to the destruction of the city in 256 C.E. Cf. DEP VII–VIII, 82; Francis, "Mithraic Graffiti," 442. In many ways the expansion of the mithraeum itself in phase 3 followed natural lines of physical adaptation, as in the extension of the left *podium*, which left an asymmetrical line to the hall. Clearly much more care was taken in the remodeling of the naos.

114. In phases 2 and 3 the mithraeum had become a separate, public building, identifiable to anyone passing by the pronaos on the street. Yet, the basic architectural form and the building's idiosyncrasies are seen in the continuity of the plan of the room from the original house and in the preservation in situ of the two original tauroctone reliefs from the first mithraeum. Thus, the spatial articulation of the building was determined by three discernible sets of factors: (1) the original plan of the building, adapted to cultic use through successive renovations; (2) some minimal notions of mithraic "cave" iconography effected through interior remodeling and decoration; and (3) the social circumstances of the group.

115. M. I. Finley, *The Ancient Economy* (Berkeley 1973) 21.

116. Cf. inter alia CIMRM 133, 161, 246, 255, 273, 313, 648, 876; R. MacMullen, *Paganism*, 107–11, 129.

117. F. Cumont, *Mysteries of Mithra*, 40f; M. J. Vermaseren, *Secret God*, 30–32. Cf. J. Helgeland, "Roman Army Religion," ANRW II.16.2 (1978) 1470–505; E. Birley, "The Religion of the Roman Army, 1895–1977," ANRW II.16.2, 1506–41. A cautionary analysis of the question is offered by C. M. Daniels, "The Role of the Roman Army in the Spread and Practice of Mithraism," in *Mithraic Studies*, II:249–74.

118. The outlying provinces are more representative, especially in garrison towns such as Procolitia (Carrawburgh) in Britannia (CDEE, no. 95), and Carnuntum (Deutsch-Altenburg) in Pannonia Superior (CIMRM 1664–722; cf. Daniels, "Role of Roman Army," 250), Lambaesis in Numidia, Africa (CIMRM 134ff.; cf. Daniels, "Role of Roman Army," 271), or Dura-Europos in Syria (see above). These cases suggest that the spread via the military continued in certain areas through the time of Constantine.

119. The monuments are catalogued in CIMRM 1487–618. Cf. L. Campbell, "Typology of Mithraic Tauroctones," *Berytus* 11 (1954) 32–39; Daniels, "Role of Roman Army," 260–61. Among the military personnel attached to the late Mithraeum III was one Aurelius Justinianus, a *vir perfectissimus* and the *dux* of the garrison, CIMRM 1614 (= CIL III, 4039).

120. So Vivienne J. Walters, *The Cult of Mithras in the Roman Provinces of Gaul* (Leiden 1974) 31–45.

121. The dedicant of a tauroctone at Mons Seleucus was a wealthy romanized Gaul, M. Julius Meternianus (Walters, 32 and 73 no. 14 = CIMRM 899). While Greek and theophoric names are common among mithraists, in the later provincial capital of Trier the *pater* of the local mithraeum, Martius Martialis, was still of Gallic origin (Walters, 33 and 111 nos. 40–41 = CIMRM 987 and supplement). Among the higher offices (*pater*), where higher social standing is indicated, it seems to have made little difference whether the individual was of oriental or Gallic descent (Walters, 36).

122. R. MacMullen, *Paganism*, 127–29. Phrases such as *vetustate conlapsum . . . fanum restauravit* ("so-and-so restored the sanctuary which had collapsed with age") are found regularly as in other types of temples; cf. CIMRM 308, 648 (= CIL IX, 4110), 1485 (= CIL III, 11676), 1661 (= CIL III, 4540), 1673 (= CIL III, 4420).

123. CIL III, 4796, 4800. The texts and the reconstruction of this sequence are given in CDEE, no. 78.

124. CIMRM 1434 (= CIL III, 408): *Ulpius Valeri/us specul(ator) leg(ionis) primae Nor(icorum)*.

125. CDEE, no. 78, CIMRM 1431 (= CIL III, 4796): Aurelius Hermodorus, a *vir perfectissimus*. The date (ca. 311) and titles correspond to provincial reorganization under Diocletian and Constantine. Cf. Andre Chastagnol, *La préfecture urbaine à Rome sous le bas Empire* (Paris 1960) 26–29.

126. CIMRM 1438 (CIL III, 4800), dated 239 C.E.; CIMRM 1432 (= CIL III, 4797); CIMRM 1439 (= CIL III, 4802).

127. Cf. R. MacMullen, *Paganism*, 107–8, 125–26.

128. Ibid., 129, cf. 111.

129. CIMRM 223 (= CIL XIV, 4314); 422; 235 (= CIL XIV, 403); 273. As in CIMRM 422 (CDEE, no. 87), there are several cases where the major benefactor held several different titles, where it does not appear that they represented successive grades of initiation. Cf. CIMRM 311, 313, 315, 714, 803.

130. CIMRM 1438 (CDEE, no. 77), CIMRM 652 (CDEE, no. 91).

131. CIMRM 1315 (CDEE, no. 94).

132. See especially CIMRM 688 (CDEE, no. 92), where a long list of *cultores* are also called "patrons of Mithras." Apparently the cell was organized as a collegium under a president (*prosedente*), Gaius Propertius Profuturus (the only person in the list who carries a *trinominum*), while the usual Mithraic ranks are noticeably absent.

133. Cf. M. J. Vermaseren, *Secret God*, 56. Thus, I am in basic disagreement with the recent study of Reinhold Merkelbach, *Mithras* (Königstein/Ts 1984), which attempts to reassert the sacramental view of Cumont, especially in terms of an overtly literal reading of the seven grades of initiation and the sacred meal (cf. 86–132). See also the suggestion made above in n. 89.

134. Thus, one ought to expect the title *pater* often to designate the leading patron and benefactor. Cf. Vermaseren-Van Essen, *Santa Prsica Mithraeum*, 125. It seems to me that the social implications of the organization of mithraism have not been fully recognized. For peculiar combinations see CIMRM 367, 803. Functionally, at least, there may have been only two or three grades of members, with the *pater* and *sacerdos* clearly at the top both ritually and socially. For a similar suggestion see Francis, "Mithraic Graffiti," 440–42.

135. R. MacMullen, *Paganism*, 131–37; *Christianizing the Roman Empire*, 48–49.

4. Synagogues in the Graeco-Roman Diaspora

1. See M. Stern, "The Jewish Diaspora," in CRINT I.1:117–83 and S. Applebaum, "The Organization of the Jewish Communities in the Diaspora," in CRINT I.1:464–503. On the status of Jewish freedmen see S. Treggiari, *Roman Freedmen during the Late Republic* (Oxford 1969) 205–7. For the catalogues of Diaspora enclaves see George LaPiana, "Foreign Groups in Rome," HTR 20 (1927) 225–338; H. J. Leon, *The Jews of Ancient Rome* (Philadelphia 1960) passim; Ramsay MacMullen, *Roman Social Relations* (New Haven, CT, 1974) 60–67; E. M. Smallwood, *The Jews Under Roman Rule* (Leiden 1976) passim; Emil Schürer, *A History of the Jewish People in the Age of Jesus Christ*, rev. ed. M. Black, G. Vermes, and F. Millar, 2 vols. (Edinburgh 1973) II:85–183; J. Juster, *Les Juifs dans l'empire romaine*, 2 vols. (Paris 1914) I:208, 414–47.

2. The term *synagogue*, like *church* (*ekklesia*), comes to mean both the assembled congregation and the building as place of assembly. Cf. Martin Hengel, "Proseuche und Synagoge: Jüdische Gemeinde, Gotteshaus, und Gottesdienst in der Diaspora und in Palästina," in *The Synagogue: Studies in Origins, Archaeology, and Architecture*, ed. J. Gutmann (New York 1975) 27–54. On language and culture see E. M. Meyers and J. F. Strange, *Archaeology, the Rabbis, and Early Christianity* (Nashville, TN, 1981) 62–90; Wayne A. Meeks, *The Moral World of the First Christians* (Philadelphia 1987) 48–90; Joseph Blenkinsopp, "Interpretation and the Tendency to Sectarianism: An Aspect of Second Temple History," in *Jewish and Christian Self-Definition, Vol. II: Aspects of Judaism in the Greco-Roman Period*, ed. E. P. Sanders et al. (Philadelphia 1981) 1–26.

3. 3 Macc. 6; *Testament of Moses* 8–9; *Testament of Levi* 14.5–8; Qumran Rule IQS VIII.4–5. Among later documents cf. 4 Ezra 10.19–56; *bAboth* V.20; *ySukkah* 41a. See S. Safrai, "Relations between the Diaspora and the Land of Israel," in CRINT I.1:184–214, and "The Temple," in ibid., I.2:865–906.

4. H. J. Leon, *The Jews of Ancient Rome*, 167ff. and J. Z. Smith, "Fences and Neighbors: The Contours of Early Judaism," in *Approaches*

to the *Study of Ancient Judaism* II, ed. W. S. Green (BJS 9; Chico, CA, 1980) 1–25.

5. On the vexed question of synagogue origins see J. Gutmann, "The Origin of the Synagogue: The Current State of Research," in *The Synagogue: Studies in Origins, Archaeology, and Architecture*, 72–76, and I. Sonne, "Synagogue," *Interpreter's Dictionary of the Bible* Vol. IV (Nashville 1976), 477ff.

6. Most attempts at architectural classification, like theories of origins, have been based almost entirely on later Palestinian evidence and sources. Thus, for Diaspora studies see L. M. White, "The Delos Synagogue Revisited: Recent Fieldwork in the Graeco-Roman Diaspora," HTR 80 (1987) 133–60; A. T. Kraabel, "Unity and Diversity among Diaspora Synagogues," in *The Synagogue in Late Antiquity*, ed. L. I. Levine (American Schools of Oriental Research, Philadelphia 1986) 49–60; E. M. Meyers and A. T. Kraabel, "Archaeology, Iconography and Nonliterary Written Remains," in *Early Judaism and its Modern Interpreters*, ed. R. Kraft and G. Nickelsburg (Atlanta, GA, 1986) 175–210. For the traditional classifications see M. Avi-Yonah, "Ancient Synagogues," in *The Synagogue: Studies in Origins, Archaeology, and Architecture*, 95–109; E. M. Meyers, "Synagogue Architecture," *Interpreter's Dictionary of the Bible*, supplement (1976) 842ff; "Ancient Gush Ḥalav (Gischala), Palestinian Synagogue and the Eastern Diaspora," in *Ancient Synagogues: The State of Research*, ed. J. Gutmann (BJS 8; Chico, CA, 1981) 61–78; A. R. Seager, "Ancient Synagogue Architecture, An Overview," in ibid., 39–47; Marilyn Joyce Chiat, "First Century Synagogue Architecture: Methodological Problems," in ibid., 49–60; *A Handbook of Synagogue Architecture* (BJS 29; Chico, CA, 1982) passim.

7. M. Hengel, "Proseuche und Synagoge," 29–46.

8. CDEE, Appendix B, Table 2. Meyers and Kraabel, "Archaeology, Iconography, and Nonliterary Written Remains," 183–89; A. T. Kraabel, "The Diaspora Synagogue: Archaeological and Epigraphic Evidence since Sukenik," ANRW II.19.1 (Berlin 1979) 475–510; "Unity and Diversity among Diaspora Synagogues," in *The Synagogue in Late Antiquity*, 49–60. We note here the less fully known archaeological discoveries of synagogues (generally of later date) from Aegina (Insula Graeca) and Hamman Lif (North Africa). Both are discussed in E. R. Goodenough, *Jewish Symbols in the Graeco-Roman Period*, 12 vols. (New York 1953–1968) II:70–100. Most recently, new discovery of a mosaic floor indicates the presence of a synagogue in Roman Philippopolis, which as yet has not been excavated.

9. Edicts relating to the rights of Jews in Josephus, *Antiquities* XIV.231ff. (pertaining to Delos, Ephesus, Halicarnassus, and Sardis).

10. A. T. Kraabel, "The Social Systems of Six Diaspora Synagogues," in *Ancient Synagogues: The State of Research*, 89.

11. Cf. J. Gutmann, "Origins of the Synagogue," 76 n. 40; "The Diaspora Synagogue: Archaeological and Epigraphic Evidence since Sukenik," 500–2.

12. CDEE, no. 70; L. M. White, "The Delos Synagogue Revisited," HTR 80 (1987) 133–60.

13. 1 Macc. 15.15–23; Josephus, *Ant.* XIV.231f.

14. Cf. figures and detailed analysis in CDEE, no. 70, and in L. M. White, "Delos Synagogue Revisited," 148ff.

15. Cf. A. T. Kraabel, "The Diaspora Synagogue," 493, 501.

16. Discussed above in chap. 2, n. 49; cf. L. M. White, "Delos Synagogue Revisited," 157–60.

17. CDEE, no. 71; cf. P. Bruneau, "'Les Israélites de Délos' et la juiverie délienne," *Bulletin de Correspondance Hellénique* 106 (1982) 465–504.

18. The texts and issues of dating and social setting are discussed in detail in my article "The Delos Synagogue Revisited," HTR 80, 141–47, and reflect some differences from the reading of P. Bruneau.

19. Josephus, *Ant.* XIV.213f.: *hoi Ioudaioi en Dēlo kai tines tōn paroikōn Ioudaiōn* ("The *Jews in Delos* and some other Jews *sojourning* there"). The phrase "Jews in Delos" suggests an official status of resident foreigner, while the *paroikōn* indicates alien, nonresident status. The phrase "in Delos" is also applied to the Samaritan enclave in the later of the two inscriptions. There are, therefore, several groups of "Jews" on the island, each with its own social standing. See White, "Delos Synagogue Revisited," 145–47, and Marie François Baslez, "Déliens et étrangers domiciliés à Délos (166–155)," REG 89 (1976) 343–60.

20. See CDEE, no. 69.

21. See chap. 3 (at n. 68). On the oecus/prostas house plan see J. W. Graham, "Notes on Houses and Housing-Districts at Abdera and Himera," AJA 2nd ser. 76 (1972) 295ff.

22. Compare the circumstances regarding acquisition of adjacent property for the later synagogue at Dura-Europos, below n. 32 and CDEE, no. 60b. On Priene, see also A. T. Kraabel, "Judaism in Western Asia Minor under Roman Rule" (Ph.D. Thesis, Harvard University 1968) 22–25.

23. So concluded by the principle excavator, M. Floriana Squarciapino, "La Sinagoga di Ostia: secondo campagna di scavo," in CIAC VI, 299ff. A. T. Kraabel ("The Diaspora Synagogue," 498f.) basically follows this conclusion, but suggests a different building history. The following discussion is based on my recent examination of the site, as reflected also in the description of CDEE, no. 83.

24. The dining hall addition is indicated by the change in masonry from the earlier shell of the building in *opus reticulatum* to the new construction in *opus vitatum*. Also, for dining halls connected with

synagogues, see the epigraphic evidence from Aphrodisias, discussed below.

25. On the aedicula see A. T. Kraabel, "Diaspora Synagogue," 499, and the discussion of the inscription from Side, Pamphylia (CIJ 781); cf. L. Robert, "Inscriptions grecques de Side," *Revue Philologique* 32 (1958) 36–47. In the light of recent discoveries of synagogue arks from the Galilee, it seems that further work needs to be done on the date and factors surrounding the introduction of the ark into synagogue architecture. Cf. E. M. Meyers, J. F. Strange, and C. L. Meyers, "The Ark of Nabratein," *Biblical Archeologist* 44 (1981) 237–43.

26. See CDEE, no. 84.

27. See CDEE, no. 72; cf. Martin Hengel, "Die Synagogeninschrift von Stobi," ZNW 57 (1966) 145–83, repr. in *The Synagogue: Studies in Origins, Archaeology, and Architecture*, 110–48.

28. Cf. Dean Moe, "The Cross and the Menorah," *Archaeology* 30 (1977) 148ff.

29. See CDEE, no. 66; cf. A. R. Seager, "The Building History of the Sardis Synagogue," AJA ns 76 (1972) 425ff.; A. T. Kraabel, "*Hypsistos* and the Synagogue at Sardis," *Greek, Roman and Byzantine Studies* 10 (1969) 81–93, and "Melito the Bishop and the Synagogue at Sardis: Text and Context," in *Studies Presented to G. M. A. Hanfmann*, ed. D. G. Mitten (Cambridge, MA, 1971) 77–85.

30. See CDEE, no. 67; cf. L. Robert, *Nouvelles inscriptions de Sardes* (Paris 1967) passim; A. T. Kraabel, "The Impact of the Discovery of the Sardis Synagogue," in *Sardis from Prehistoric to Roman Times*, ed. G. M. A. Hanfmann (Cambridge, MA, 1983) 178–86.

31. See CDEE, no. 60. The primary excavations are published in DEP VI; DEF VIII.1; E. R. Goodenough, *Jewish Symbols in the Graeco-Roman Period* vols. 9–11 (New York 1952–1965). Cf. also A. R. Seager, "The Architecture of the Dura and Sardis Synagogues," in *The Dura-Europos Synagogue, A Re-appraisal 1931–1971*, ed. J. Gutmann (Missoula, MT, 1972) 79–116.

32. Thus C. H. Kraeling (DEF VIII.1, 329) suggests that the Jews had come into possession of several other houses in Insula Block L7, especially Houses B, C, and D. The block, then, had become something of a Jewish quarter as the synagogue grew in public stature. It must be remembered that the House of the Roman Scribes also occupied a prominent position in this block, having taken over and adapted House A and part of House B.

33. E. R. Goodenough, *Symbols*, 9:15, 28.

34. DEF VIII.1, 332f.

35. Here (among other places) C. H. Kraeling and E. R. Goodenough disagree sharply. Goodenough (*Symbols* 9:28) argues that Samuel lived in the annexed House, H, while Kraeling (DEF VIII.1, 11) argues for the contiguous House, C, whose party wall with the syna-

gogue was breached in the remodeling. The nature of the renovations suggests that Kraeling is correct, but we may go further to suggest that House C, as the house of the presbyter, priest, and patron, played an integral part in the life of the Jewish community, especially during the renovation of House H. See my discussion in CDEE, no. 60.

36. Of course in the earliest synagogue edifices (such as the one on Delos), which were operative well before 70 C.E., no Torah ark is to be found. The evidence points to the introduction of the Torah ark as a fixed and permanent architectural feature by the late second century C.E. A good example may well be the indications that a false aedicula was a secondary addition to the early synagogue at Dura-Europos (ca. 150–200), replacing or working in concert with some sort of portable repository. It is all the more significant, then, that in the renovation of the later synagogue at Dura such conscious articulation of a formal Torah shrine was planned into the construction of the new hall of assembly (ca. 244).

37. See the collection of inscriptions by Baruch Lifshitz, *Donateurs et Fondateurs dans les Synagogues juives* (abbreviated LD hereafter; published as Cahiers de la Revue Biblique 7; Paris 1967) passim. Recently on the role of women in such matters, see Bernadette Brooten, *Women Leaders in the Ancient Synagogue* (BJS 36; Chico, CA, 1982) passim. Cf. my "Adolf Harnack and the 'Expansion' of Early Christianity: A Reappraisal of Social History," *The Second Century* 5 (1985/6) 97–127.

38. See CDEE, no. 72.

39. For *hagios topos* and similar terms as designations for the synagogue edifice see CIJ 754 (Philadelphia, Lydia, third cent. C.E.); 964 (Ascalon, fifth cent.); 867 (Gerasa, fifth cent.); 1436–37 (Egypt, date uncertain, perhaps first cent. B.C.E.).

40. See CDEE, no. 84.

41. On the Samaritans of the Hellenistic Diaspora see E. Schürer, *A History of the Jewish People at the Time of Jesus*, rev. ed. (Edinburgh 1978) 3:51f.; M. Hengel, *Judaism and Hellenism* (Philadelphia 1977) 2:59; C. R. Holladay, *Fragments from Hellenistic Jewish Authors*, vol. I: *Historians* (Chico, CA, 1983) 157–65; B. Lifshitz and J. Schiby, "Une Synagogue samaritaine à Thessalonique," *Revue Biblique* 75 (1968) 368–78.

42. See CDEE, no. 71; L. M. White, "Delos Synagogue Revisited," HTR 80:141–44.

43. L. M. White, "Delos Synagogue Revisited," 145–47.

44. Josephus, *Ant.* 14.213f.; see above n. 19.

45. See B. Brooten, *Women Leaders in the Ancient Synagogue*, 103–38; cf. A. R. Seager, "Architecture of Dura and Sardis Synagogues," 88 and n. 35.

46. See CDEE, no. 75; CIJ 720 (= IG V. 2,295; third cent.).

47. CIJ 739 (fourth cent.).

48. Cf. S. Applebaum, "The Organization of the Jewish Communities in the Diaspora," CRINT I.1:498.
49. See CIJ 619d, where *pater* equals *patron;* cf. B. Brooten, *Women Leaders*, 62.
50. Generally on the growth of synagogue offices see M. Hengel, "Die Synagogeninschrift von Stobi," 126f.; A. T. Kraabel, "Jews in Western Asia Minor," 44f.; H. J. Leon, *The Jews of Ancient Rome* (Philadelphia 1960) 168–75. The sense of office is especially noteworthy in the Roman period, where collegia of all types tended to ape the official terminology of local administration or of the imperial bureaucracy. Thus, offices tend to appear in far greater number in Jewish donation inscriptions from the Roman period, in contrast to those of Ptolemaic Egypt. See also B. Brooten, *Women Leaders*, 57–72. I must differ with Brooten on her use of the term *honorific* (esp. 64). She treats it as synonymous with *honorary* and as the antithesis to *functional* leadership roles. In reality, however, honorific titles were widely conferred on men and women of status and leadership in the reciprocal relationship owed to benefactors. Merely honorary titles are yet another matter. Cf. R. P. Saller, *Personal Patronage under the Early Empire* (Cambridge, England, 1982) 22–27; J. M. Reynolds and R. Tannenbaum, *Jews and Godfearers at Aphrodisias, Greek Inscriptions with Commentary* (Cambridge, England, 1987), 41 and 71 n. 170.
51. See CDEE, no. 68.
52. Cf. L. M. White, "Delos Synagogue Revisited," 143.
53. On *proedria* see Ramsay MacMullen, *Roman Social Relations* (New Haven, CT, 1974) 76; F. Poland, *Geschichte der griechische Vereinswesens* (Leipzig 1960) 425, 436; cf. L. M. White, "Delos Synagogue Revisited," 153 and n. 81.
54. It might also be a case of intermarriage, but as is often the case, this is difficult to determine with surety. For the sympathizers see Louis H. Feldman, "Jewish Sympathizers in Classical Literature and Inscriptions," *Transactions of the American Philological Association* 81 (1950) 200–8; Heinz Beilen, "*Synagoge ton Ioudaion kai theosebon*, Die Aussage einer bosparanischen Freilassungsinschrift (CIRB 71) zum Problem der 'Gottfürchtigen.'" *Jahrbuch für Antike und Christentum* XVIII–IX (1965–1966) 171ff. More recently the discussion has revolved around the notion of a special class of "god-fearers" in the synagogue. Cf. A. T. Kraabel, "The Disappearance of the 'Godfearers,'" *Numen* 28 (1981) 113–26. See also below concerning the Aphrodisias inscription.
55. See CDEE, no. 65.
56. *Paulys Real-encyclopädie der klassischen Altartumswissenschaft* X.1 (ed. G. Wissowa and W. Kroll; Stuttgart 1917), 947; S. R. F. Price, *Rituals and Power: The Roman Imperial Cult in Asia Minor* (Cambridge, England, 1984) 62–64.
57. IGRR IV.655. The name Tyronnius Rapo is also attested

among the family members of Julia's household. Since slaves or freedmen might well have taken the name as members of the household, it suggests that the lines of contact to Julia came from these household relations. Cf. S. Applebaum, "The Organization of the Jewish Communities in the Diaspora," CRINT I.1:501.

58. R. MacMullen, *Roman Social Relations*, 75–85.

59. CIJ 1441, 1447; CPJ II.149; III, Appendix 1, no. 1441; John Chrysostom, *Adv. Judaeos* VI.5. Cf. A. T. Kraabel, "The Diaspora Synagogue," 501f.

60. LD 11 (Olbia on the Black Sea) and no. 31 (Mysa, Caria). Cf. P. M. Fraser, "Inscriptions from Graeco-Roman Egypt," *Berytus* 15 (1964) 71f.; 84 (no. 14 = IGRR I, 1106) for the terms *synodos* and *synagogē* used in pagan collegial contexts.

61. CPJ I, 138 (= P.Ryl. 590; ca. mid-first cent. B.C.E.); cf. CPJ I, 139 (first cent. B.C.E.; Apollinopolis Magna), a collegial banquet held in the synagogue hall.

62. See the Ophel synagogue inscription (CDEE, no. 62), begun and completed by a father and son who successively held the office of *archisynagogos*; cf. LD 31; CIJ 682, 735, 744.

63. For renovations and additions see CDEE, nos. 65, 66, and 72; CIJ 682, 735, 739 (= CIG IV, 9897), 1433, 1441, 1442, 1444.

64. See CDEE, no. 63. Shim'on Applebaum, *Jews and Greeks in Ancient Cyrene* (Studies in Judaism in Late Antiquity 28, Leiden 1979) 160–67; Applebaum, "The Organization of the Jewish Communities in the Diaspora," CRINT I.1:486f.

65. CRINT I.1:486; cf. below n. 105.

66. See CDEE, no. 74a (CIJ 722 = IG IV, 190). On community building projects and matters of ownership cf. S. Applebaum, "The Organization of the Jewish Communities," CRINT I.1:501.

67. CDEE, no. 74a, line 3 note; cf. L. Robert, "Inscriptions grecques de Side en Pamphylie," *Revue Philologique* 32:39. Compare the inscriptions from Sardis, CDEE, no. 67a, and L. Robert, *Nouvelles inscriptions de Sardes*, 49 n. 2.

68. See CDEE, no. 74b (CIJ 723 = IG IV, 190); compare Side, CIJ 781, and L. Robert, "Inscriptions grecques de Side," 36–38.

69. Cf. L. Robert, *Nouvelles inscriptions de Sardes*, nos. 3–8, 13–17.

70. See CDEE, no. 67b.

71. See CDEE, no. 67a.

72. A. T. Kraabel, "The Social Systems of Six Diaspora Synagogues," *Ancient Synagogues*, 85.

73. CIJ 766 (CDEE, no. 65).

74. CDEE, nos. 67b, 74; cf. CIJ 803–18 (from Apamea, Syria = LD 38–55).

75. CDEE, no. 67a; cf. LD 30 (Tralles); CIJ 781 (Side); 653 (Syracuse).

76. CIJ 754 (Philadelphia, Lydia); cf. LD 37 (Side).
77. CIJ 781 (Side); LD 12 (Pergamum). Several menoroth were found at Sardis. One, in particular, was an intricately carved marble approximately 1 m wide, with the name Socrates carved on the face. It probably represents the inscription of the donor. Cf. D. G. Mitten, *The Ancient Synagogue at Sardis* (New York 1965) 4 and fig. 11.
78. LD 12 (Pergamum).
79. See LD 64–68 (Caesarea Maretima), 69 (CIJ 961, Azotos), 70, 71 (CIJ 964–65, Ascalon), 72, 73 (CIJ 966–67, Gaza), 74 (CIJ 991, Sepphoris), 75 (CIJ 983, Capharnahum), 76 (Tiberias), 77 (CIJ 1166, Beth-Alpha), 77a–c (Scythopolis), 78 (Gerasa), 81 (Huldah).
80. Especially those of Hammath-Gadar, Sussiya, and Beth-Alpha; cf. E. L. Sukenik, "The Ancient Synagogue of El-Hammeh," *Journal of the Palestine Oriental Society* 15 (1935) 136–37. A number of those from the Galilee also reflect bilingual usage, as at Hammath Tiberias and Beth-Alpha.
81. S. Levy, "The Ancient Synagogue of Maʿon (Nirim)," *Bulletin of the Louis M. Rabinowitz Fund* 3 (1960) 6–40, esp. 27. A. D. Trendall, *The Shellal Mosaic* (Canberra 1942) passim.
82. A. T. Kraabel, "*Synagoga Caeca:* Systematic Distortions in Gentile Interpretations of Evidence for Judaism in the Early Christian Period," in *To See Ourselves as Others See Us: Christians, Jews, and "Others" in Late Antiquity*, ed. J. Neusner and E. S. Frerichs (Chico, CA, 1985) 219–46.
83. Cf. Josephur, *Ant.* 14.213–32 (noted above).
84. Luke 7.3–5: *hoi de paregenomenoi pros ton Iēsoun parekaloun auton* **spoudaiōs**, *legontes hoti* **axios estin** *hō parexē touto,* **agapa** *gar to ethnos hēmōn kai* **tēn synagōgēn** *autos ōikodomēsen hēmin* ("They came to Jesus exhorting him *diligently* and saying, 'He is *worthy* to have this done, because *he loves* our nation and *he built us our synagogue'* "). [The emphasis has been added to indicate terms that come from the technical vocabulary used in honors to benefactors.]
85. The term *synagōgē* occurs in Luke 4.15, 16, 20, 28, 33, 38, 44; 7.5; 8.41; 11.43; 13.10; 20.46; 21.12; Acts 6.9; 9.2, 20; 13.5; 14.1; 15.21; 17.1, 10, 17; 18.4, 7, 19, 26; 19.8; 22.19; 24.12; while *proseuchē*, or *oikos proseuchēs*, occurs in Luke 19.46 and Acts 16.13.
86. Acts 18.7–8: *eisēlthen eis oikian tinos onomati Titiou Ioustou, sebomenou ton theon, hou hē oikia hēn synomorousa tē synagōgē. Krispos de ho archisynagōgos episteusen tō kyriō syn holō tō oikō autou* ("he went into the house of a certain man named Titius Justus, a worshipper of God, whose house was contiguous to the synagogue. And Crispus, the archisynagogos, believed in the Lord, together with his whole household").
87. 1 Cor. 7.18; Gal. 2.7; cf. Wayne Meeks, *The First Urban Christians: The Social World of the Apostle Paul* (New Haven, CT, 1983) 26, 33. Often the assumption is drawn, on the basis of 2 Cor. 11.24 (the "39

lashes"), that Paul suffered what was a regular form of synagogue discipline. So cf. Josephus, *Ant.* 4.8.21-23; however, in the pre-70 period there is little evidence for this practice outside of near-Palestine and Coela Syria (perhaps as far north as Antioch). We should also note the apparent distinction made in 2 Cor. 11.26 (*ek genous*) between Diaspora Jews and those of Judea. (Compare also 1 Thess. 2.14.) Too many assumptions are drawn from the later rabbinic practice as described in *Makkot* 3.1-14. In fact it is often noted that the reference in 2 Cor. is the first to indicate the practice of stopping one short of the maximum 40. Cf. V. Furnish, *Second Corinthians* (Anchor Bible, New York 1986) 517.

88. On the organization of the Jewish communities at Antioch and Alexandria, and the problems of overgeneralization, cf. Wayne Meeks and Robert Wilken, *Jews and Christians at Antioch* (Missoula, MT, 1981) 1-57; S. Applebaum, "The Organization of the Jewish Communities," CRINT I.1:473-76, 480-501; Aryeh Kasher, *The Jews of Hellenistic and Roman Egypt: The Struggle for Equal Rights* (Tübingen 1985) 106-67; E. M. Smallwood, *The Jews under Roman Rule*, 358ff.

89. M. Hengel, "Synagoge und Proseuche," passim.

90. J. Gutmann, "The Origins of the Synagogue: The Current State of Research," in *The Synagogue: Studies in Origins, Archaeology, and Architecture* (New York 1975) 72-76; Ellis Rivkin, *A Hidden Revolution: The Pharisees' Search for the Kingdom Within* (Nashville, TN, 1978) 248-51. To this general view of Pharisaic origins, however, it is yet necessary to correlate the implications of Jacob Neusner's suggestions regarding the nature of the pre-70 Pharisaic *haburoth*; cf. his *From Politics to Piety: The Emergence of Pharisaic Judaism* (New York 1979) 83-90.

91. See CDEE, no. 62, esp. the note on line 6.

92. Acts 6.9.

93. See Joachim Jeremias, *Jerusalem at the Time of Jesus* (Philadelphia 1975) 65f. On the basis of talmudic references Jeremias would prefer to call this the "Synagogue of the Alexandrians" or the "Synagogue of the Tarsians." Cf. S. Safrai, "Relations between the Diaspora and the Land of Israel," CRINT I.1:184-215, esp. 192.

94. See CDEE, no. 64; J. M. Reynolds and R. Tannenbaum, *Jews and Godfearers at Aphrodisias* (Cambridge, England, 1987) passim.

95. On Jewish charitable agencies at Antioch see John Chrysostom, *Adv. Judaeos* VIII.6 (a hospital).

96. For discussion of the term *dekania* see Reynolds and Tannenbaum, *Jews and Godfearers*, 28-30.

97. Cf. ibid., 26-38, 101. Here I see more separation between the *dekany* (and its charitable enterprise) and the synagogue proper.

98. On the names and trades, ibid., 93-111, 117-22.

99. The acknowledged public standing of the Jewish community of

Aphrodisias is indicated by two inscriptions from the odeon (in Blocks b and d), which reserved seating areas: *topos Benetōn Hebreōn tōn paleiōn.* Connections with a political faction, the Blues, are also indicated. Cf. J. M. Reynolds and R. Tannenbaum, *Jews and Godfearers*, 132.

100. It seems to me that R. Tannenbaum has overstressed the rabbinical connections of the text by restricting the term *philomathōn* to mean "study of Torah" (J. M. Reynolds and R. Tannenbaum, 32–34), so that the *dekany* is identical to the *bet ha-midrash*. Nothing in the text itself suggests this. The dekany and the charitable agency seem rather to have been separate from the worshipping synagogue community, and the amalgamated titles (*panteulogōn*) suggest public, collegial designations of a common sort. It seems to me that the term *philomathōn*, then, is intentionally ambiguous, so as to connote either philosophy or Torah piety, depending upon context or inclinations.

101. Here compare the Miletus theater inscription which uses the term *theosebōn* in a similar fashion, as a neutral, pagan designation for the Jews: *topos Eioudeōn tōn kai theosebiōn* ("the place of the Jews, who are also called the god-fearing"). (For the text see A. Deissmann, *Light from the Ancient East*, 4th ed. [London 1924] 451–52.) The usage suggests that "god-fearers" was a positive designation of Jews by pagans in the culture at large. For Jewish participation in public theater events at Aphrodisias, see the inscriptions cited above, n. 99.

102. See above n. 54. Though there were certainly pagan sympathizers who were attracted to Jewish worship, I think A. T. Kraabel is correct in asserting that the term *theoseboi* does not indicate a uniform designation for a "class," a penumbra of "near-proselytes," in all synagogues. Each synagogue community would have handled the problem of the status and participation of such sympathizers in different ways, owing to their degree of social acceptance and cultural accommodation. Clearly, some non-Jewish sympathizers in certain localities were granted full status in and access to the worshipping community (as appears at Sardis). It cannot be assumed, therefore, that the term at Aphrodisias designates such a penumbra to the synagogue (so J. M. Reynolds and R. Tannenbaum, 48–65). Instead, it may represent the non-Jewish members in the collegial association, some of whom were sympathizers to Jewish worship as well. Cf. John Gager, "Jews, Gentiles, and Synagogues in the Book of Acts," in *Christians among Jews and Gentiles, Essays in honor of Krister Stendahl*, ed. G. W. E. Nickelsburg and G. W. MacRae (Philadelphia 1986) 91–99.

103. J. M. Reynolds and R. Tannenbaum, *Jews and Godfearers*, 133ff., inscr. nos. 2 and 9.

104. Jael seems to be a man's name, rather than a woman's. (So J. M. Reynolds and R. Tannenbaum, 41, 101, contra B. Brooten, *Women Leaders*, 151.) If Jael was a woman *prostates* here, it is all the more significant, since she would be the only woman in the entire list. By the

same token, the apparent exclusion of women from the *dekany* lists further suggests to me that this group was some sort of men's club, a collegia, made up of Jews and pagans, and set apart from the synagogue proper.

105. S. Applebaum, *Jews and Greeks in Ancient Cyrene*, 160–67; "The Organization of the Jewish Communities in the Diaspora," CRINT I.1:486.

106. CIG III, 5362; cf. G. and J. Roux in REG 62 (1949) 290–94. Dated 8–6 B.C.E.

107. CIG III, 5361; cf. REG 62 (1949) 283–89. Dated 24–25 C.E.

108. See above chap. 2, n. 18.

109. S. Applebaum, "Organization," CRINT I.1:475–77.

110. See CDEE, no. 63 and above at n. 64.

111. S. Applebaum, "Organization," CRINT I.1:476, 479. Cf. V. Tcherikover, *Hellenistic Civilization and the Jews* (New York 1970) 322–32, 410–15.

112. Cf. A. T. Kraabel, "Melito the Bishop and the Synagogue at Sardis: Text and Context," in *Studies presented to G. M. A. Hanfmann*, 77–85. We should be somewhat careful, however, in that there is no direct evidence for activity of the Jewish community of Sardis at the precise time of Melito.

113. H. J. Leon, *The Jews of Ancient Rome*, 168ff.; on the *gerousia* of the Jews at Ostia see CIJ 533 (from Castel Porziano, probably second cent. C.E.).

114. See CDEE, no. 73. Hengel, "Die Synagogenischrift von Stobi," 126f.

115. See CDEE, no. 72b (an inscribed donor plaque, Stobi INV. no. I-70-61).

116. See CDEE, no. 72b, and D. Moe, "Cross and Menorah," 148f.

117. DEF VIII.1, 326.

118. Probably in the period after the Roman takeover, thus between 166 and 200 C.E. Cf. DEF VIII.1, 327.

119. Ibid., 274f.; Inscr. nos. 20–22.

120. Ibid., 275, 328.

121. Despite the fact that some walls or room partitions may have been altered in order to create the arrangement of the Early Synagogue, the building plan and the exterior finishing remained typically domestic, especially on the eastern side of the court.

122. The Torah shrine of the Early Synagogue was probably added later and did not include a niche in the west wall. Some of its components were preserved beneath the construction of the later synagogue, as was a grafitto depicting an aedicula structure. It has also been suggested that the secondary addition of the small Torah shrine to the existing layout of the Early Synagogue makes it a replacement for another edifice, perhaps one that sat in the center of the room. It is

likely, however, that no such edifice served as the permanent repository for the Torah scrolls. See CDEE, no. 60a, and Kraeling in DEP VI, 334.

123. The traditional assumption regarding the layout held that Room 2 was the hall of assembly, while Room 7 was set aside for women. This segregation seems highly unlikely, especially since no such place was set aside in the later synagogue. E. R. Goodenough argues persuasively that Room 7 served instead as a "sacristy" of sorts, perhaps where the scrolls were kept. Cf. his *Symbols* 9:32f. (contra C. H. Kraeling, DEF VIII.1, 31f.). Goodenough's argument is also followed by B. Brooten, *Women Leaders*, 126.

124. Cf. DEF VIII.1, 19–23. Though lost, we might well expect that the ownership of the first synagogue house came from the same type of source as the later renovation, a private benefaction. It is possible, then, that the family of Samuel bar Yeda'ya had owned this property, too, and gave it over to the congregation.

125. On hostelleries see also the Ophel synagogue inscription (CDEE, no. 62) discussed above; cf. S. Klein, "Das Fremdhaus der Synagogue," *Monatschrift für Geschichte und Wissenschaft des Judentums* 77 (1932–1933) 545–57; J. Jeremias, *Jerusalem in the Time of Jesus*, 65f.

126. See above nn. 25, 36. There is no archaeological evidence of a fixed Torah shrine or ark prior to the late second century (at Dura and Priene) or in the third to fourth centuries (at Ostia, Sardis, and en Nabratein). See also C. Wendel, *Der Thoraschrein in Altertum* (Halle 1950); Rachel Hachlili, "The Niche and Ark in Ancient Synagogues," *Bulletin of the American Schools of Oriental Research* 223 (1976) 43–54.

127. See CDEE, no. 61.

128. See CDEE, no. 60 and figs. 24–26.

129. See CDEE, no. 60b for detailed discussion. Contrast E. R. Goodenough, *Symbols*, 9:28f.

130. The dates for the later synagogue edifice are firmly fixed by (a) the inscriptions that date the completed building project to the year 244/245 C.E. (CDEE, no. 61) and by (b) the destruction of the city in 256 C.E.

131. Cf. DEF VIII.1, 329f. For documentary evidence of provisions for disposition of property with shared party walls see the Dura parchment Inv. D, in DEF V.1, no. 19.

132. See CDEE, no. 61e. Cf. the suggestion of E. R. Goodenough (*Symbols* 9:28) that Samuel lived in the domestic suite of House H (contra C. H. Kraeling, DEF VIII.1, 11).

133. DEF VIII.1, 332f. C. H. Kraeling also suggests that the Greek- and Aramaic-speaking groups within the Jewish community might have had different responsibilities in the remodeling project.

134. We might wish to call this a "regional cosmopolitanism," since it largely represents influences from the Roman levant. Cf. DEF VIII.1,

269. The inscriptions of the later synagogue represent Aramaic (Syrian-Babylonian, rather than Palestinian), Greek, Middle Iranian, and Palmyrene. The artistic style is often called proto-Byzantine and is likened to painting style from Antioch, but it is ultimately an eclectic blend of western tendencies with an eastern base. See Ann Perkins, *The Art of Dura-Europos* (Oxford 1973) 114–26.

135. There are suggestions by Du Mesnil of direct connections between Greek-speaking Jews and the Greek-speaking Christian group down the street: Comte Du Mesnil du Buisson, "L'inscription de la niche centrale de la synagogue de Doura-Europos," *Syria* 40 (1963) 310–14; see CDEE, nos. 61a and 61f.

136. E. R. Goodenough, *Symbols*, 9:15, 28.

137. Josephus, *Ant.* 14.231. The Roman official named by Josephus is known to have served in Asia in 48 B.C.E. (cf. OGIS 448). Cf. A. T. Kraabel, "Judaism in Western Asia Minor," 200; S. Krauss, *Synagogale Altertümer* (Berlin 1922) 182.

138. See CDEE, no. 66a. The municipal complex was begun after about 17 C.E., when much of the city had been damaged in an earthquake. Previously the area was occupied by a Hellenistic cemetery. It is not impossible that an earlier synagogue edifice might have been affected, but the Jews only came into possession of the hall after completion of the entire complex, sometime well after 166 C.E.

139. The prosopography is summarized in CDEE, no. 67b. See L. Robert, *Nouvelles inscriptions de Sardes*, passim; A. T. Kraabel, "Judaism in Western Asia Minor," 218–19; A. R. Seager, "The Architecture of the Dura and Sardis Synagogues," 84–85.

140. See CDEE, no. 67b for one such text. For the *Constitutio Antoniana* see Smallwood, *The Jews under Roman Rule*, 502–4; A. N. Sherwin-White, *The Roman Citizenship* (Oxford 1939) 216–27.

141. Several donors use the epithet *theosebēs* (L. Robert, *Nouvelles Inscriptions*, nos. 3–5), but it is difficult to know whether it means "pagan sympathizer," "proselyte," or just "pious" Jew. In any case, there does not seem to have been any restriction on the areas of participation by such individuals, and their donations show high social status and prominence within the community. Among the donations given by 27 named benefactors to the building are mosaic floors, marble revetments, paintings, a gold menorah, a marble menorah, the crater of the atrium, and the construction itself. A survey is found in BASOR 187 (1967) 32.

142. Sardis Inscr. 62.111 [= *Bulletin of the American Schools of Oriental Research* 187 (1967) 27; LD 27]: *Ananeōsis Hippasiou hui[ou . . .]*. Cf. L. Robert, *Nouvelles Inscriptions*, no. 17.

143. See CDEE, no. 67a. A. T. Kraabel, "Judaism in Western Asia Minor," 222–23.

144. That is, if the second stage of the building (the conversion

from an *apodyterion* for the gymnasion to a hall) was already completed prior to the Jewish acquisition. It is possible that this second stage was in progress, but incomplete, or that the Jews were involved in the conversion almost from the beginning of stage 2. See CDEE, no. 66a; A. R. Seager, "The Building History of the Sardis Synagogue," AJA ns 76 (1972) 432.

145. The dating of the Jewish acquisition prior to 212 is based on Robert's analysis of the prosopography. The names in stages 2–3 show much less evidence of the *Constitutio Antoniana*. See CDEE, no. 67a.

146. See CDEE, no. 66d. At some point a major structural modification occurred, when the columns of stage 2 were replaced with piers. It suggests that changes were also made in the exterior and elevation of the building as well. Again, the renovation was not a private matter only.

147. The mosaic work and, perhaps, the lions were private donations, while the "Eagle Table" was a spoil with pagan symbolism. See A. T. Kraabel, "Judaism in Western Asia Minor," 227–28.

148. The aediculae were introduced only after stage 4 construction was complete. The reversal of orientation is observable in the pattern of the floor mosaics, as those of stage 3 were set so as to be read facing west toward the apse, while those of stage 4 were made to be read facing east, toward the new aediculae.

149. Several factors point to public access in the hall, at least at certain times. Cf. A. T. Kraabel, "Judaism in Western Asia Minor," 238; "The Social System of Six Diaspora Synagogues," 86. It should be noted that the south face of the hall on the street front was lined with shops, several of which belonged to Jewish merchants (as identified by inscriptions). At least by stage 4, then, the synagogue had become a public landmark, and it continued in use until the city was destroyed in 616 C.E.

5. From House Church to Church Building

1. Tacitus, *Annals* XV.44. Cf. Pliny, *Epp.* X.96, 97, see CDEE, no. 25.
2. Cf. Robert Wilken, *The Christians as the Romans Saw Them* (New Haven, CT, 1985) passim; A. D. Nock, *Conversion, the Old and the New in Religion from Alexander the Great to Augustine of Hippo* (London 1933) 48–71; *Early Gentile Christianity in its Hellenistic Background* (New York 1964) 23f.
3. Gerd Theissen, *Sociology of Early Palestinian Christianity* (Philadelphia 1978) 1.
4. L. M. White, "Shifting Sectarian Boundaries in Early Christianity," *Bulletin of the John Rylands University Library of Manchester* 70:3 (1988) 7–24. See also Matt. 15.24 and the parallel passage in Mark 7.24–

30; cf. Rudolf Bultmann, *History of the Synoptic Tradition* (rev. ed., New York 1968) 145; Norman Perrin, *Rediscovering the Teachings of Jesus* (London 1967) 201–3; John Gager, *Kingdom and Community: The Social World of Early Christianity* (Englewood Cliffs, NJ, 1975) 19–41.

5. Jacob Neusner, *From Politics to Piety: The Emergence of Pharisaic Judaism* (2nd ed., New York 1979) 81–96.

6. Cf. *mShabbath* 1.4; *bMenahoth* 41b; S. Safrai, "Home and Family," CRINT I.2:728–92, esp. 731; Marcel Simon, *Jewish Sects at the Time of Jesus* (Philadelphia 1967) 32, 56.

7. The phrase *kat' oikon* in Acts (2.46; 5.42) is regularly rendered "from house to house," more or less at random, a sense that is traceable to the Vulgate (*circa domos*). It would be more consistent with the inferred customary action in Acts 12.12 as well as with the Pauline usage simply to render it "at home" (cf. 1 Cor. 16.19 and esp. Philem. 2). This seems to be more in keeping with the distinction being made in Acts between the private gathering "at home" versus the public worship "in the Temple." Cf. Marlis Gielen, "Zur Interpretation der paulinischen Formel *he kat' oikon ecclesia*," ZNW 77 (1986) 109–25.

8. Cf. Gerd Theissen, "Wanderradikalismus," *Zeitschrift für Theologie und Kirche* 70 (1973) 245–71; *Sociology of Early Palestinian Christianity*, 8–16; G. Kretschmar, "Ein Beitrag zur Frage nach dem Ursprung früchristlicher Askese," *Zeitschrift für Theologie und Kirche* 61 (1964) 27–67.

9. Cf. Wayne A. Meeks, *The Moral World of the First Christians* (Philadelphia 1986) 97–107.

10. Theissen, *Sociology of Early Palestinian Christianity*, 17–25; "Legitimation and Subsistence: An Essay on the Sociology of Early Christian Missionaries," in *The Social Setting of Pauline Christianity: Essays on Corinth* (Philadelphia 1982) 27–53.

11. L. M. White, "Sociological Analysis of Early Christian Groups: A Social Historian's Response," *Sociological Analysis* 47 (1986) 249–66; "Shifting Sectarian Boundaries in Early Christianity," *Bulletin of the John Rylands University Library of Manchester* 70:3 (1988) 7–24; Gager, *Kingdom and Community*, 19–41.

12. Wayne Meeks, *The First Urban Christians: The Social World of the Apostle Paul* (New Haven, CT, 1983) 9–50; *The Moral World of the First Christians* 108–23; cf. John H. Elliott, *A Home for the Homeless: A Sociological Exegesis of 1 Peter* (Philadelphia 1981) 59–84.

13. Wayne Meeks and Robert Wilken, *Jews and Christians at Antioch* (Chico, CA, 1981) 13–22; L. M. White, "Adolf Harnack and the 'Expansion' of Early Christianity: A Reappraisal of Social History," TSC 5 (1985/1986) 97–127.

14. White, "Harnack and the Expansion," 111–15; Cf. A. J. Malherbe, *Paul and the Thessalonians* (Philadelphia 1987) 5–33; A. T. Kraabel, "Greeks, Jews, and Lutherans in the Middle Half of Acts," *Chris-*

tians Among Jews and Gentiles: Essays in Honor of Krister Stendahl on His Sixty-fifth Birthday (HTR 79, Philadelphia 1986) 147–57.

15. *Passio Pauli* 1 (cf. CDEE, no. 9b).

16. See CDEE, nos. 8, 10, 11, among others. Many, of course, are legendary episodes modeled after the canonical book of Acts; however, it should be noted that the household setting is simply assumed to be "typical" and that the role of these house church meetings often has theological import for the particular document. Noteworthy here is the house of the Marcellus in the *Acts of Peter,* cf. Robert Stoops, "Patronage in the Acts of Peter," in *The Apocryphal Acts of the Apostles,* ed. Dennis McDonald (*Semeia* 39, Atlanta 1986) 78–94.

17. Cf. Calvin Roetzel, *The Letters of Paul* (2nd ed., Atlanta 1982) 79; Helmut Koester, "The Purpose of the Polemic of a Pauline Fragment," *New Testament Studies* 8 (1962) 317.

18. Cf. Victor Paul Furnish, *Second Corinthians* (Anchor Bible, Garden City, NY, 1984) 26–35.

19. Acts 18.2–4; 1 Cor. 16.19.

20. Rom. 16.5 (see below n. 26).

21. 1 Cor. 16.15; cf. 1.11, 15 (compare Acts 18.8).

22. Rom. 16.2, 23.

23. Gal. 2.9; Rom. 16.16.

24. Philem. 22.

25. Chan-Hie Kim, *The Form and Structure of the Familiar Greek Letter of Recommendation* (Missoula, MT 1972) passim; S. K. Stowers, *Letter Writing in Greco-Roman Antiquity* (Philadelphia 1986) 51–70; A. J. Malherbe, *Social Aspects of Early Christianity* (2nd ed., Philadelphia 1983) 94–103; *Ancient Epistolary Theorists* (Atlanta 1988) 1–13, 30–41; Peter Marshall, *Enmity in Corinth: Social Conventions in Paul's Relations with the Corinthians* (Wissenschaftliche Untersuchungen zum Neuen Testament 23, Tübingen 1987) 91–117.

26. Rom. 16.2. I am assuming here (as above in n. 20) that Rom. 16 is integral with the rest of the letter. Cf. Harry A. Gamble, *The Textual History of the Letter to the Romans: A Study in Textual and Literary Criticism* (Grand Rapids, MI 1977) passim; W. A. Meeks, *First Urban Christians,* 16; A. J. Malherbe, *Social Aspects,* 64–65.

27. I base this suggestion, first, on the proximity of the letter of recommendation for Phoebe to the greeting to Prisca and Aquila and, second, on the assumption that Phoebe herself would have known or known of Prisca and Aquila from their earlier stay in Corinth. The other cells at Rome are noted in Rom. 16.5b–19; cf. W. A. Meeks, *First Urban Christians,* 57, 60, 143.

28. Rom. 15.22–30.

29. Cf. A. G. MacKay, *Houses, Villas, and Palaces in the Roman World* (London 1975) passim, and with regard to exegetical issues cf. L. M. White, "Scaling the Strongman's Court (Lk. 11.21): An Index of Social

Facets," *Foundations and Facets Forum* 3 (1987) 3–28. By contrast note the assumptions of homogeneity in housing in J. Murphy-O'Connor, *St. Paul's Corinth: Texts and Archaeology* (Wilmington, DE 1983) 153–60.

30. See above chap. 1.

31. I am not convinced by the study of N. Afanasieff, "L'assemblée eucharistique unique dans l'église ancienne," *Kleronomia* 6 (1974) 1–36, which argues for a single eucharistic gathering for each city, based largely on the reference in Rom. 16.23. Because the eucharist was still thoroughly a part of the common meal in the house church gathering, there would probably have been diverse gatherings (and practices) within any given locality where there were multiple house church cells. This seems to be precisely the case (and the source of some of the problems) at Corinth, cf. 1 Cor. 11–14; Meeks, *First Urban Christians*, 76, 221 n. 7.

32. G. Theissen, "Social Integration and Sacramental Activity," in *Social Setting of Pauline Christianity*, 145–73; A. J. Malherbe, *Social Aspects*, 81; Dennis E. Smith, "Meals and Morality in Paul and his World," *Society of Biblical Literature Seminar Papers* 1981 (Chico, CA, 1981) 319–40.

33. W. A. Meeks, *First Urban Christians*, 158–63; cf. Hans-Josef Klauck, *Hausgemeinde und Hauskirche im frühen Christentum* (Stuttgart 1981) 30–40. Stephen C. Barton ("Paul's Sense of Place: An Anthropological Approach to Community Formation in Corinth," *New Testament Studies* 32 [1986] 225–46), I think, goes a bit too far in drawing a radical distinction between the household and the "church," but the discussion of boundary definition and "sacred space/sacred time" is useful.

34. Cf. A. J. Malherbe, "The Inhospitality of Diotrophes," in *Social Aspects*, 2nd ed., 92–112.

35. Ibid., 95–99; Elliott, *A Home for the Homeless*, 165–219; William R. Schoedel, *Ignatius of Antioch* (Hermeneia, Philadelphia 1986) 12–19.

36. See CDEE, no. 36. The dating of the renovation to 240/241 C.E. is established by C. H. Kraeling, DEF VIII.2, 34–37.

37. *Passio Sancti Justini et Socii* 3 (CDEE, no. 7b). For the dating (ca. 164/165, under the prefect Q. Junius Rusticus) see H. Musurillo, *The Acts of the Christian Martyrs* (Oxford 1971) xviii, 43 n. See also A. J. Malherbe, "Justin and Crescens," in *Christian Teaching: Studies in Honor of L. G. Lewis* (Abilene, TX, 1981) 312–27.

38. According to one line of tradition from this text, the place "above the baths" has been linked with the *titulus Pudentis*, upon which the basilica S. Pudenziana presumably rests. This tradition is based on the two names attached to the bath (Martinus and Timotheus) that appear in Recension B of the text (see CDEE, no. 7b, n. 3.3). Cf. R. M. Grant, *Early Christianity and Society* (New York 1977) 149. It must be

noted, however, that the names differ in the other recensions and make such an identification impossible, while the architectural history of S. Pudenziana does not present clear evidence of Christian usage in the levels below the present basilica (cf. CDEE, Appendix A, no. 10). The more likely candidate, where a securely identified pre-Constantinian meeting place is located in a residential complex containing both baths and upper-story rooms, is the *titulus Byzantis* beneath the basilica SS. Giovanni e Paolo (CDEE, no. 52).

39. Justin Martyr, *Apology* I.61.3 (see CDEE, no. 7a).
40. As suggested above in n. 38 for the insula of SS. Giovanni e Paolo. Cf. James E. Packer, "Housing and Population in Imperial Ostia and Rome," JRS 57 (1967) 80–95; Jerome Carcopino, *Daily Life in Ancient Rome* (New Haven, CT, 1940) 22f. It is perhaps significant of incipient changes in attitude toward the location (becoming a more formal sense of "church") that Justin refers to the "meeting place" (*syneleusis*). The term is a synonym for *koinon* and begins to move in the direction of identifying the congregation (as "church") with the regular place of assembly. So, also, note the regular use in Justin of the Pauline phrase *synerchesthai epi to auto* almost as a specialized technical term for the eucharistic assembly. Compare Justin, *Apol.* I.67.3 and *Mart.* 3.1 (Rec. B), 2.4 (Rec. C, see CDEE, no. 7b, n. 3.1) with Ignatius, *ad Eph.* 5.2, 13.1; *ad Mag.* 7.1 (CDEE, no. 6a–b), and Origen, *De orat.* 31.5 (CDEE, no. 15).
41. See CDEE, no. 53.
42. See CDEE, no. 52b; cf. CBCR I:293ff.
43. CDEE, no. 50.
44. CDEE, no. 41 and Appendix A, no. 8.
45. See above chap. 3 and CDEE, no. 72.
46. CDEE, no. 57b.
47. See CDEE, Appendix A, no. 12.
48. See above chap. 1.
49. For the text see CDEE, no. 26.
50. The reference is much debated, especially since the work of Walter Bauer, *Orthodoxy and Heresy in Earliest Christianity* (English transl., Philadelphia 1971) 12–15. In keeping with his view of the development of Christianity in Syria (much as in Egypt) Bauer argued that the two references of the *Edessene Chronicle* were a product of later orthodox Christianity in an effort to project an episcopal succession back on the earlier period. Thus, rather than reflecting one of the diverse forms of heterodox Christianity of that earlier period, the flood account was taken to be a fabrication. See also DEF VIII.2, 137–38.
51. For such combinations in Jewish usage, although rare, see CIJ 682 (Olbia on the Black Sea, as restored by LD 11); CIJ 694 (Stobi, CDEE, no. 73); CIJ 867 (Gerasa). Cf. above chap. 3.
52. While we should take W. Bauer's criticisms of a literalistic

reading seriously, we should give more credence to the historical evidence, since other records attest to the flood disaster in Edessa. For me, however, the seeming redundance of the phrase "temple of the church" is less problematic. The term *haikla* in the earlier period could be "temple," "holy place," or just "palace/hall," i.e., any public building. At this period, *church* (like synagogue) probably still had the ambiguous sense of either building or congregation. Hence, the title cited in the text sounds very much like a lintel inscription or public census designation. The building had come to be known as the "holy place of the Christian congregation." Moreover, this is the kind of notice we might well expect to be preserved in a court record (perhaps using official census records) of the list of buildings destroyed by the flood of 201, as suggested by Hallier. For *topos* used in this way of the Christian institution see the late third century papyrus letter from bishop Sotas (P. Oxy. XII, 1492; cf. CDEE, no. 45).

53. See CDEE, no. 26 for text. See also A. Harnack, *Mission and Expansion*, II:142–45.

54. Cf. W. Bauer, *Orthodoxy and Heresy*, 14–15. Bauer, of course, saw this monumentalization as a reflection of the orthodox victory and suppression of the earlier heterodox varieties. Yet, he does discuss the activities of the nascent orthodox from as early as ca. 190 (under the bishop Palut) alongside the other groups; cf. ibid., 20–21.

55. Graydon F. Snyder, *ANTE PACEM: Archaeological Evidence of Church Life before Constantine* (Macon, GA 1985) 163–65; compare ECBA, 24.

56. 1 Cor. 11.17–34. For Paul both the problem and the corrective arose out of the integral nature of the meal setting for worship and eucharist. Cf. Günther Bornkamm, *Early Christian Experience* (English trans., New York 1969) 127–38, 155. P. Neuenzeit, *Das Herrenmahl* (Munich 1960) 70–73; Gerd Theissen, "Social Integration and Sacramental Activity," in *The Social Setting of Pauline Christianity: Essays on Corinth* (Philadelphia 1982) 145–74. Also on the bracketing effect of the words of institution before and after the meal proper see H. Conzelmann, *First Corinthians* (English trans., *Hermeneia*, Philadelphia 1975) 199.

57. So following G. Theissen (note above); cf. his "Social Stratification in the Corinthian Community: A Contribution to the Sociology of Early Hellenistic Christianity," in *Social Setting of Pauline Christianity*, 69–120. Here I would not take the phrase "one is hungry and another is drunk" (v. 21) as a literal reflection of the problem. Rather it is part of Paul's stylized characterization of the situation. Thus, "hungry" and "drunk" are to be read as part of the overall parallel structure of the passage built around the terms *eat/drink, bread/cup*, and *body/blood*. See also W. A. Meeks, *First Urban Christians*, 67–68, 157–62.

58. Cf. Joachim Jeremias, *The Eucharistic Words of Jesus* (English

trans., London 1966) 115–17; Dennis E. Smith, "Social Obligation in the Context of Communal Meals" (Ph.D. Thesis; Harvard University 1980) passim; "Meals and Morality in Paul and his World," *SBL Seminar Papers 1981* (Missoula, MT 1981) 327, 337.

59. D. E. Smith, "Meals and Morality," 325; cf. G. Bornkamm, *Early Christian Experience*, 176 n. 2. The key phrase is *synerchesthai epi to auto* in 1 Cor. 11.20 and 14.23, which suggests that the activities discussed in chaps. 12–14 were also conducted in the same meal setting.

60. N. Afanasieff, "L'assemblée eucharistique unique dans l'église ancienne," *Kleronomia* 6 (1974) 1–36.

61. Thus, I would disagree with Gregory Dix and others who maintain that the eucharist was from the beginning a separate sacramental act. If anything, Paul himself sowed the seeds of this separation in 1 Cor. 11. Cf. G. Dix, *The Shape of the Liturgy* (2nd ed., London 1945) 77–79; Josef Jungmann, *The Early Liturgy to the Time of Gregory the Great* (Notre Dame, IN, 1959) 32–33.

62. The earliest evidence comes from the Epistle of Jude (v. 12) and from the *Epistula Apostolorum*, dated to the middle of the second century; cf. Jeremias, *Eucharistic Words of Jesus*, 115–16.

63. Did. 9–10. Contra Jeremias (118–20), however, I see no evidence for a separation or sequencing of agape and eucharist based on the two sections in Did. 9–10 and 14 read back as a parallel on the idealized Jerusalem church in Acts. 2.42. Cf. Willy Rordorf, "The Didache," in *The Eucharist of the Early Christians* (New York 1978) 1–23. On the Didache I would follow more along the lines of Hans Lietzmann, *Mass and Lord's Supper* (Leiden 1972) 123, 187–88, who argues for a change of function over time in the two originally integral acts of worship.

64. Cf. Pliny, *Ep.* X.96 (CDEE, no. 25); Tertullian, *Apol.* 39 (CDEE, no. 13b); Justin, *Apol.* I.61–66 (CDEE, no. 7a).

65. Cf. Tertullian, *De exhortatione castitatis* 11; Cyprian, *De opere et eleemosyne* 15. Compare Jungmann, *The Early Liturgy*, 116–17; however, I would argue that the new practice was more a result of gradual changes in the eucharistic assembly than just theological formality.

66. *Paedagogus* II.1 (= 4.3–7.3 in the GCS edition of Staehlin). Cf. the third century Coptic *Acts of Paul* (in *New Testament Apocrypha*, ed. Hennecke and Schneemelcher [Philadelphia 1965] II:388), which reflects the tendency of reading later developments back into Pauline practice. See also the fourth century commentators, such as Amphilochius of Iconium (bishop from 376–395); cf. Harnack, *Mission und Ausbreitung* (4th German ed., Leipzig 1924) II:611.

67. *Apostolic Tradition* (ed. G. Dix) XXIV, XXVI.1–12 (CDEE, no. 14b); cf. Dix, *Shape of the Liturgy*, 82–84 (though he tends to push the evidence of Hippolytus back as identical to that of Justin's time).

68. See CDEE, no. 36, based on the archaeological reports of C. H. Kraeling, *The Christian Building* (= DEF VIII.2) 34–38.
69. For the inscriptions see CDEE, no. 37. On the legal issues see DEF VIII.2, 139 or ECBA, 25 in contrast to the traditional view reflected in G. Bovini, *La proprieta ecclestici e la condizione giuridica della chiesa in eta preconstantiniana* (Milan 1948), and by Marta Sordi, *Il cristianesimo e Roma* (Bologna 1965) 468–71; cf. Sordi, *The Christians and the Roman Empire* (Norman, OK, 1986) 188.
70. DEF VIII.2, 153–54. Compare the layout of the Lullingstone chapel (CDEE, no. 57b) and others which suggest the beginning of an orientation on the long axis of the room toward a bema or dais on one of the shorter sides. This development is consistent with the evidence noted above regarding changes in eucharistic practice.
71. Dura is the earliest known case where baptism was consciously integrated into the ecclesiastical setting by means of architectural adaptation. A similar process seems to have been involved in the second phase adaptation of the Parentium villa (CDEE, no. 50).
72. While there is no archaeological evidence that the house was used by the Christians prior to renovation, the level of planning in movement and articulation of liturgical space may suggest a familiarity with the space. Thus, note the window emplacements for communication between Rooms 4 and 5 and the courtyard (discussed by C. H. Kraeling, DEF VIII.2, 19). The planning shows formal liturgical considerations and larger community considerations (cf. DEF VIII.2, 153). These factors may point to some short-term use of the building by the Christians prior to the renovation project. This would suggest the role of a major patron or donor, as I have suggested for the inscriptions of the baptistry (cf. CDEE, no. 37, notes).
73. Other sites include the villa at Parentium, Istria (CDEE, no. 50), the so-called Julianos' Church at Umm el-Jimal, Syria/Arabia (CDEE, no. 41), and perhaps the house at Hinton St. Mary's, Britannia (CDEE, Appendix A, no. 12).
74. The text, now called the *Acta Munati Felicis*, is preserved untitled in the *Gestae apud Zenophilum* (CDEE, no. 31).
75. Cf. W. H. C. Frend, *Martyrdom and Persecution in the Early Church* (New York 1967) 372–73; A. H. M. Jones, *Constantine and the Conversion of Europe* (New York 1948, repr. 1978) 53–56.
76. P. Gen. Inv. 108, dated ca. 298–341. See CDEE, no. 44.
77. Ibid., column D, line 11. For possible reconstructions of the lacuna see the notes to CDEE, no. 44.
78. P. Oxy. I (1898) 43 verso, dated ca. 295 (text at CDEE, no. 46).
79. P. Oxy. XXXIII (1968) 2673, dated 304 (text at CDEE, no. 47). The document, preserved in triplicate, is an official declaration of church property written by a court official and attested by a church official (who was apparently illiterate in Greek).

80. Cyprian, Ep. 39.4.1 (text at CDEE, no. 16a).

81. Compare Ep. 38.2 and the reference to the ordination of the confessor Numidius in Ep. 40. By contrast we should remember that in Tertullian's day, acts of worship were still conducted without clerical distinction and simply "in the midst" of the assembly (*Apol.* 39; text at CDEE, no. 13b). Thus, we may be able to mark the chronological parameters of the development, at least for Carthage, so that prior to Cyprian's time the larger scale of worship had not appeared. As to its nature in the days of Tertullian, I doubt that the reference in *Adv. Valentinios* 3 to "the house of the dove [Christ]" which "is high up and close to the light" is to be taken literally. Hence I would not read it, as some have, to indicate a "house church" assembly in Tertullian's day. Rather, the references in Tertullian to assembly during persecution (*De fuga* 3.2, 14.1; CDEE, no. 13d) and to patterns of penitential discipline (which place the offender outside the door of the church) would suggest a move toward a domus ecclesiae type of structure around the beginning of the third century in Carthage (cf. *De pudicitia* 3.5, 4.5; CDEE, no. 13e).

82. Cyprian, Ep. 59.18.1 (text at CDEE, no. 16d).

83. The information comes from the synodal letter of Malchion of Antioch (who helped to depose Paul) as preserved in Eusebius HE VII.30.9 (see text at CDEE, no. 20).

84. The bema must have been a raised platform or *pulpitum* (as in Cyprian), on which Paul had built (probably at his own initiative and expense) the *secretum*. Both terms come from the vocabulary of Roman civil architecture, as indicated by the use of the Latin word *secretum* in the Greek text. The *secretum* was an enclosure for magistrates and officials in court buildings and audience halls.

85. It would appear from the wording of Malchion's letter that the bema itself was already present in the church building and was not viewed as part of Paul's innovation. It is comparable, then, to the development at Carthage and to the analogous period in synagogue development, when the bema became more of a regular feature.

86. See J. B. Ward-Perkins, "Recent Work and Problems in Libya," CIAC VIII, 219–36; J. B. Ward-Perkins and R. G. Goodchild, "The Christian Antiquities of Tripolitania," *Archaeologica* 95 (1953) 39–41. Most recently, archaeological work in Greece has begun to suggest that basilical church building was a rather late innovation, commencing in the late fourth or fifth centuries.

87. The most distinctive feature of the Lullingstone chapel decoration is the incorporation of three large Chi-Rho monograms in the form of a *labarum* with encircling wreath and flanking doves. This design clearly suggests familiarity with mid-fourth-century Roman interests especially associated with the Constantinian revolution. Also, the orant figures on the rear wall of the Lullingstone chapel have been

described as "Byzantine" in artistic style and in dress. Cf. G. W. Meates, *Lullingstone Roman Villa* (London 1955) 132–34; *Excavations of the Lullingstone Roman Villa* (2 vols; London 1986–88) passim.

88. On Cirta see the suggestion of C. H. Kraeling, DEF VIII.2, 140 n. 3, although it appears to me to be a suggestion made on slim evidence save the fact that when the authorities went to search the church the bishop was there and watched the proceedings from his chair. On Hippo cf. H. I. Marrou, "La basilique chrétienne d'Hippo d'après le résultat des derniers fouilles," *Revue des Études Augustiniennes* 6 (1960) 109ff.; Jean Lassus, "Les édifices du culte autour de la basilique," CIAC VI, 588. More recently an episcopal residence has been excavated as part of the complex associated with the earliest (i.e., the Octagon) of the several churches at Philippi, Greece. The episkopeion was renovated from an existing insula adjoining the octagonal complex that had been built over an earlier fourth century "hall" church. Cf. CDEE, Appendix A, no. 4; Charalambos Bakirtzis, *"TO EPISKOPEION TON PHILIPPON"* in *Proceedings of Symposium on Kavala and its Region* (Kavala 1987) 149–57.

89. Augustine, *Contra Crescionum* III.30 (PL VIII, 744).

90. Optatus, *On the Donatist Schism* I.14: *quia basilicae necdum fuerunt restitutae, in domum Urbani Carisi* (Corpus Scriptorum Ecclesiasticorum Latinorum XXVI; Vienna 1893). On the name of the owner, a variant appears between Augustine (above) and Optatus. Optatus also says (*De schism.* I.15–19) that this same assembly initiated the Donatist schism a little later at a gathering in Carthage in 312/313, but it is noteworthy that at that point the church building at Carthage was still standing apparently untouched.

91. *Acta Saturnini* 8–9 (text at CDEE, no. 21). Cf. W. H. C. Frend, *The Donatist Church* (Oxford 1952) 9–10; A. H. M. Jones, *Constantine and the Conversion of Europe*, 52–53.

92. The text (*Acta Sat.* 2) also mentions the house of Octavius Felix as the meeting place. The text is considerably later (perhaps by a century) than the event; therefore, the phrase *dominicas basilicas* should be read with some caution, either without technical architectural significance on the word *basilica* or as an anachronism (as in Optatus). There is growing evidence that the former was possible, as in the inscription from Altava, Mauretania (cf. CDEE, no. 56) and in the inscription from the simple fourth-century "hall" church, called the "Basilica of St. Paul," found under the Octagonal complex at Philippi (cf. CDEE, Appendix A, no. 4). Also on the use of *basilica* in literary texts of this period see L. Voelkl, "Die konstantinischen Kirchenbauten nach dem literarischen Quellen des Okzidents," RDAC 30 (1954) 99–136; "Die konstantinischen Kirchenbauten nach Eusebius," in RDAC 29 (1953) 60–64.

93. Cf. Tertullian, *De fuga in persec.* 14.1 (text at CDEE, no. 13d).

94. Cf. W. H. C. Frend, *Donatist Church*, 53–54. Optatus seems to have referred to the simple mudbrick buildings of the Donatists as *basilicas non necessarias*. See also J. B. Ward-Perkins, "Memoria, Martyr's Tomb, and Martyr's Church," *Journal of Theological Studies* ns 17 (1966) 20–25.

95. ECBA, 38. Compare the developments in the Dura-Europos Synagogue by the mid-third century (CDEE, no. 60).

96. Eusebius, HE VIII.1.5 (text at CDEE, no. 23b). This section of text comes, in all probability from the first edition of Eusebius' work; cf. H. J. Lawlor and J. E. L. Oulton, *Eusebius: The Ecclesiastical History and the Martyrs of Palestine* (London 1954) II:5f.; H. J. Lawlor, *Eusebiana* (Oxford 1912) 211–35; R. M. Grant, "Eusebius H.E. VIII: Another Suggestion," VC 22 (1968) 16–18.

97. So A. Harnack, *Mission and Expansion* II:88; and R. M. Grant, "Temples, Churches, and Endowments," in *Early Christianity and Society* (New York 1977) 150; but contrast ECBA, 38 and n. 50, and above chap. 2.

98. H. J. Lawlor and J. E. L. Oulton, *Eusebius*, II:30ff., 268, 275; Norman Baynes, *Eusebius and Constantine* (New York 1984) 15ff.

99. The phrase is common in inscriptions, as in the Aegina synagogue (CDEE, no. 74) as well as in LD 11 (CIJ 682, Olbia) and no. 72 (Joppa); CIJ 744 (Teos); and CIJ 735 (Golgoi, Cyprus). For mithraea compare Virunum, discussed above in chap. 3, nn. 122–27.

100. The term *aula ecclesiae* is coined here after A. Harnack's *Saalkirche* (cf. *Mission und Ausbreitung*, 4th German ed., II:615). See above chap. 2.

101. CDEE, no. 50.

102. Text of the inscription at CDEE, no. 51.

103. *Monumenta Asiae Minoris Antiqua*, vol. I.1 (Manchester 1928), 170; text of the inscription at CDEE, no. 49. M. Julius Eugenius had been a soldier in the military officium of the province but was forced into retirement as a Christian confessor during the persecution of Diocletian. He was apparently from a prominent local family as his marriage and his position in the local decurionate later attest. Thus, his role as confessor and bishop who rebuilt the church must be seen in light of local circumstances as well.

104. CDEE, no. 39. That the church building was built de novo as a Christian aula ecclesiae was a result of the peculiar local circumstances of the village, apparently just being settled at the beginning of the fourth century. Georges Tchalenko (*Villages antiques de la Syrie du Nord* [Paris 1953–1958] I:319–32) postulated that this period of settlement corresponded to the beginning of private estate farming in the region. The owner of the house next door to the church was the founder of the village/estate and would have served as patron of the free villagers. As

he also built the church complex adjacent to his own house, he was the patron of Christianity in the village.

105. Porphyry, *Adversos Christianos* frag. 76 (text at CDEE, no. 29).

106. Eusebius, HE VII.30.18–19 (text at CDEE, no. 20b). Cf. Fergus Millar, "Paul of Samosata, Zenobia, and Aurelian: The Church, Local Culture, and Political Allegiance in the Third Century," JRS 61 (1971) 126–34.

107. apud Lampridius *Historia Augusta, Severus Alexander* 49. 6 (text at CDEE, no. 27). Cf. R. Syme, *Ammianus and the Historia Augusta* (Cambridge, England 1968) passim; R. J. Penella, "Alexander Severus 43.6–7: Two Emperors and Christ," VC 31 (1977) 229–30.

108. Lactantius, *De mortibus persecutorum* 12.4–5 (text at CDEE, no. 24).

109. See above nn. 74–75, 79, 88.

110. See CDEE, no. 52b. We must begin to recognize too that such renovations must have had enormous socioeconomic impact. In addition to the cost of acquisition and renovation of an entire urban insula property, the renovations of the upper floors for exclusive ecclesiastical use would have displaced the residents (both commercial and domestic). On the implication for population at Rome cf. James E. Packer, "Housing and Population in Imperial Ostia and Rome," JRS 57 (1967) 80–95.

111. See CDEE II, nos. 53, 54.

112. ECBA, 37–39; CBCR I;144–65. Cf. CDEE, no. 55.

113. For texts see CDEE, nos. 32–35.

114. See CDEE, Appendix A.8. Much has been made of the supposed house church under the later cathedral; however, the evidence is slim. Yet it must be noted that the elaborate double hall edifice begun under bishop Theodore was not basilical when it was first built in ca. 314–317. The North Hall seems to have had a chancel and bema on the east end, but there was no apse or aisle construction.

115. *Monumenta Asiae Minoris Antiqua*, vol. I.1 (Manchester 1928), 170; text at CDEE, no. 49.

116. Eusebius, HE X.4.1, 37ff. (text at CDEE, no. 23d).

117. Eusebius, HE X.4.33–36. Cf. Paul Corbey Finney, "TOPOS HEIROS und christlicher Sakralbau in vorkonstantinischer Überlieferung," *Boreas* 7 (1984) 217–25. I have suggested elsewhere that the section in Eusebius, HE X.2–4, is a thematic composition intended to tie the first period of reconstruction directly to themes in the earlier edition of the work, especially in bk. VIII.1–2, but prior to the more elaborately developed Constantinian panegyric of later Eusebian works. Hence I see the grandiose descriptions of the church more as a product of Eusebian "triumph" metaphor than as a reflection of an immediate transition to monumental basilical architecture. Cf. L. M.

White, "The Glory of this House: Church Building and Church History in Eusebius" (forthcoming).
118. Cf. R. Krautheimer, "The Beginnings of Early Christian Architecture," RER 3 (1939) 134–36.
119. This fact has often been overlooked, since the text refers to side *stoai* on the main building (HE X.4.42). Most scholars have assumed this to reflect an internal basilical aisle with colonnade. Careful analysis of the text, however, shows that this terminology is precisely parallel to that used to describe the external portico of the atrium (X.4.39). It is not unlikely, then, that the long sides of the building were flanked by lateral *stoai* or promenades, which communicated with exedrae and other external structures (X.4.45). Read in this way the description is more similar to Krautheimer's reconstruction of the first building of S. Crisogono at Rome (ca. 310; see fig. 24) and is in some measure comparable to the description of M. Julius Eugenius' rebuilt church at Laodicea Combusta and bishop Theodore's church at Aquileia, both of which come from the same period (ca. 314–319). Finally, it should be noted that each of these was rebuilt by the bishop himself as patron of the project. Compare also the hall church under the Octagon at Philippi (see fig. 27).
120. See CDEE, no. 41.
121. See above chap. 3. Cf. E. M. Meyers and J. F. Strange, *Archaeology, the Rabbis, and Early Christianity* (Nashville, TN 1981) 140–54; E. M. Meyers and A. T. Kraabel, "Archaeology, Iconography, and Nonliterary Written Remains," in *Early Judaism and Its Modern Interpreters*, eds. R. A. Kraft and G. W. E. Nickelsburg (Atlanta 1986) 175–93.
122. Thus, we should note that both S. Clemente and SS. Giovanni e Paolo at Rome are the reverse of the normal orientation of church architecture, precisely because their development was determined by the existing structures and their earlier use. By the same token, we should note that in both the Ostia and Sardis synagogues the Torah shrine seems to have been a later addition that resulted in a reversal of the existing orientation of each building to fit more of a normative pattern. Thus, on the Torah shrine see E. M. Meyers and A. T. Kraabel, *Early Judaism* (1986) 194–96; on orientation see F. Landsberger, "The Sacred Direction in Church and Synagogue," in *The Synagogue: Studies in Origins, Archaeology, and Architecture*, ed. J. Gutmann (New York 1975) 239–60.
123. Compare Eusebius, HE X.4.44 (CDEE, no. 23d: on the introduction of the chancel to guard the "holy of holies" in the Church at Tyre). Contra Dix (*Shape of the Liturgy*, 28–29), I do not see evidence of a fully segregated area for bishops and clergy at the beginning of the second century (i.e., in Rev. 4.1–7 and Ignatius, *ad Mag.* 6.1). The earliest evidence comes from the end of the second century and

through the third, as in Tertullian and Cyprian or the apocryphal Acts literature. In the case of the latter, a cathedra was often placed in lofty position for the apostle, but they most likely reflect the beginnings of such arrangements in their own day, telescoped backward onto the apostolic period. Cf. Clementine *Recognitions* X.71 (text at CDEE, no. 11). Also on Carthage and the development of clergy see Albano Vilela, *La condition collegiale du Prêtres au IIIe siècle* (Paris 1971) 286–88 (with special reference to Cyprian, Epp. 12.1, 16.1, 40, and 55.11).

124. There is no evidence for the processional liturgy prior to the fourth century. J. A. Jungmann (*The Early Liturgy*, 117) posits as a starting point a procession of laity in conjunction with the newly formalized offertory in the third century. But, as noted above (n. 65), the offertory was also a liturgical byproduct of architectural renovation. There were, however, substantial variations in each locality. For example, most Syrian churches of the fourth century were entered through two (or three) side portals. H. C. Butler argues that these were designated for segregated entry (laity on the west end, clergy on the east); cf. *Syria: Publications of an American Archaeological Expedition to Syria in 1899–1900*, ed. R. Garrett et al., vol. II (New York 1903), 89.

125. Edited by R. H. Connolly (Oxford 1929), chap. XII (= II.57–58; text at CDEE, no. 18). While this document was dependent upon the Didache, it shows considerable development in liturgical forms. Later it was taken over directly into the still more highly ordered procedures of the *Constitutio Apostolicorum* dating from the fourth to fifth centuries.

126. Cf. H. Selhorst, *Die Plätzanordnung im Gläubigenraum der altchristlichen Kirche* (Münster 1931) passim; Klaus Gamber, "Die frühchristliche Hauskirche nach *Didascalia Apostolorum* II.57.1–58.6," *Studia Patristica* X (1970) 337–45. Gamber must be taken with some caution, however, given his treatment of the evidence in relation to Dura-Europos and Aquileia in *Domus Ecclesiae: Die ältesten Kirchenbauten Aquilejas sowie im Alpen- und Donaugebiet bis zum Beginn des 5 Jahrhunderts liturgeschichtlich untersucht* (Regensburg 1968) passim.

127. On the date and situation supposed see Connolly, *The Didascalia Apostolorum* (Oxford 1929) xxx, lxxxvii–xci.

128. Eusebius, HE X.4.44; see above n. 123, and CDEE, no. 55 and Appendix A, no. 10; ECBA, 40; on the altar see also Eusebius, HE VII.15.4 (text at CDEE, no. 23a).

129. For the third century see Hippolytus' *Apostolic Tradition* 16–18 (CDEE, no. 14b) and Gregory Thaumaturgus' *Canonical Letter* 11 (CDEE, no. 19). In the Pauline period, however, there seems to have been no effort to exclude the unbaptized, so Bornkamm, *Early Christian Experience*, 171; cf. B. Capelle, "L'introduction du catéchumenat à Rome," *Recherches de théologie ancienne et medievale* 5 (1933) 120–54. The

development of the baptismal liturgy, and especially its articulation within ecclesiastical architecture, remains a complex problem. The shift from natural settings (Acts 8.36, 16.33; Did. 7.1-3) to indoor settings (Justin, *Apol.* I.61; Tertullian, *De bapt.* 4) would result, by the early third century, in more formalized practice. Thus, see *Acts of Thomas* 132; Tertullian, *De bapt.* 20.5; Hippolytus, *Apost. Trad.* 21.20; Cyprian, Ep. 73.9-10). Of course the earliest visible evidence for the integration of baptism into church architecture is Dura-Europos; cf. DEF VIII.2, 146-47. Cf. T. Klauser, "Taufet in lebendigem Wasser," in *Pisciculi, Festschrift für F. J. Dölger* (Münster 1939) 157-65; Jean Lassus, *Sanctuaires chrétiennes de Syrie* (Paris 1947) 17-19; A. F. J. Klijn, "An Ancient Syriac Baptismal Liturgy in the Syriac Acts of John," in *Charis kai Sophia, Festschrift für Karl Heinrich Rengstorf* (Leiden 1964); A. Vööbus, "Regarding the Background of the Liturgical Relations in the Didache," VC 23 (1969) 81-87; J. Quasten, "The Blessing of the Baptismal Font in the Syrian Rite of the Fourth Century," *Theological Studies* 7 (1946) 309-13; J. G. Davies, *The Architectural Setting of Baptism* (London 1962) passim; W. M. Bedard, *The Symbolism of the Baptismal Font in Early Christian Thought* (Washington, D.C. 1951) passim.

130. ECBA, 28, 40; Ramsay MacMullen, *Paganism in the Roman Empire* (New Haven, CT, 1981) 126-30; *Christianizing the Roman Empire* (New Haven, CT, 1984) passim.

6. Conclusions

1. *Epistle to Diognetus* 5.1-2, 4-9 (trans. after K. Lake, LCL). Cf. R. A. Markus, "The Problem of Self-Definition: From Sect to Church," in *Jewish and Christian Self-Definition, Volume I: The Shaping of Christianity in the Second and Third Centuries*, ed. E. P. Sanders (Philadelphia 1980) 1-15.

2. ECBA, 26; Davies, *Secular Use of Church Buildings*, 2. Cf. Origen, *Contra Celsum* III.55; VIII.17; Minucius Felix, *Octavius* 32; Arnobius of Sica, *Adv. Nationes* I.4, VI.3.

3. Cf. Tertullian, *Ad Scapulam* 5; *Apol.* 2, 37; Pliny Ep. X.96.9; L. M. White, "Adolf Harnack and the 'Expansion' of Christianity: A Reappraisal of Social History," TSC 5 (1985/1986) 97-127.

4. Porphyry, *Adv. Christianos*, frag. 76; Lactantius, *De mortibus persecutorum* 12.5 (see CDEE, nos. 29, 24). Robert L. Wilken, *The Christians as the Romans Saw Them* (New Haven, CT, 1984) 117ff. et passim.

5. Mikhail Rostovtzeff, *Social and Economic History of the Roman World* (2nd ed., Oxford 1957) I:17, 31; Moses I. Finley, *The Ancient Economy* (Berkeley 1973) 52-53; Richard Duncan-Jones, *The Economy of the Roman Empire, Quantitative Studies* (Cambridge, England 1974) 21.

6. Ernest Renan, *Paulus* (Leipzig 1869) 257, noting esp. the text of

CIL VI,9148: *collegium quod est in domu Sergiae Paullinae*, which was suggested to be related to the Sergius Paulus of Acts 13.7. See also the discussion in chap. 3, nn. 80 and 82.

7. Johannes Weiss, *Earliest Christianity, A History of the Period A.D. 3–150*, ed. F. C. Grant, 2 vols. (New York 1959) II:620f.; cf. his commentary *Der erste Korintherbrief*, 10th ed. (Meyer Kommentar 5; Göttingen 1925) 307.

8. Adolf Harnack, *The Mission and Expansion of Christianity in the First Three Centuries* (London 1908) I:443.

9. Ibid., II:85–86 (cf. chap. 1, n. 36 above). Harnack's was one of the first attempts to use church building as a guide to the expansion of Christianity. His periodization in four phases may have been a source for Krautheimer (cf. ECBA, 481 n. 2). Unfortunately Harnack was dependent upon architectural views of his own day. Thus, he calls for the introduction of the basilica in the third century. It is interesting, however, that Harnack describes a simpler hall structure, which was usually a rectangle (German: *Oblong*), with a niche "on one of the short sides" (*an der einem Schmalseite*).

10. L. M. White, "Harnack and Expansion," 97–105.

11. Floyd V. Filson, "The Significance of the Early Christian House Church," *Journal of Biblical Literature* 58 (1939) 105–112, esp. 109f. Some of the archaeological data cited by Filson is, of course, outdated and erroneous.

12. 1 Cor. 4.12; 2 Cor. 11.7f.; 1 Thess. 2.9f.; Acts 18.3. For references see n. 2 above and Robert M. Grant, "The Social Setting of Second Century Christianity," in *Jewish and Christian Self-Definition*, ed. E. P. Sanders, I:16–29.

13. Adolf Deissmann, *Light from the Ancient East*, English trans. from 4th German ed. by L. Strachan (London 1927; repr. Grand Rapids, MI 1978) 8ff.; *Paul: A Study in Social and Religious History*, trans. W. Wilson, 2nd ed. (New York 1957) 47f. Still Deissmann notes that there must have been at least a few wealthier people, in order to host the churches in their homes; cf. *Paul*, 243 n. 3. Cf. A. J. Malherbe, *Social Aspects of Early Christianity*, 2nd ed. (Philadelphia 1983) 31ff. Karl Kautsky, *Foundations of Christianity, A Study in Christian Origins*, 13th ed. (New York 1972) 323f. It should be noted that Deissmann was adamantly opposed to the Marxist appropriation of his views; cf. his *Light*, 465f. and C. L. Lee, "Social Unrest and Primitive Christianity," in *The Catacombs and the Colosseum*, ed. S. Benko and J. O'Rourke (Valley Forge, PA 1971) 121–38.

14. J. G. Davies, *The Secular Use of Church Buildings* (New York 1968) 1–3; cf. ECBA, 26.

15. E. A. Judge, *The Social Pattern of Christian Groups in the First Century* (London 1960) 60.

16. Ibid., 58f.; idem., "The Early Christians as a Scholastic Com-

munity," *Journal of Religious History* I (1960/1961) 129ff.; cf. Wilhelm Wuellner, "The Sociological Implications of 1 Cor. 1.26–28 Reconsidered," *Studia Evangelica* VI (Berlin 1973) 666–72; A. J. Malherbe, *Social Aspects*, 31, 61.

17. Gerd Theissen, *Social Setting of Pauline Christianity: Essays on Corinth*, 83ff.

18. John C. Gager, *Kingdom and Community: The Social World of Early Christianity* (Englewood Cliffs, NJ 1975) 19–48. Cf. L. M. White, "Shifting Sectarian Boundaries in Early Christianity," *Bulletin of the John Rylands University Library of Manchester* 70:3 (1988) 7–24.

19. G. Theissen, *Social Setting of Pauline Christianity*, 145–62; cf. 125ff. Cf. A. J. Malherbe, *Social Aspects*, 71ff. and W. A. Meeks, *First Urban Christians*, 69f.

20. D. W. Riddle, "Early Christian Hospitality: A Factor in the Gospel Transmission," *Journal of Biblical Literature* 57 (1938) 141–54; J. B. Matthews, "Hospitality and the New Testament Church: An Historical and Exegetical Study," (Ph.D. Thesis, Princeton Theological Seminary, 1965), 198–228; Peter Marshall, *Enmity in Corinth: Social Conventions in Paul's Relations with the Corinthians* (Wissenschaftliche Untersuchungen zum Neuen Testament 23, Tübingen 1987) 133–50; A. J. Malherbe, *Social Aspects*, 92ff.

21. Elizabeth Schüssler-Fiorenza, *In Memory of Her: A Feminist Theological Reconstruction of Christian Origins* (New York 1983) 163–235. Cf. W. A. Meeks, *First Urban Christians*, 23f., 55ff.

22. Dennis Smith, "Social Obligation in the Context of Communal Meals"; L. E. Keck, "On the Ethos of the Early Christians," *Journal of the American Academy of Religion* 42 (1974) 446f.; Willy Rordorf, "Was wissen wir über die christlichen Gottesdiensträume der vorkonstantinischen Zeit?" ZNW 55 (1964) 111f.; Hans-Josef Klauck, *Hausgemeinde und Hauskirche im frühen Christentum* (Stuttgart 1981) 101 et passim.

23. W. A. Meeks, *First Urban Christians*, 74ff. Cf. A. D. Nock, *Conversion: The Old and the New in Religion from Alexander the Great to Augustine of Hippo* (Oxford 1933) 66ff.

24. E. A. Judge, "The Early Christians as a Scholastic Community," *Journal of Religious History* I (1961) 126f.; R. L. Wilken, "Collegia, Philosophical Schools, and Theology," in *The Catacombs and the Colosseum*, 268–91; A. D. Nock, *Conversion*, 53f., 75ff.; R. M. Grant, "Temples, Churches and Endowments," in *Early Christianity and Society* (New York 1977) 146ff.

25. George LaPiana, "Foreign Groups in Rome in the First Centuries of the Empire," HTR 20 (1927) 183–403; Ramsay MacMullen, *Roman Social Relations* (New Haven, CT, 1974) 68–76.

26. H.-J. Klauck, *Hausgemeinde und Hauskirche*, 15–20; John H. Elliott, *A Home for the Homeless: A Sociological Exegesis of First Peter*

(Philadelphia 1981) 165ff.; Marlis Gielen, "Zur Interpretation der paulinischen Formel, *hē kat' oikon ekklēsia*," ZNW 77 (1986) 109–125.

27. W. A. Meeks, "The Image of the Androgyne: Some Uses of a Symbol in Earliest Christianity," *History of Religions* 13 (1974) 165–79; Bernadette Brooten, *Women Leaders in the Synagogue* (Chico, CA, 1982) 145–48.

28. See CDEE, nos. 58, 60.

29. DEF VIII.1, 326–36; A. R. Seager, "The Architecture of the Dura and Sardis Synagogues," in *The Dura-Europos Synagogue: A Re-Evaluation 1932–1972* (Missoula, MT 1973) 79–116; E. D. Francis, "Mithraic Graffiti from Dura-Europos," in *Mithraic Studies*, ed. J. Hinnels, 2 vols. (Manchester 1975) II:428ff.

30. A. T. Kraabel, "The Social Systems of Six Diaspora Synagogues," in *Ancient Synagogues: The State of Research*, ed. J. Gutmann (Chico, CA, 1981) 79–91; idem., "The Roman Diaspora: Six Questionable Assumptions," in *Essays in Honor of Yigael Yadin*, ed. G. Vermes and J. Neusner, *Journal of Jewish Studies* 33 (1982) 445–64; H. J. Leon, *The Jews of Ancient Rome* (Philadelphia 1960) 167ff. Ramsay MacMullen, *Paganism in the Roman Empire* (New Haven, CT, 1981) 112ff.

31. R. MacMullen, *Roman Social Relations*, 62, 94. Cf. R. Duncan-Jones, *Economy*, 3, 12.

32. R. MacMullen, *Social Relations*, 89; cf. Duncan-Jones, *Economy*, 4, 11, and 343f. (for a list of major fortunes in the early Empire).

33. R. Duncan-Jones, *Economy*, 17–32, 118. Cf. Cicero, *Letters to Friends* V.6.2; M. I. Finley, *Ancient Economy*, 53, 142.

34. R. MacMullen, *Social Relations*, 168 n. 15; cf. J. Carcopino, *Daily Life in Ancient Rome*, 23.

35. James E. Packer, "Housing and Population in Imperial Ostia and Rome," JRS 57 (1967) 80–95; A. G. MacKay, *Houses, Villas, and Palaces in the Roman World* (London 1977) 64–99; MacMullen, *Social Relations*, 62–63.

36. Cf. J. Carcopino, *Daily Life*, 24–26, 32, 44; Cicero, *Pro M. Caelio* 7; Justinian, *Digest* XIX.2.3; Juvenal, *Sat.* 3.165–67, 223–25; Martial, *Epigr.* XII.31. On relative costs cf. R. Duncan-Jones, *Economy*, 345–47, 366.

37. M. I. Finley, *Ancient Economy*, 21. Cf. B. Laum, *Stiftungen in der griechischen und römischen Antike* (Berlin 1914) I:134–40; R. Grant, *Early Christianity and Society*, 149–55.

38. For Pliny's benefactions, see R. Duncan-Jones, *Economy*, 156, 220; Pliny, Epp. V.7, VII.18, CIL V, 5262.

39. R. P. Saller, *Personal Patronage under the Early Empire* (Cambridge, England 1982) passim; F. W. Danker, *Benefactor: Epigraphic Study of a Graeco-Roman and New Testament Semantic Field* (St. Louis, MO, 1982) passim; compare the quip by Plutarch, *Lives: Cato Maior* 18.4.

40. On honors for the patron see R. MacMullen, *Social Relations*, 67,

76 and compare the cases of Cl. Tiberius Polycharmos, Julia Severa, and Tation discussed above in chap. 4.
41. See above chap. 5.
42. So A. J. Malherbe, *Social Aspects of Early Christianity* (2nd ed., Philadelphia 1983) 92–112, which also discusses the situation in the Pastorals. Cf. L. M. White, "Social Authority in the House Church and Eph. 4.1–16," *Restoration Quarterly* 29 (1987) 209–28.
43. See esp. 2 John 7–10 and 3 John 9–10. Cf. Shepherd of Hermas, *Vis.* II.4.3; *Sim.* IX.27.2; Justin, *Apol.* I.61, 65; Tertullian, *Apol.* 39.5 (for the use of *prostates*); Robert Wilken, "Collegia, Philosophical Schools, and Theology," in *The Catacombs and the Colosseum*, 268–91.
44. Cf. CDEE, no. 37 and discussion in chap. 4 above.
45. See CDEE, no. 8 (Acts of Peter); no. 10 (Acts of Thomas); no. 11 (Clementine Recognitions); cf. Gregory of Tours, *History of the Franks* I.29.
46. Tertullian, *De praescr. haer.* 30; *Contra Marcionem* I.4; cf. Walter Bauer, *Orthodoxy and Heresy in Earliest Christianity* (Philadelphia 1971) 121–23; Adolf Harnack, *Marcion: Das Evangelium vom Fremden Gott* (2nd ed., Texte und Untersuchungen zur Geschichte der altchristlichen Literatur 45; Leipzig 1924) 17*–23*.
47. On Cyprian's fortune cf. L. William Countryman, *The Rich Christian in the Church of the Early Empire* (New York 1980) 183–86. Compare the situation at Alexandria in the third century, L. M. White, "Scholars and Patrons: Christianity and High Society in Alexandria," in *Christian Teaching: Studies in Honor of L. G. Lewis* (Abilene, TX 1981) 328–42.
48. Eusebius, HE III.18.4; Cassius Dio, *Hist.* 67.14; CBCR I:117–20.
49. See CDEE, no. 52; CBCR I:267–303; ECBA, 29–30.
50. Cf. J. Carcopino, *Daily Life*, 43, 67, and n. 33 above.
51. R. MacMullen, *Paganism in the Roman Empire* (New Haven, CT, 1981) 128; cf. *Acta Phileae* (CDEE, no. 22); P. Bas. I (1917) 16; P. Amh. I (1900) 3a (dated 264–282, from the Fayyum); cf. R. M. Grant, *Augustus to Constantine* (New York 1970) 241–42; P. Flor. I (1906) 71/87; cf. E. A. Judge and S. R. Pickering, "Papyrus Documentation of Church and Community in Egypt," JAC 20 (1980) 61–62; Peter Brown, "Aspects of the Christianization of the Roman Aristocracy," in *Religion and Society in the Age of St. Augustine* (New York 1972) 161–82; Ramsay MacMullen, "The Power of Bishops outside the Church," in *The Role of the Christian Bishop in Ancient Society* (Center for Hermeneutical Studies, 35; Berkeley 1980) 25–29; A. H. M. Jones, *The Later Roman Empire* (Norman, OK, 1964) II:920–24; F. D. Gilliard, "The Social Origins of Bishops in the Fourth Century: (Ph.D. Thesis, University of California, Berkeley 1966).
52. L. M. White, "Harnack and Expansion," 125–27.

Index

▲ ▲ ▲

Agapē meal. *See* Eucharist
Aleppo, 23
Alexandria (Egypt), 82, 87, 91
Antioch (Syria), 23, 82, 87, 91–92, 103, 104, 124, 136
Apuleius of Medauros, 102
Aquileia (Istria), 22, 115, 136, 138
Archisynagōgos, 81, 83, 86, 87
Archon, 77, 81, 83, 88; title of, 91
Atrium, 13, 16, 17, 100, 107
Atrium House Theory, 13–17, 152 n.15, 153 n.21; rejection of, 17–18. *See also* Basilical form
Aula ecclēsiae, 127–39; architectural style of, 137–38, 199 n.123, 200 n.124; defined, 22, 128, 155 n.49, 197 n.100; persistence of, 23

Basilical form, 11, 118, 136; adaptation to, 114, 115–16, 134; early theories of, 12–17; Krautheimer's theory, 18–21; liturgy and, 11, 14–17, 18, 25; origins of, 128, 130, 138, 195 n.86. *See also* Constantine
Basilicas, 4–9, 23, 24, 114, 134, 166 n.80; *Basilica Hilariana*, 46; liturgy of, 14; renovated from synagogue, 114. *See also* Roman churches
Benefactor, 29, 30, 31, 53, 57, 78
Bequests. *See* Patronage

Bishops, 114, 118, 124, 126, 129, 134, 136, 146; as patrons, 147; residences of, 126, 196 n.88

Carthage, 126, 136, 138
Cassius Dio, 27, 156 n.3, 157 n.8
Church (*Ekklēsia*), 15, 17–20, 21, 23, 24, 123, 136
Churches at Rome: St. John Lateran, 17, 20, 23; St. Peter's, 23; San Clemente, 7–8, 22, 23, 114, 115–16, 134, 199 n.122; San Crisogono, 20, 22, 23, 132–34, 136, 138; San Martino ai Monti, 134; SS. Giovanni e Paolo, 22, 23–24, 112–13, 114, 199 n.122. *See also* Rome; *Tituli*
City council. *See* Decurionate
Clement of Alexandria, 120
Clement of Rome, 7, 114
Clients, 37, 82
Clubs, 32, 39, 59; benefaction toward, 82, 145; confraternity, 41; Greek models of, 37; guilds, 29, 43, 44; halls of, 43. *See also* Collegia
Collegia, 29, 46–47, 165 n.80; Christian organization and, 143; halls of, 32, 39, 47, 98, 145, 166 n.82; Mithraic organization and, 57, 173 n.132; officers of, 82; renovation by, 44; synagogue organization and, 82–83, 88, 89, 183 n.102

▲ 207 ▲

INDEX

Constantine, 4, 18, 139, 150 n.9; and origins of basilica, 18, 20, 23, 128, 136, 137, 139, 147–48
Corinth, 105, 106, 109, 119
Cults, 26, 37; buildings of, 31–32, 145; Egyptian, 26, 31, 33–35, 39; household, 44–46, 59, 143; mystery cult chapels, 15; official, 29, 38, 59. *See also* Isis/Sarapis
Cybele (Magna Mater), 26, 45–46
Cyprian, 124, 125, 127, 146, 195 nn.80–82

Decoration, of Christian buildings, 117; donations for, 80–81, 85, 92, 99, 186 n.141; of mithraea, 49, 53, 57, 169 n.107; of synagogues, 66, 77, 79, 84–85, 89, 100
Decurionate, 31, 74, 88, 89, 90, 99
Dekany, 88, 89–90
Delos, 39, 158 n.21; cult of Sarapis, 31, 33, 37–40; Samaritan enclave on, 66–67, 80, 81; synagogue on, 39, 62, 64–67, 79
Didache, 119
Didascalia Apostolorum, 138, 200 n.125
Dining. *See* Meals
Dining rooms, 35, 40–41, 44, 94, 121; in house church and *domus ecclesiae*, 107, 119–20, 122, 190 n.31; in synagogues, 69, 176 n.24. *See also* Meals; *Triclinium*
Domus ecclēsiae, 20, 111–23, 154 n.36; adaptation to *aula ecclesiae*, 123–26, 128, 147; adaptation from house church, 22, 24, 110, 120, 145–47, 194 n.72; transformation to basilica, 22–23, 24, 156 n.57. *See also* Dura-Europos, Christian building at
Donations. *See* Patronage
Dura-Europos (Syria), 12, 17, 131, 144, 151 n.18; Christian building at, 7–8, 15, 21–22, 24–25, 44, 108–9, 110, 111, 116–18, 120–21, 125, 127, 131; mithraeum at, 44, 50, 54–55, 164 n.67; synagogue at, 62, 74–77, 83, 93–97, 127, 146; temples at, 40–44, 163 nn.64–65

Emperors of Rome, 27; Augustus, 1, 69; Aurelian, 129; Caracalla, 99; Claudius, 91; Constantine, (s.v.); *Constitutio Antoniana*, 99; Diocletian, 123, 127, 130; Hadrian, 37, 40; Julius Caesar, 71; Lucius Verus, 40; Nero, 28, 102, 156 n.6; Severus Alexander, 130; Titus, 27–28; Trajan, 40, 102, 120
Ephesus, 39, 105
Eucharist, 15, 16, 17, 107, 119; separation from *agapē* meal, 15–17, 107, 119, 193 nn.61–63
Eusebius of Caesarea, 124, 127–28, 129–30, 134, 136, 150 n.10, 197 n.96, 198 n.107, 198 nn.116–17, 199 nn.119, 123, 200 n.128

Gerousia, 91
God-Fearers, 88–90, 179 n.54, 183 nn.100–103
Guilds. *See* Clubs; Collegia

Harnack, Adolf, 6, 141, 150 n.15, 154 n.36, 202 nn.8–9
Hippolytus, 16–17, 120
Hospitality, 106–7, 109, 143; provisions for, in synagogues, 87, 95, 185 n.125
House church, 4–9, 12–19, 21, 47; development to *domus ecclesiae*, 24, 110, 119–20, 145–47; social status of, 142
Household, 45, 143, 144–45, 165 n.71, 179 n.57
Household assemblies, 6, 11, 12, 13, 15, 17, 45, 93, 109, 142. *See also* House church; Cults, household
Houses, 13, 29–30, 35–37, 122;

▲ *208* ▲

INDEX

at Dura-Europos, 7–8, 40–41, 43–44, 74–77, 144, 146; transformed for religious purposes, 15, 19, 41, 43, 64, 67, 69, 74, 93, 110, 114, 116–17, 118–21, 122, 143–44; used for cultic activity, 15, 18, 44–46, 47, 48, 50, 71, 78–79, 93–94, 104–5, 111. *See also* Atrium House Theory; House church; Insula; Villas

Inscriptions, 31, 32, 33, 35, 46, 53, 56, 66, 69, 70, 74, 78, 81, 84, 85, 86, 88–89, 90–91, 94, 95, 97, 99, 118, 120, 129, 136, 165 n.74, 170 n.107, 171 n.108, 172 n.116, 173 nn.121–22, 176 nn.17–18, 177 nn.25, 30, 180 n.60, 182 n.94, 183 n.101, 185 n.125, 186 n.142, 194 n.69
—CIG: III,5361–62, 90–91, 184 nn.106–7
—CIJ: 619d, 81, 178 n.49; 720, 80, 178 n.46; 739, 81, 178 n.47; 754, 867, 1436–37, 178 n.39; 682, 722, 723, 735, 744, 754, 766, 781, 803–18, 964–65, 1441, 1447, 180 nn.59–79
—CIL: II,3229, 166 n.80; III,408, 56–57, 173 n.124; III,4038, 4779, 166 n.80; III,4796, 4800, 56–57, 173 nn.123–26; VI,494, 46, 165 n.76; VI,641, 46, 165 n.77; VI,9149 + 10260–64, 46, 166 nn.81–82; VI,10295, 10350, 166 n.80; X,187, 794, 908, 158 n.18; X,846, 31, 157 n.18; XI,5749, 165 n.80; XIII,1747, 166 n.80; XIV,70, 49, 168 n.103; XIV,403, 4314, 57, 173 n.129; XIV,408, 56–57, 173 n.124; XIV, 4310–4313, 49, 168 nn.101–2
—DEF VII-VIII (Dura): 847, 50, 171 n.110; 867–69, 44, 163 n.66; 871, 873, 41, 163 n.56; 886, 888, 41, 163 n.58; 907–8, 43, 163 n.63
—ID: 1510, 38, 162 nn.47–48; 1519, 1774, 162 n.49; 2610, 38, 161 n.46
—IG: IV.1,659, 45, 165 n.72; XI.4,1299, 33, 35, 36, 158 nn.23–24, 160 n.33, 37–38, 161 n.39
—IGRR I,1106, 180 n.60; IV,655, 179 n.57
—Inscr. Cret. IV.249, 162 n.52
—MAMA I.1,170, 129, 136, 197 n.103, 198 n.115
—OGIS 594, 595, 32, 158 nn.20–21
—SIG 985, 45, 165 n.70
Insula, 35, 67, 74, 94, 107, 110, 114, 145, 146
Isis/Sarapis, 27, 30–31, 33–37, 38–40, 158 n.23. *See also* Cults, Egyptian

Jerusalem, 4, 15, 87, 103. *See also* Temple, at Jerusalem
Jesus movement, 102–3
Josephus, 62, 67, 85–86, 98
Justin (martyr), 110–11, 118, 119, 191 n.40
Juvenal, 29, 157 n.11

Krautheimer, Richard, 7, 18–21, 22, 25, 114, 136, 150 n.17, 154 n.33

Living room, 44, 117. See also *Tablinum*
Lord's supper. *See* Eucharist
Lucian, 102
Luke-Acts. *See* New Testament

Martial, 1, 28, 149 n.3
Matēr synagogēs, 80, 81. *See also* Patrons
Meals, 17, 19, 47, 107–9, 119–20; in cult of Mithras, 48; in cult of Sarapis, 40. *See also* Dining rooms; Eucharist
Mithraeum, adaptation of, 48–59, 171 n.112, 172 nn.13–14;

▲ 209 ▲

INDEX

Mithraeum (*cont.*)
  architecture of, 47–48, 51–52, 107, 166–67 nn.86–90; at Dura-Europos, 8, 44, 50, 169 nn.4–5
Mithraism, 9, 47, 53, 56–59, 125, 173 n.33
Money, 30, 93, 157 n.14; for churches, 146; donated to synagogues, 71, 83; in Pauline letters, 105; for rent, 32, 146
Mosaics, in Christian buildings, 117; in synagogues, 84, 85, 100, 175 n.8, 187 n.147. *See also* Decoration

New Testament, 4–5, 11, 12–13, 15, 17, 19, 141, 142. *See also* Paul
—Colossians, 149 n.7
—1 Corinthians, 17, 105, 107, 109, 119, 142, 149 n.7, 181 n.87, 188 n.7, 189 n.21, 190 n.31, 192 n.56, 202 n.12
—2 Corinthians, 181 n.87, 202 n.12
—Galatians, 181 n.87, 189 n.23
—2–3 John, 110, 145
—Luke-Acts, 4, 15, 19, 47, 85–88, 103–6, 141, 149 n.6, 181 nn.84–86, 182 n.92, 188 n.7, 189 n.19, 202 n.6
—Mark, 187 n.4
—Matthew, 103, 187 n.4
—Pastorals, 110
—1 Peter, 110
—Philemon, 106, 149 n.7, 188 n.7, 189 n.24
—Philippians, 105
—Romans, 22–23, 27–28, 106–7, 149 n.7, 189 n.20

Oecus. See *Tablinum*
Ostia, synagogue at, 62, 69–71
Oxyrhynchus (Egypt), 123, 130. *See also* Papyri

Papyri, 122–23, 180 n.59, 61, 194 nn.77–79, 205 n.51

Parentium (Istria), 22, 114, 117, 128–29. *See also* Aquileia
Pater, 49, 57, 58, 79, 81, 174 n.134; *patēr familias*, 16; *patēr synagogēs*, 80. *See also* Patrons
Patronage, 4, 18, 37, 38–39, 144–47; of Christians, 86, 139, 144–47; of mithraea, 49, 53, 57–59; of Samaritans, 66, 79–80; of synagogues, by Jews, 78, 79, 81, 83–89, 94–97, 99–101; of synagogues, by non-Jews, 78, 79–83, 84, 88–91, 99
Patrons, 4, 37, 45, 49, 78–79, 80, 83–84, 90, 97, 145; patronesses, 45, 81–82, 106. See also *Matēr synagogēs*; Pater, *Patēr synagogēs*; *Prostatēs*
Paul, 17, 105–7, 119, 142, 192 nn.56–57; "basilica" of (at Philippi), 134; house churches of, 104–10, 127, 141. *See also* New Testament
Paul of Samosata, 124–25, 127, 129, 146
Philippi (Macedonia), 22, 39, 105, 134–35
Philo, 60
Pliny the Younger, 30, 102, 144, 156 n.2, 157 n.15
Politeuma, 90–91
Pompeii, 12–13, 16, 17, 27, 30–32
Proedrion, 81
Proseuchai, 62, 66, 87, 118, 181 n.85
Prostatēs (*Prostatis*), 82, 88
Provinces of Roman Empire
—Asia Minor, 87; Bithynia-Pontus, 102, 130; Caria, 88–89; Lydia, 81, 98; Phrygia, 81
—Britannia, 22, 24, 48, 116–17, 125
—Egypt-Cyrenaica, 83, 90, 123, 130
—Gallia, 48, 56
—Germania, 48
—Greece, 87
—Hispania, 24, 107

▲ *210* ▲

INDEX

—Italia, 29, 48
—Noricum, 56
—North Africa-Numidia, 23, 24, 122, 123, 126, 130
—Pannonia, 56
—Syria-Arabia (includes Coela-Syria, Phonicia, Palestina), 13, 22, 23, 111, 115, 129; Palestina, 61, 85
—Tripolitania, 24, 125

Rome, 6, 7, 12, 17, 18–19, 20, 151 n.2; Christian assemblies in, 106, 111, 114, 131–34; mithraea in, 48, 49–50, 52; synagogues in, 61; temples of Magna Mater in, 46. *See also* Churches at Rome

Samaritans, 66–67, 79–80, 81, 178 n.41. *See also* Delos
Sanctuary, 26, 32, 43, 44; in mithraea, 48, 49–50, 53, 57. *See also* Temple
Sarapeion, 32, 33–37, 38–40, 159 nn.30–33; 161 n.46. *See also* Cults, Egyptian; Isis/Sarapis
Sardis, Christians at, 92, 184 n.112; synagogue at, 62, 71, 73–74, 83, 84, 90, 98–101
Scholē, 12, 105
Suetonius, 27–28, 149 n.2, 156 nn.5–6
Synagogues, 12, 61–62, 87, 107; at Aegina, 83–84; at Aphrodisias, 88–90, 101; collegial organization of, 82–83, 88, 90, 92, 179 n.50; at Delos, 64–67, 78, 79; at Dura-Europos, 8, 74–77, 83, 86, 93–98; at Jerusalem, 87; origins of, 61–64, 85–92, 104, 175 n.5, 182 n.90; at Ostia, 69–71, 79; at Priene, 67–69, 78, 86, 101; renovation of, 64, 67, 69, 71, 74, 77, 83–84, 92–93, 95–98, 101; role of patrons in, 77–85, 94–97, 99–101; at Sardis, 62, 71, 73–74, 83, 84, 90, 98–101; at Stobi, 71, 72, 78, 79, 80, 92; types of, 12, 62, 80, 98–99, 137, 175 n.6

Tablinum, 13, 14, 117. *See also* Living room
Tacitus, 102, 156 n.6, 157 n.10
Temple, 26, 30, 39, 47; of Christians, 129, 130, 136, 141, 201 n.4; of Church at Edessa, 118; at Dura-Europos, 40–44; at Jerusalem, 60, 61, 64, 66, 85, 103, 136; mithraic, 56. *See also* Cults; Isis/Sarapis
Tertullian, 119, 193 n.65, 196 n.93, 201 n.129, 205 n.46
Tituli, 19, 114, 131, 146, 190 n.38. *See also* Churches at Rome
Torah shrine, 66, 67, 69, 78, 100, 177 n.25, 178 n.36; in Dura synagogue, 95, 131, 184 n.122, 185 n.126
Triclinium, 16, 19, 41, 122, 166 n.80. *See also* Dining rooms

Villas, 13, 17, 22, 107, 114, 116–17, 125, 128–29. *See also* Houses

Wealth, 50, 53, 77, 84, 94, 96–97, 126, 141–43, 144, 202 n.13. *See also* Benefactor; Money; Patronage
Women, 45; donations by, 80–83; in early Christianity, 105–6, 143; in synagogues, 80–82, 90, 179 n.57, 183 n.104. *See also Matēr synagogēs*; Patrons, patronesses
Worship, 47, 97–98, 100; and architecture, 17, 25, 97, 107, 109, 119, 121

NA 4817 .W55 1990 $27.50
White, L. Michael.
Building God's house in the
Roman world